# Managed Health Care *in the* New Millennium

## Innovative Financial Modeling for the 21st Century

# Managed Health Care *in the* New Millennium

## Innovative Financial Modeling for the 21st Century

### David I. Samuels

CRC Press
Taylor & Francis Group
Boca Raton   London   New York

CRC Press is an imprint of the
Taylor & Francis Group, an **informa** business

A PRODUCTIVITY PRESS BOOK

CRC Press
Taylor & Francis Group
6000 Broken Sound Parkway NW, Suite 300
Boca Raton, FL 33487-2742

© 2012 by Taylor & Francis Group, LLC
CRC Press is an imprint of Taylor & Francis Group, an Informa business

No claim to original U.S. Government works

Printed in the United States of America on acid-free paper
Version Date: 20111102

International Standard Book Number: 978-1-4398-4030-6 (Hardback)

### Library of Congress Cataloging-in-Publication Data

Samuels, David I.
 Managed health care in the new millennium : innovative financial modeling for the 21st century / David I. Samuels.
    p. ; cm.
  Includes index.
  Update of: Capitation / David I. Samuels. c1996.
  Summary: "Thoroughly exploring how capitation has evolved domestically and internationally in recent years, this book discusses actuarial assumptions and the difficulties in payers transitions from community-based underwriting to experience-based ratings. It explores what the future holds in the areas of clinical pathways and population-based risk assumption tools and approaches. It covers what happens when the underlying actuarial and risk assumptions are ignored or trivialized. The author also discusses the challenges capitation-based pricing faces from an international perspective, including Latin America and the Caribbean"--Provided by publisher.
  ISBN 978-1-4398-4030-6 (hardcover : alk. paper)
  I. Samuels, David I. Capitation. II. Title.
  [DNLM: 1. Managed Care Programs--economics--United States. 2. Capitation Fee--United States. 3. Marketing of Health Services--United States. WI 735]

  LC classification not assigned
  368.38'2--dc23
                                                                                    2011026257

**Visit the Taylor & Francis Web site at**
**http://www.taylorandfrancis.com**

**and the CRC Press Web site at**
**http://www.crcpress.com**

# Contents

# Preface

This book, *Managed Health Care in the New Millennium: Innovative Financial Modeling for the 21st Century*, is a nearly 20-year reassessment since my first book, *Capitation: New Opportunities for Healthcare Delivery* (Probus, 1995), whose manuscript was first written between 1992 and 1994.

Over particularly the last 15 years, I heard reports from colleagues both inside and outside the managed care and health care service industries that capitation was "dead." Not only was this thinking untrue—managed Medicare and Medicaid have been contracting with providers, practitioners, integrated networks, and all types of managed care organizations (and especially health plan contractors to the U.S. Department of Health and Human Services [DHHS]), continually via capitation—but also I really wondered how anyone could have come to such a ridiculous assertion. I was particularly surprised to hear this thinking coming from my consultant colleagues. That is when I first knew I had to revisit and update my *Capitation* work for the 21st century.

To be sure, hospitals and other institutional-type provider organizations experimented with capitated pricing in select U.S. markets but recognized that their lack of control over key demand drivers (such as physician referrals, emergency department visits, hospital admissions from the emergency and/or outpatient department(s), maternity- and neonatal-related demands) did not allow them to avoid becoming surprised when utilization grew, all without the ability to be paid for actual services rendered. As I mention in Chapter 10, there are all sorts of blame to go around for hospitals getting into capitated contracts, and I would argue that because institutions are generally built on "The Illness Model" rather than "The Wellness Model" (see Chapter 5), there was no real place for them in these types of contracts. I, for one, am certainly glad that most hospitals have gotten out of all capitation contracting—even (or especially) for Medicare Advantage, with or without hospitalists—but just because they extricated themselves from them does not mean that it was because capitated pricing itself was "dead." That is, however, a pretty convenient face-saving explanation, rather than to acknowledge that hospitals did not plan accordingly for capitation and had no business entering into such contracts from the outset.

Part of the problem, I have come to realize, is the rationale for such a wide price disparity between capitation pricing under Medicare Advantage (and under both Medicare+Choice and Medicare Part C plans before it) and for commercial risk products. In Chapters 9 and 10, I show how the calculations for provider pricing (see Chapter 2) under Medicare Advantage can literally be 100 times higher relative to commercial risk pricing for overlapping scopes of work. While it is true that health care consumption by Medicare beneficiaries can be some seven to eight times higher than for those covered under commercial risk, the factor is not 100-fold, and such benchmarking studies were hardly risk adjusted. In other words, does a Type 2 diabetic over age 65 consume eight times as many resources as a 45-year-old with the same chronic disease and of comparable health status? It is hardly distinguishable, even under the worst circumstances. But a 100-fold disparity is absurd.

The obvious answer is that there is profiteering occurring and, by my estimation, quite a bit of it. So, what is the real differential regarding commercial risk? Well, I do know that many actuarial and health status assumptions of most commercial risk markets are completely unregulated (except by the insurance/MCO industry itself and, starting in 2010, in accordance with key provisions of so-called health reform) and had seldom been updated since the 1950s. While managed care products had been rerated many times over, there is no evidence that the actuarial assumptions of health care consumptive behavior have kept pace. Therefore, I was particularly troubled that Congress never took up this issue in expanding commercial risk coverage for 31 million Americans who will be covered under an expanded Medicaid program and by a select group of providers vetted to participate in accountable care organizations. The Affordable Care Act also made underwriting procedures more transparent in rate setting for commercial risk, an apparent rationale for private health plans to have raised commercial risk premiums since health reform was enacted in April 2010, but never apparently challenged any underlying actuarial assumptions for consumption in 2011 compared to consumption in 1951. Even on its face, I find it difficult to write this without laughing hysterically.

But, what has been happening in other health care sectors since the mid-1990s has been anything but funny. As mentioned in Chapter 10, we have seen self-styled managed care experts who have bankrupted entire nations by misunderstanding the difference between contracting and actuarial modeling. A consultant writes a book, shops his knowledge to the country of Colombia to be engaged to design a health care delivery system for its Ministry of Health, only to have so severely understated health care consumption to have bankrupted the health care delivery system for the entire country. The true culprit was his misunderstanding of a "contact capitation" methodology used to weight payments to physicians based on the acuity or volume of services provided, based on as few as one prior year's consumption patterns. Apparently, no consideration was given for the obvious fact that providing citizens vouchers for receiving free care would increase consumption well above prior utilization statistics! That is why the omission of actuarial mathematics—based on incidence and prevalence statistics reflecting many years of data—was critical in destroying the health voucher program in Colombia. Here, also, the fault was not so much the capitation payment methodology itself, but that the same rules about actuarial basis and stringency of underwriting that we have in America were not actually part of the engagement to Colombia. The biggest blame was on the unsophistication of the legislators engaging this consultant and in improperly vetting this consultant simply because he wrote a book (present company excluded of course).

So, I have been worrying that not enough simple-to-understand content has been published that puts all of these disparate concepts under consideration. How does actuarial mathematics work, and how is underwriting performed? If underwriting were better understandable, could specialty groups of practitioners bearing capitated risk be able to determine what they should be paid, rather than just what the market will bear? Of course, if practitioner organizations do not understand their activity-based costs, then what does a given price represent, except what the market will bear? (I will leave that topic for a different book.)

And, while I introduced the role of the member in operationalizing capitation, I have recognized that key roles and responsibilities have never been required before. In fact, nothing I have seen in the Affordable Care Act—other than Medicare beneficiaries currently being covered for wellness exams, but with no apparent strategy to encourage them to be seen when they are not sick (again, the persistent preference for The Illness Model)—makes Americans more accountable for their personal health status and the lifestyle choices they make to improve it or destroy it. Have you ever wondered, for example, why bad drivers pay higher auto insurance premiums—or are relegated to assigned risk policies—but the only accountability for obese, diabetic smokers relative to their health insurance is how large their employer is? Where is the equity in that relationship? That is why I devote a significant portion of Chapter 5 to this topic and to improving lifestyles as part of a capitated disease management model described in more detail in Part B of Chapter 9. I also take a wider swipe in Chapter 10 at the situations that have perpetuated such disparities and challenged the betterment of the managed care industry, and there is plenty of blame to go around. Rather than focusing on the blame game in my own book, I explore new ways that the managed care industry can improve its market positioning when state health exchanges start competing in 2014 (and possibly as early as late 2013) and where the market opportunities will be to lower underwriting and premium expenses within this new construct.

Strap your seatbelts, dear readers, because the road ahead is still rather bumpy.

# Acknowledgments

Of course, any book-writing effort does not just appear out of nowhere and without many months and even years of thankless and largely uncompensated efforts. First and foremost, I thank my wife, Lori, who always finds it difficult to believe that I can be so detailed and meticulous about managed care while completely oblivious to coffee stains left on the kitchen counter. After 33 years of marriage, she comes to expect me to leave the coffee stains but make sure my manuscripts, report write-ups, and lectures are as detailed as they end up being. Of course, as a nurse, I do not think she understands my world all that well, or has ever fully read any of my books, but I know she loves me and supports me just the same. As far as the coffee stains, I just chalk it up to "male-pattern blindness." (I know most every spouse can relate.) I also thank her father, Max, who has been living with us for part of the duration that the manuscript was being put together, for his wisdom and good counsel. (Did I say that right, Honey?)

I also thank "my boys"—now adults and professionals in their own rights—who constantly encourage me to fulfill my dreams and my legacies and who have kept the name-calling to a minimum. I love you, Aaron and Josh, and I am sure you know it, too. I also thank my parents, Melvin and Charlotte, who loved me for more than 55 years and instilled in me the endless curiosity and ability to see the world not as it is, but how it could be improved.

Thanks again to Kristine Mednansky (JTS) at CRC Press, who continues to encourage my best work. For the first time in three books written with her, Kris did not have to resort to bloody knives and threatening to whack my kneecaps (as per her reputation) to get my manuscripts in by final deadline. She was also particularly accommodating when the initial enactment of the Affordable Care Act forced me to rethink the content of my entire book, and CRC was gracious enough in granting me a well-needed manuscript extension. I look forward to many future book-writing projects with Kris (if she can truly stomach the thought).

Thanks as well to my colleagues Robert F. Collins, OD, as well as Lawrence "Lan" Lievense, FHFMA, FACMPE, who have been great friends to me, and together we have caused each other to reconsider the true value of managed care contracts. Dr. Collins, and in collaboration with his optometrist and ophthalmologist colleagues, has been integral to my appreciation of the greater roles that optometrists can play in improving primary care access. In addition, much of the discussion topics of new perspectives on current financial modeling for managed care in Chapter 10 owes to my ongoing collegial relationship with Lan. One day, I hope to convince Lan to write his own book, particularly once the Hanif decision is officially overturned in California.

I also thank my other friend and colleague—and fellow CRC Press author—Maria K. Todd, PhD. Maria has encouraged me over the years, back from our first books writing for Kristine Mednansky with Probus, Richard D. Irwin, and McGraw-Hill, and we have considered innovative financial models together for the future of managed care. I am also fortunate that Maria asked me to consult for her when the opportunity to respond to a request for proposal from the Colombia Ministry of Health first arose. We have also been collaborating in the field of improving the contractual provisions of medical practice organizations, and I look forward to other such opportunities with Maria and in future book projects that may result from them.

**David I. Samuels**

# About the Author

**David Samuels** received his Bachelors of Science in Gerontology and Masters of Public Administration degrees, as well as post-graduate certification in both Health Services Administration and Comprehensive Health Planning from the University of Southern California. Mr. Samuels was appointed to the program faculty of USC's Center Of Excellence in Health Care Management of its School of Pharmacy from 1992–1997 and has also held an adjunct appointment with the Masters of Healthcare Administration program within the Health Sciences Department of Chapman University (Orange, CA) from 1992–1998. Mr. Samuels also received a 3-year appointment to the Board of Examiners for the Healthcare Financial Management Association's Managed Care Specialty Section, and has also written managed care content for BoE's other specialty groups, including Patient Financial Services, Accounting & Finance, as well as Physician Practice Management.

Over 35 years of health care experience has offered Mr. Samuels valuable experience in such positions as Chief Financial Officer of a 30-physician medical group, Director of Product Development for a prior unit of Catholic Healthcare West, Vice-President of Development for a behavioral health services MSO representing over 1 million lives at the time (which had begun to wrap-around behavioral health comorbidity management into disease management contracts for medical conditions), strategic and senior hospital line management assignments with Tenet HealthCare Corporation, as well as a manager of physician marketing services for UCLA Medical Center. Mr. Samuels also served as a board director of a non-profit health plan serving 135,000 Medicaid lives in Southern California, and started his own firm in the field of detecting undercharges for hospitals on an at-risk basis. In his work for a revenue cycle consultancy, Mr. Samuels gained expertise in revenue cycle redesign and management, as well as re-engineering the revenue cycle with a focus on improving managed care contractual relationships. Mr. Samuels has also been principal of his own consulting firm since 1992.

Mr. Samuels' newest book is *Managed Care in the New Millennium: Innovative Financial Modeling for the 21st Century*, to be available in December 2011 and published by CRC Press. His four prior book credits include *Capitation: New Opportunities in Healthcare Delivery* (Probus/Irwin Professional Publishing, 1996) and *The Healthcare Financial Management & Budgeting Toolkit* (McGraw-Hill Healthcare Education Group, 1998), a complete correspondence course in managed care published for HFMA by MGI Management Institute (March 1999) and a complete managed care self-study guide published by Healthcare Financial Management Educational Foundation, November 2000.

Mr. Samuels received his HFMA Fellowship in 1998, with a specialization in managed care, and is a Past-President of HFMA's Nevada Chapter, having served as its President from November 2008 through June 2010. Mr. Samuels has been an active member of HFMA's Nevada Chapter since 2001, having previously provided 15 years of active service to its Southern California Chapter as well. The Southern California Chapter bestowed HFMA's highest Founder's Award, Medal Of Honor, on David in May 2000.

David has two adult children, Aaron (a resident of Chicago) and Joshua (a PhD candidate in biomedical engineering at Drexel University). David's wife of 33 years, Lori, is a registered nurse performing concurrent case management for the NICU Team's Western Region for Aetna Insurance.

# 1 An Updated Introduction to Managed Care and Capitation

## INTRODUCTION

One of the greatest ironies since writing my first book, *Capitation: New Opportunities in Healthcare Delivery*, was that so many people claimed to have read it, but never really did so. And, it wasn't like I hid my work either! During the period before I reclaimed the rights to that work, it had gone through five publication runs, I went on multiple nationwide book promotion and educational tours, and I cross promoted my work during every lecture or workshop at which I spoke. My work became required reading for health care finance and managed care classes and seminars in which I taught and was even incorporated into managed care self-study courses for the Healthcare Financial Management Association, a professional association that graciously allowed me to reclaim my authorship rights to—and to incorporate my original ideas, financial models, and insurance industry operational knowledge in—this new book. But more on that in just a bit.

The basic problem in terms of managed care and capitation knowledge is that the key drivers of managed care, and its specialized and hybridized payment forms (including various flavors of "capitation"), were neither truly understood nor applied. I cannot even begin to count the number of self-styled managed care experts I have met, both before and after *Capitation* was published, who unfortunately knew only as much as they were privy to know, but never believed it was important to understand other important drivers of care and financial modeling that they did not know. Moreover, quite a few of such self-styled experts were truly unaware of the drivers of their particular insights, however narrow they were. This selective ignorance typically encompasses an entire universe of mathematical relationships, operational assumptions, and interactive mechanisms that they did not apparently care to ask about to enhance their own "theories." As we will see in other chapters, this gross level of managed care knowledge gaps—bordering on intellectual incompetence in certain cases—needs to be addressed, and there is really no time like the present to do so.

As shown in this chapter, and per *Capitation*, the term *managed care* means different things in both the private and public sectors. I went into great length in my first book to describe the insane syllogism of defining the term in the private sector. In a nutshell (consider this a "spoiler alert" if you did not read my first book), through much of the 1980s, private-sector managed care involved little management, the least care that was absolutely necessary (and sometimes even less), little actual management of patient care on a concurrent basis, and a raft of contracting maneuvers designed to indemnify successful levels of providers from having to perform any care at all, much of it through a very adult version of the childhood game "hot potato." Whoever got stuck with the hot potato (that is, the obligation to provide actual care, typically at the lowest market price), after all middle-man provider groups took their respective cuts off a successively lower price for a given risk obligation, was the loser. And, it is not hard to fathom why.

A modern example, also discussed in Chapter 5 and Chapter 9, concerns the field of medically certified optometrists. From my experiences since 2007, the field is poorly understood in general medical primary care fields, even though optometrists are trained not only in many of the same disciplines as medical general practitioners but also in the field of general medical eye care, in which general practitioners (GPs) are poorly trained, if at all. Yet, the majority of the problem surrounding optometry is that its members are trained to be primary care providers (PCPs) with in-depth knowledge of the eyes, but health insurance actuaries have mistakenly classified optometry as a specialty and have done so since the 1960s. The irony is not without precedence. Consider that one typical type of PCP in managed care plans, obstetricians/gynecologists (OB/GYNs), are considered both a surgical subspecialty (gynecology), and its expertise in delivering babies largely covered by the primary care field of family practitioners. Yet wouldn't it seem odd that optometrists, who in most states are not allowed to perform treatments that penetrate the skin, are considered specialists under most every medical care insurance risk plan?

In so doing, the insurance folks who actually rate insurance policies, set premium prices for different classes of medical risk, and dictate at what price points providers can be paid for different levels of service risks (medical actuaries and underwriters), for both private- and public-sector health insurance policies (including all forms of managed care), have created a bizarre twist to the process of primary care physicians referring patients to other primary care physicians for general medical eye care examinations that are medically necessary. As seen in Figure 1.1, any underwritten policy that requires a primary care physician to refer to another primary care physician (optometrist) via a specialty referral to a higher-cost eye care surgeon to perform identical services only serves to roughly triple the costs of providing primary medical eye care by an ophthalmologist relative to an optometrist. This convoluted pathway for medical eye care is the primary reason that underwriters tolerate paying surgical eye care pricing for largely primary eye care risk, which is a pattern that is unfortunately perpetuated under the Patient Protection and Affordable Care Act of 2010 and excludes a potential pool of some 45,000 medically certified optometrists from helping to alleviate a critical shortage of primary care physicians as a result. (This topic is discussed in far more detail in Part A within Chapter 9.)

The last point I wish to underscore at this juncture of this book, knowing that there will be far more in-depth discussion in Chapter 9 and Chapter 10

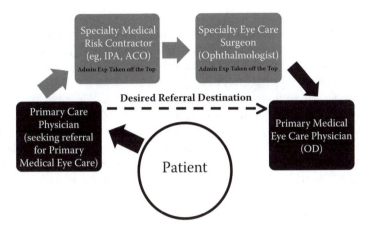

**FIGURE 1.1** Is this any way to refer for primary medical eye care?

of optometry and the financial and mathematical models that can be used to address the issues raised here, is that optometrists—as a discipline—is dissimilar from other allied health care practitioners who can be considered "physicians" by the Centers for Medicare and Medicaid Services (CMS) per Social Security Act §1861(r). Chiropractors are limited by CMS to treat specific spinal misalignments, even though a substantial portion of the population, particularly in America, treat with them on a primary care basis for other spinal conditions. Dentists are limited by their professions to treat only the structures of the oral cavity, even though a tremendous amount of the scope of their profession is in preventive dentistry and hygienics. By contrast, optometrists' scope of practice is not limited to the eye, but *includes* the eye and treatment through various visual accommodations.

Finally, and also with respect to Figure 1.1 above, this is another example of the "Hot Potato" game. Using a fee-for-service model, let's say the primary care physician (PCP) were able to refer a "commercial" (non-governmental) patient directly to the optometrist for a general medical eye exam (see broken line titled "Desired Referral Destination" in Figure 1.1.) that is considered medically necessary. Since most optometrists readily take walk-ins, a referred patient can often be treated on the same day, with little if any waiting required. Now follow Figure 1.1's gray arrow sequence before it turns solid black, which represents the indirect process required by most managed care plans. If the PCP has to refer to the insurance carrier or one of its contracted agents (such as an independent practice association or another at-risk provider/practitioner entity), the contractor will take a piece of the money available for its own administrative overhead (i.e., contracting and managing its own subcontractors) "off the top" of its applicable revenue stream, and will offer a smaller portion of the money available for provider payment to those contractors (e.g., its contracted ophthalmologists). However, fee-for-service ophthalmologists compete with optometrists for primary medical eye care patients, but the ophthalmologist will typically bill upwards of $400 for the same scope of care that the optometrist can perform for $100. And where ophthalmologists own or sublet retail optical stores in their offices, there is no rationale whatsoever to refer any fee-for-service patient to any subcontracted optometrist, except for very specific services (like co-managing patients after LASIK surgery).

The same pattern holds for commercial and Medicare managed care plans, where ophthalmologists similarly retain the risks for primary medical eye care, all of the surgery or referred eye care, and even some, if not all, of vision correction risk. In some contracts, optometrists are not allowed to treat any of the ophthalmologists' Medicare Advantage patients. The optometrist is therefore given the "bones," particularly for much poorer-paid commercial risk contracts, and mostly for traditional (non-medical) optometry services like refractions and lens fitting. Thus, where similar scopes of primary eye care services are performed on an at-risk basis, the eye surgeon could be paid closer to $5 per unit while the optometrist paid under 10¢ (more than a 50-fold differential).

Variants of this financial disparity have kept all but the "hungriest" optometrists away from at-risk relationships in the first decade of the 21st century. For this reason, optometrists appear receptive to innovative evidence-based approaches to "move up the managed care food chain" while surpassing both quality and clinical comparisons to ophthalmologists for comparable scopes of care at substantially lower costs. And, not surprisingly, there remain very few ophthalmologists willing to collaborate professionally with optometrists for anything but the most basic of eye care services, and whom optometrists inherently continue to distrust.

These types of misclassifications create discontinuities of care, as described more fully in Chapter 2, which has profound implications for the manner in which insurers cover medical eye care risk, for the providers who treat such patients, for patients' reasonable expectations from optometrists, and even how optometrists view their own place in current health care debates. What also needs to be considered is the societal injustices created when these misclassifications create competitiveness that should not have ever existed. These have devolved into political battles between the American Medical Association (AMA) and the American Optometric Association (and their related state associations), as well as both state and national associations representing chiropractors, acupuncturists, homeopaths and naturopaths, as well as various Eastern medicine practitioners; all routinely battle with the AMA for their rightful access to primary care for segments of the population who prefer alternative practitioners to allopaths or osteopaths. All of these battles continue, along with money paid to their respective political action groups and lobbyists, as long as insurers continue measuring their performance against the wrong risk parameters and discriminating based on a provider's degree or training. As mentioned in *Capitation*, and to some extent in Chapter 5, the more equitable benchmark is on evidence-based outcomes of care provided for risk-stratified patient populations. (But, that is probably more for a different book.)

## A SIMPLE DEFINITION—BUT NOT SO SIMPLE HISTORY—OF MANAGED CARE AND CAPITATION

One of the most frequently used, and frequently misunderstood, health care terms used today remains the phrase *managed care*. Since 2010, and even while the term remains misunderstood, a variant of this construct, "accountable care," has gained prominence and involves a far more complex infrastructure than managed care alone. Interestingly, the forces that brought accountable care to recent prominence are not so much different from those that created initial models for managed care.

A strong case can be made that the initial model for managed care was rooted in the movie industry. Prior to the mid-1980s, MCA-Universal and studios like it were in the business of producing movies strictly for their own brand. The studios hired actors beholden only to that production house to star in specific numbers of movies; at the same time, the gross and net revenues of the studio were driven solely by foreign and domestic box office receipts. Neither videocassettes nor DVDs existed in those days (perish the thought!), as well as videos on demand through cable companies or downloading movies (legally or illegally) over the Internet, neither of which comparably existed. Except for occasional rereleases of classic films (only in theaters, and usually for limited runs), each shown movie became part of the warehouse of the studio, drawing no additional revenues whatsoever. The movie reels took up warehouse space and were either considered overhead or inventory, based on the likelihood of a later rerelease to movie theaters. This business direction made studios vulnerable to heavily bankrolled movie projects that were box-office bombs and that no amount of marketing could save, except if they became "cult favorites," which could be rereleased, typically for midnight showings.

One case that could be made was how Warren Beatty, who was heavily bankrolled in 1987 for his pet project, *Ishtar* (which came after a string of highly successful movies like *Reds* and *Heaven Can Wait*), nearly ruined Paramount Studios with a disastrous box office run and poor critical reviews. The head of MCA-Universal at that time, Lew Wasserman, preempted another *Ishtar* by declaring that his company was in the entertainment business, and not just in the movie production business. With this strategic realignment, he changed the contractual relationships so that specific fees were set according to specific projects. Soon thereafter, producers became executive producers by forming their own production corporations (similar to IPAs in future forms of the U.S. health care industry) to engage different movie and television studios for inclusion in specific projects. Funded projects then hired specific directors, who contracted with specific casting companies to find specific actors for specific roles. This structure continues to dominate the entertainment industry, now with a 25-year history of doing so.

In the health care field, Lew Wasserman's restructuring of the contractual relationships of MCA-Universal was picked up by Fred Wasserman (of no known relation), the head of a Southern California-based health plan called Maxicare. Maxicare was one of the first health plans to help physicians and hospitals to form IPAs and to create managed care relationships that were initially tied to case pricing and later to "capitation." Alas, these strategic innovations were unable to keep Maxicare out of bankruptcy court, and on a repeated basis.

## UNDERSTANDING MANAGED CARE IN THE PRIVATE AND PUBLIC SECTORS: A REALITY CHECK

Managed care in the private sector is a means of overseeing health care services within a defined network of qualified providers who are given the responsibility to manage and provide certain aspects of high-quality, cost-effective health and wellness services. Nothing in this definition restricts patients to certain types of

- **Providers** (such as doctors of medicine instead of doctors of chiropractic, optometry, or dentistry or even nonmedical providers such as acupuncturists, herbalists, nutritionists, and Eastern medicine practitioners such as those practicing ayurvedic medicine),
- **Health care and wellness services** (such as injury prevention, medical tourism, disease management, inpatient hospitalization, ambulatory surgery, provider office services, home health care, online wellness assessments, lifestyle monitoring, and addiction management, to name but a few of literally thousands of specific service options),
- **Organizations or entities formed to manage provision of care** (such as IPAs, medical groups, integrated networks, or panels managed by third-party administrators),
- **Risk responsibility** (full risk, shared risk, primary care/gatekeeping risk, specialty risk, excess liability risk, malpractice risk, tertiary risk, commercial risk, governmental risk [including state/federal programs, including Medicare risk], or even responsibility that involves no risk at all),
- **Benchmark attainment or quality indicators** (whether representing satisfaction studies [whether by patients or by case managers], clinical outcomes, clinical balanced scorecard benchmarks, clinical indicators, clinical pathways, clinical practice parameters, or even as simply as evaluating intervals of returns to hospital or clinics), or
- **Networks** themselves (integrated care, primary care, specialty care, medical eye care, behavioral health care, concierge care, dental care, chiropractic care, hospice/palliative care, or even church-based care for prayer-based healing).

As mentioned in *Capitation*, the public sector is much less evasive in understanding managed care and views the concept almost literally. In the public and governmental sectors (which have become quite different over the years), managed care really is all about managing populations—whether beneficiaries (such as with Medicare, Tricare, Supplemental Security Income recipients under state Medicaid programs, or even the permanently disabled under state Workers Compensation programs) or recipients (such as the Aid to Families with

Dependent Children [or similarly termed] recipients under state Medicaid programs, who often fall in and out of respective eligibility on any extended basis)—and making sure they receive the actual care they need and do not "fall through the cracks." (Ironically, the private-sector managed care programs often hope that their covered populations fall through the cracks and do not demand actual health care during a specific fiscal year.)

Some health care leaders and educators I have met since the start of the 21st century are of the mistaken opinion that the public sector is always a step or two behind the private sector in terms of market evolution and network maturity under managed care. As that thinking goes, network managers and administrative (including civil service) middle- and senior-management leaders attend the same conferences as their counterparts in the private sector. They hear the newest buzzwords—like *managed care*—but are too embarrassed to ask for definitions or to understand the comparisons and contrasts of the understanding of the private sector of the term to their own environment and often try to figure it out on their own. This was the case in many instances, but as an educator for managed care organizations (MCOs) in both such sectors, I know I have gone out of my way to make sure my public-sector students were "on the same page" as the private-sector ones and to encourage both types of students to ask the right questions to "homogenize" their understanding of the given terms. But at the same time, I got my public-sector students to open up to the private-sector ones about their achievements in managed care that are often unnoticed in the private sector. Even in my own classrooms and conference halls, the term *managed care* has often remained as a euphemism in the private sector and an organized program in the public sector, on a somewhat concomitant basis.

But, here is why that thinking of the public sector being backward relative to the private sector is flat-out wrong, especially from the standpoint of managed care: Starting in the mid to late 1970s/early 1980s, before *Capitation* was written, the public sector developed checklists and beneficiary/recipient surveys to ensure that their beneficiaries were not *falling through the cracks*. This approach was needed based on public perceptions that Medicaid and other health care services to indigents and protected individuals (such as the blind or working poor) were substandard and poorly delivered. As a result, departments of health services became case managers to ensure that populations entitled to public assistance actually received care and, in fact, benefited from such services. Unfortunately, this type of thinking was considered revolutionary relative to the private sector, even as early as 40 years ago. This introduction by the public health sectors of state governments in the mid-1970s of case management—based more on the deployment and benefits of care rather than on their costs—actually transcended what was in place in the private sector.

It is most ironic that the public and private sectors have been on exactly the opposite sides of understanding the term *managed care*. The public sector understood *managed care* in terms of managing health care services, with far less concern regarding its costs per unit of service to do so or the collection of any per case revenue or share of cost per each unit of care provided. The opposite perspective occurs in the private sector, in which the term *managed care* refers to the overriding concerns of revenues and costs to provide any care at all, and very little of any aspect of care was (and in many cases is not even yet) actually managed.

The procedures and instruments did not always work very well and were crude by today's standards, but they were, in fact, implemented. During that same interval within the private sector, the concept of surveying patients after discharge was still being debated and not universally implemented. And, I can prove that surveying is still not universally implemented: When was the last time (or first time) that your primary care physician (or the one you see most often), and not his or her agent (like a nurse or front-office staff), *personally* called you after a visit (not a text message or one-way e-mail) to see how you were doing and if you had any questions about following any aftercare instructions or filling prescriptions? The public sector has been doing so (albeit not every time by the physician) for some 20 years. And, would you believe that aftercare phone calls are also being computerized in the public sector?

Over the ensuing 15 years since writing *Capitation*, I have witnessed firsthand the various protocols implemented by public health departments' staff members (including salaried physicians) to flag walk-in patients who had not established medical homes and those who were not keeping appointments. In Los Angeles County, appointments for clinics at public hospitals are fully computerized, and no patient is seen by a specialist until demonstrated medical necessity criteria are vetted by salaried physicians, including reviews of members' medical records, before appointments are made. Even from that point, the computer system of the county generates appointment reminders that are shared with the respective practitioners. Patients are surveyed (also computerized) on or after each visit, and feedback is provided to the respective parties as indicated. While the data collected are not necessarily in a form that lends itself to further benchmarking, at least the public sector is trying to collect it. (This is all while the private sector is working on collecting its appropriate reimbursements first, especially among for-profit groups, and also downgrading the priorities for collecting any data not directly related to getting paid.)

But, before you take the logical step to criticize the often-antiquated computer systems of a a public health system, system glitches, computer-generated appointments that are often not vetted by the patient beforehand, horrible rationing of appointments to certain specialists who are in extremely short supply, and the lack of transition to more modern technologies (such as telemedicine and use of smartphones and tablets), consider the "elephant in the room": How was the private sector behaving while all this benchmarking and process innovation was occurring in the public sector?

Well, considering I lived this period in the evolution of the health care industry, I will tell you. During the decade before *Capitation* was first written, I can say on the basis of firsthand knowledge that the private sector was wrestling with the term *quality*. While the public sector was documenting service quality of its defined populations, the private sector was launching advertising campaigns to tout their quality and how "well" their health plan members were and were creating logos, brands, products, taglines, collateral, billboards, media buys, and even public service announcements about the quality, "caring," and "reputation" of their hospitals and providers. Less attention was being paid to proving it; rather, the thinking was that if you said so long enough, loud enough, often enough, and in a "classy" manner, everyone would believe you had high quality, even if your organization could not specifically define it. And, if you cannot define it, you cannot measure it, so how did anyone know whether this strategy "worked" or that the money was well spent? Even today, those same ads from the early 1980s make occasional reappearances when health plans have open enrollment (often from late September to early November) or just before their contracts with large insurers are scheduled to be renegotiated.

But, this strategy of relegating quality to the proverbial megaphone was occurring long before anyone thought it was important to create benchmarks, indicators, clinical pathways, and (more recently) balanced scorecards to document that their service quality was statistically significant. This does not take private-sector health care payer and provider segments off the hook in defining quality, but at least in trying to be objective about it.

Ironically, and with all the benchmarking that is occurring, the private sector *still* has yet to define what quality is, as a universal indicator. If a statistically significant proportion of medical staff at a hospital attain a predetermined benchmark for a statistically valid number of such quality indicators, can anyone really say their care is of "the highest quality," which they were incidentally touting some 20 years ago? I am not going to name names, and you know who you are (including former employers of mine), but sadly this practice was universally adopted in the United States and many other countries since then. What does "highest" mean in terms of quality, especially from the standpoint of today's "balanced scorecards," used so often in managed care arrangements?

Does it mean you have to attain the sixth sigma (see Chapter 4) of preventable service errors to be considered highest in terms of quality? (Before you go there or flip chapters, realize that a sigma level of 6 means that you observe no more than 1 critical-to-quality [CTQ] error per approximately every 6 million opportunities for such CTQ errors to occur.) To my knowledge, no single health care provider is anywhere close to six sigmas of error prevention, given the lack of robotics and expert systems in providing such care at higher sigma values and always being at risk for human error. Since the improvement in sigma levels is logarithmic, getting even close to six sigmas from the level at which most health care organizations still operate (at less than two sigmas or approximately 1 error per 45,000 CTQ opportunities) is far-fetched and would take decades to engineer. Can a health care provider or network operate at less than two sigmas of process error and legitimately consider having attained the highest level of quality—again, whatever *that* means?

Or, can a health care organization legitimately say today that it has attained the highest level of quality in its managed care plan if the respective organization attains certification in compliance with ISO (International Organization for Standardization) 9001 (or later revisions)? There are health plans that are actually moving in this direction, as are hospitals and provider networks that are still "testing the water" by implementing selective ISO 9001 standards, even though ISO certification simply involves a process for qualifying an organization's quality program, but never actually defining what quality is for all such organizations. Moreover, organizations that are committed to ISO 9001 certification, in whatever industry, are actually committed to managing and measuring their quality programs—however they define the quality program itself or its outputs (each output constituting some aspect of quality performance). But here again, the definition of quality is never overtly specified.

Let us come back to health care for a moment. In Chapter 4, we explore accreditation of MCOs. In the hospital industry, we have The Joint Commission (TJC). If a hospital attains Joint Commission accreditation, can it be said it is a high-quality facility? That may in fact be true, other than the obvious caveat that TJC measures standards attainment, the sum total of which may constitute an "indicator" of high quality, other than obvious omissions of patient outcomes, hospital-specific balanced scorecards that TJC does not address, or even such simple data as results of patient and practitioner satisfaction surveys (that are also not addressed by the standards). So, if even the most basic data of recording patients' opinions about the quality of their care or hospitalization are omitted from The Joint Commission's standards, can any accredited hospital say with a straight face that attaining TJC accreditation is documentation of its being a high-quality institution? Likewise, can a health plan or ACO (accountable care organization) that attains accreditation by the National Commission on Quality Assurance (NCQA) document that—just on that basis alone—it has achieved high-quality managed care operations? Again, that is a big "perhaps." But, we all know there is no such measurement inherent in such accreditation to document that any such providers or MCOs are of the highest quality (not yet, at least).

## UNDERSTANDING CAPITATION—AND NOT JUST FINANCIALLY

As a former educator to the Los Angeles County Department of Health Services (after *Capitation* was written), the term *capitation* was easily understood the same way in both the private and public sectors, even while both were wrestling with a universal understanding of managed care and how one proves the quality of their services. The term is sometimes mistaken as a form of reimbursement, but this misperception stems from the fact that capitation was defined financially long before it was defined operationally. In fact, this was the basic premise of *Capitation: New Opportunities in Healthcare Delivery*: How did one actually implement capitated pricing, and where were the opportunities to improve service delivery?

Think of it from my point of view. Here is a physician who, by training and experience (and those god-awful tests), has learned how to provide care when a person walks into his or her office and becomes a patient. Here is a hospital with federally required assurances that every person walking into an emergency room (ER) is actually evaluated, if not treated, in a life-threatening emergency, and that every pregnant woman dilated to 9 centimeters who is brought into an ER is admitted and the physician attempts to deliver her baby—all of this occurring with no questions being asked about U.S. citizenship or ability to pay (at least prior to care being rendered). And, here is a health plan, which is organized and licensed as a type of insurance entity, that offers capitation to the hospital or physician entity for a population of people, irrespective of their actual need for care. An insurer sells premiums and indemnifies itself against risks (such as paying physicians and hospitals for care) and prices capitation payments on the basis of the actuarial wellness of the population being "sold" via capitation. But, the medical or hospital provider cannot even define *wellness* and instead sees members as patients only when they require primary or acute levels of care. Both parties to these capitation contracts are nearly the exact opposite of each other. Just because you know how you are compensated for wellness does not mean you understand how to completely transform your operation from one that is compensated based on degrees of illness or incident requiring care. And, even more basic than that, must a successful physician's practice become a quasi-insurance company to be successful at capitation? What happens to the health maintenance organizations (HMOs) after they capitate their customers?

First, I will describe the term financially. Capitation occurs when periodic (e.g., monthly) fixed or semifixed payments are made on some type of a *per capita* basis (the "capita" part of the term *capita*tion, refers to per person—literally per head—pricing) and are continually paid over the life of a specific contract regardless of work actually performed. When such payments are made monthly, they are often known as "per member, per month" payments, or just the acronym PMPM. The operational nuances of capitation financial modeling are discussed in greater detail in Chapters 2, 3, 9, and 10.

Second, and to reiterate the nature of capitation nonfinancially, capitation is not just another financial model to compensate health care providers for the work they performed. Rather, it is the exact opposite, because providers are paid a fixed or semifixed fee each period (month) irrespective of the actual care or wellness-oriented services that a given member may require or that the practitioner may actually provide. In such a model, physicians are transformed from actually providing care and then billing for reimbursement of the services provided to quasi-insurance companies: They are put into the role of influencing how and when patients see a physician for care and to say "no" to members who insist on being treated excessively. This is hardly a model of care delivery taught in medical school and was the basis of a term I coined as "the art of managed care" that successfully transitioned providers would need to know to succeed under capitation.

I also went into some depth in 1994 to describe the payers' expectation that physicians would eschew the so-called illness model (in which a patient seeks care when ill—actually "death bed ill" if they have to miss work to be seen) in favor of the wellness model embraced by payers (in which a member's health is managed by the provider, and the patient is seen on a preneed basis when not actually sick or *in need* of care), but even today not fully embraced by primary care physicians. And, since capitation is paid prospectively (prior to the need for care actually arising), any provider is hard-pressed to justify that capitation is just a form of reimbursement (which is retrospective). The basic reason that insurers capitate a given population of members, to a network of providers who assume nearly the entirety of a certain classification of risk pretty much on a sight-unseen basis, is simple: The insurer is taking the risk off their books and selling it to the lowest bidder.

But, I also correctly predicted the contraction of the plethora of HMOs in the mid-1990s that were selling their customers via capitation, especially once they realized that the fundamental nature of their own business model had radically changed. Sure, the health plans were still selling and collecting a premium from their customers, except they signed away their assurances to their customers that they were receiving all of the services promised. If HMOs did it themselves (and they did so before the mid-1980s), they would review the patients' records, contact the respective providers, and address the members' concerns internally and strive for high satisfaction. But, what could an HMO really review if the capitated providers did not share their encounter data, let alone the actual medical records? And, you must understand that even 15–20 years later, physicians are still not sharing their encounter data with payers who have effected capitation contracts with them.

The real contraction started occurring as HMOs continued to ignore their new business model. When they capitated their customers to third parties, the HMOs themselves became *distributors*. Unlike the customers of the health plan industry, a distributor's customers are guided by service, convenience, and efficiency and not at all on the basis of price. We already know that many physicians and hospitals failed under capitation because they refused (or ignored the need) to recognize their need to adapt their operations accordingly and to influence which members needed to be seen as (A) in-house patients, (B) via less-personal tactics (like phone calls and e-mails, which sadly are still not being implemented appropriately), or (C) not at all. Please understand that not seeing a disruptive or non-compliant patient is still inappropriate if there is a true need for care, irrespective of the practice expense in doing so.

But in much the same manner, HMOs similarly failed to retain their largest employers as clients simply because they could not transform themselves from insurers offering a premium at the lowest price to distributors who were attentive to their clients' specific needs and helped them to document the cost-benefit of their contracts (with far less attention paid to price of premium). They never really shifted the discussion to the price of care and the cost-benefit of premium collected versus reductions in employee sick days and preventable job site injuries. So, what happened? Many of the clients the HMOs capitated for their employees realized they could do just as well, if not better and cheaper, by self-funding their employees' health benefits and even redefining which benefits they wished to offer to achieve their own health and wellness objectives. Many of these self-funded plans chose to be covered under the Employee Retirement Income Security Act of 1974 (ERISA), and many of which continue to contract with HMOs, but only for certain employee populations and mostly based on past experience. But even in this construct, the ERISA plan becomes the entity to select with which HMOs, if any, it *chooses* to continue doing business. Where the HMOs had the opportunity to influence their customers' contract preferences as distributors, the contraction of the market and the mass exodus of their largest customers to ERISA plans had the effect of relegating HMOs to purveyors of niche services to self-funded plans, without any assurance of the longevity for which the HMOs would be contracted by the self-funded plans. And, if the ERISA plan contracts with its own third-party administrator, the HMO often has little access to decision makers within the self-funded plan itself.

In *Capitation*, I went into great depth of the rationales for insurers to capitate and for providers to accept capitated payments, most all of which has not changed after all these years. There actually was a trend, during the first 5 years after *Capitation* was first published in 1995, for hospitals to chase capitation payments and negotiate their own capitation arrangements with insurers. The misdirection was their belief that since the primary care physician was given capitation to become a quasi-payer, hospitals needed to bond better with the PCP members of their medical staffs. It was a misdirection because PCPs have a generally terrible record in influencing hospital use, in directly referring patients for admission (outside the ER), and for contributing significantly to the bottom line of a hospital with respect to income from operations. Not only was the PCP the wrong target, but also hospitals lost significant money for every capitated patient who crossed the threshold of a hospital waiting room or ER in hopes of receiving care. From a financial perspective, it was truly a bottomless pit of service obligations for prepaid members for whom hospitals could not bill a penny for services provided.

However, the timing of these capitation deals with hospitals would prove to be particularly lousy due to the increased enforcement of the Emergency Treatment and Active Labor Act of 1986 (EMTALA). With the Office of the Inspector General promising to decertify from public funding (through Medicare and Medicaid, for example) any hospital that violated EMTALA statutes, hospitals became obligated to accept every pregnant woman in active labor (regardless of U.S. citizenship or ability to pay) and provide medical screening examinations by physicians (not triage nurses, per the letter of the law) to anyone presenting in any emergency department whose life could be considered in danger (whether the patient knows it or not, also regardless of both the patient's ability to pay and the citizenship of the patient being seen). There were famous cases of hospitals shown on video transporting "skid row" patients in need of care to public hospitals and even directly back to the streets and threats of Medicare decertification (which essentially bankrupts a hospital when 50–60% of its payer funding goes away). And unbeknownst to many hospitals within 200 miles of the Mexican border, lay health educators known as *promotoras* were famously known for teaching Latinas how to tell when they were about to go into active labor, but with enough lead time to call a cab and be driven directly to the ER of a border hospital; this way, the hospital could not turn them away (because of EMTALA), their babies born would become U.S. citizens (per the 14th Amendment to the U.S. Constitution), and the mother, as necessary for the health of the infant, would later also gain a path to U.S. citizenship)—all this for the cost of a cab ride.

## EFFECTS OF PUBLIC POLICIES ON CAPITATION AND CAPITATED RELATIONSHIPS

As anyone familiar with health policy knows, EMTALA created an unfunded obligation for hospitals to provide care for everyone living in America, nearly 25 years before this obligation was expanded under PPACA (Patient Protection and Affordable Care Act), which also (again) neglected to include financial provisions to compensate health care providers for these additional financial and risk obligations. As such, EMTALA was a mechanism for the U.S. government to offload a significant component of emergent care risk created by the statute to emergency departments nationwide with little to no financial compensation in doing so. To this day, hospitals are largely uncompensated for any care they provide that is required only by EMTALA, let alone for so-called anchor babies, whose care may cost hundreds of thousands of dollars in a neonatal intensive care unit (NICU), particularly for drug-addicted mothers and as a result of poor standards of prenatal care that are pervasive in Mexico and throughout much of Central America. EMTALA simply became yet another fixed cost for hospitals to do business.

Here are my questions (which I address in more detail in Chapter 2): What impact does EMTALA place on the underwriting of any capitation offered to a hospital or physician entity servicing the ER when federal mandates for incurring losses without any remuneration for this added obligation effectively skew their cost behavior? And, how should such contracts be rectified to exclude governmentally required services thrust on providers without remuneration?

Of course, much of this argument is moot due to the implementation of so-called health reform, but I also doubt that the actuaries of CMS have similarly accounted for EMTALA, state- or locally mandated programs for which any compensation offered is far from commensurate with the depth and breadth of health care services that the providers are obligated to perform. Examples of such inequalities of risk versus remuneration exist for victims of violent crime, local police or sheriff contracts obligating hospitals to perform blood alcohol testing for suspected impaired drivers, mandatory indigent care for the most destitute and at-risk individuals of an area who are not covered by Medicaid, and so on. Even PPACA has created insurance risk obligations that themselves do not involve any increases in provider payments, except as implemented by Congress. Is it not probable that the PPACA statute overadjusted provider risk, especially for providers servicing EMTALA-compliant ERs, in calculating how such providers should be paid under capitation, such as within an ACO?

In the first 10 years after EMTALA was implemented—during the same interval that the Justice Department began onerous enforcement of compliance and promising loss of Medicare certification for turning indigent patients away from ERs without evidence of medical screening exams or even "dumping" them into ERs of public hospitals before medically clearing them for ambulance transport—some hospitals actually closed their ERs, dropped their maternity beds and closed their labor and delivery units, or downgraded from licensed trauma centers or even from basic-level ERs to stand-by emergency departments that do not accept patients arriving via rescue ambulances responding to 911 dispatches. Through much of the first decade of the new millennium, hospitals have again adjusted to providing more services for less money, with EMTALA and PPACA just newer hurdles. Conversely, implementation of PPACA initially increased funding to ACOs that established patient-centered medical homes (PCMHs) in conjunction with their primary care services, and the American Recovery and Reinvestment Act of 2009 established tax incentives for physician practice organizations that converted to electronic health care records (that met certain eligibility criteria) and even established bonus potentials for those practices with installed electronic health records (EHR) systems that registered for the Patient Quality Reporting Initiative, also under the enactment of the American Recovery and Reinvestment Act of 2009 (ARRA). Clearly, and consistent with my 15-year-old recommendations from *Capitation*, the availability of EHR in conjunction with an improved deployment of primary care services make capitation models easier to manage operationally, with less-adverse or preventable patient care events, and with the greater opportunity for achieving profitability in balance with quality benchmarks under an appropriately negotiated capitation contract.

But, one of those hurdles was capitation, particularly where it was contracted inappropriately, and hospitals were caught by the more vigilant enactment of EMTALA at the same time that they were trying to adapt to suboptimal capitation contracts. Both "hurdles" had a common thread, however: The hospital could not really control who came through the door because it was the primary care physician who received the capitation. And—with the notable exception of obstetricians and more recently of the new category of primary care physicians known as "hospitalists"—the primary care physician does not typically admit patients to hospitals. So, hospitals bore significant managed care risk for patients they did not directly control and for physicians they rarely saw admitting patients or even treating inpatients of theirs at a particular hospital. In the second decade of the 21st century, we are seeing a greater proportion of capitation patients, particularly for Medicare risk plans, whose care is transferred to hospitalists and "intensivists" almost from the minute they first arrive in the ER.

The logical response, of course, was that hospitals started running for the exits with whatever capitation contracts they were remiss to initiate. The financial burden initially placed on them contemporaneously by the escalated enforcement of EMTALA along with capitation contracts in any contractual form being clearly a "double whammy." When renegotiation periods arose for those capitation contracts, hospitals were only too happy to make unrealistic demands for concessions from payers, just so that they could be released from their capitation contracts.

For much of the first decade of the 21st century, hospitals had extricated them-selves from almost all of their capitation deals, with the exception of a smattering of Medicare and Medicaid managed care risk plans, and the dominant contracting payment mechanism reverted back to per diem arrangements initially and later to certain case pricing arrangements that have become increasingly "low balled" as the recession first hit in earnest in 2008/2009. Amazingly, by the autumn of 2010 (when accountable care organizations first started forming between payers and hospitals), some contracting discussions started shifting back to a capitation model, and early indications appear to be that hospitals are seriously considering reestablishing some form of capitation tied to performance benchmarks and to shares of cost savings. If hospitals actually do reenter capitated relationships with payers in time for the January 1, 2012 launch date of ACOs, it will have been less than a decade between the frantic dash of hospitals to the exits of their capitation contracts and their rush back to embrace such contracts under the ACO umbrella set by PPACA of 2010 (which is probably a record for such a complete turnaround in contracting philosophies).

## A SIMPLIFIED UNDERSTANDING OF MANAGED CARE MODELS

Under the traditional roots of allopathic medicine (on which the majority of U.S. medical practice is still largely based), health care consumers still demand "services" and demand them through either the "wellness-based" or the "ill-ness-based" demand model. Either model presumes that practitioners and pro-viders exist to provide services to their respective customers. Oddly, the extent of innovation in online and virtual technologies to manage patients without requiring them to be seen in any respective physical setting did not originate in the cash-strapped public sector with ample public investments in online technologies, or even in the large integrated networks of the private sector, but mostly in small "boutique" medical practices, particularly those involved in "concierge-type" medical services on largely a cash-paid or otherwise non-risk-bearing insured basis. Under capitation, however, new relationships between risk-bearing practitioners and their respective populations at risk are based on advocacy of healthiness rather than traditional service providers, particularly in the emerging ACO setting.

## TWO BASIC DEMAND MODELS OF MANAGED CARE: ILLNESS-BASED VERSUS WELLNESS-BASED

With few exceptions in the early 21st century, the health care industry is man-aged entirely on the illness-based demand model. This model presumes both that health care consumers demand "care" when they are sick, injured, or oth-erwise in pain and that physicians are available to these consumers once they become patients. Beyond this presumption, a person covered by insurance does not become a patient until he or she actually seeks care in a practitioner's office, at a clinic, in an urgent care center, or in a hospital's emergency department. In other words, prior to arrival at a hospital, an individual member gets progressively sicker to the point that medical or hospital care is required. Yet, with the exception of chance occurrences, this member is not identified until the actual care is consumed. Moreover, the perpetuation of traditional office-, clinic-, ER-, and hospital-based practitioner settings necessarily involves practice expenses, even if one setting is less expensive than another. Even in a world that includes Skype (and other free and low-cost streaming video calling competitors) and certain regulatory or billing allowances for certain practitioners to utilize these emerging technologies in the performance of health care, much of the health care practitioner industry remains rooted in the traditional face-to-face encounter, despite its occurrence at far greater fixed costs relative to voice-over-Internet-protocol-based telecommunication alternatives. Also to this day, the illness-based demand model is the cornerstone of emergency services (at either a clinic or hospital location) and inpatient U.S. health care. In such settings, "case management" (see further discussion in this chapter) becomes a managed care operational strategy to "lose less money" per incidence of health care consumption.

An alternative model to the illness model is the wellness-based demand model. The wellness model presumes that health care consumers access physicians and hospitals not, primarily, as patients. In this alternative model, therefore, covered individuals enter the managed care system when they are not sick, injured, or otherwise in pain. The wellness model is the basis for the creation of HMOs (which are also discussed in this chapter, as well as in more detail in Chapter 5) and is the paragon by which managed care consumers more appropriately demand health care services. By extension, therefore, provider and practitioner managed care contracts offered by HMOs are based on a wellness model of service delivery, not on an illness model. To this day, illness model operations under managed care are focused on providing fewer services and losing less money; by contrast, the operations of the wellness model are based on providing appropriate and cost-effective health care services that are the least acute. One way the managed care plans attempt to do so is to make preventive, early care, and wellness services inexpensive or free to enrollees.

## UNDERSTANDING HEALTH PLANS

The HMO is the cornerstone of the managed care finance and operations of a health plan. HMO products were the third type of insurance that payers covered, and the inclusion of health maintenance insurance (after both indemnity and preferred providers) was also known as the third option as part of a payer's marketing use of the term *triple option*.

The earliest HMOs competed with both providers and practitioners under the "staff model" delivery system. Few HMOs continue to operate this way as the staff model compromises the ability of an HMO to expand into new markets since a health care campus and an entire infrastructure of physicians and employees would have to be hired prior to receiving even one new subscription in an entirely different marketplace. A key component of understanding the relationship of an HMO to managed care providers and practitioners necessitates some basic background information.

Once actuarially measured and rated (see next paragraph), managed care has typically existed in the United States as insurance products, operating similarly to other such policies as casualty, automobile, and life insurance, for which cost-related factors enter into decision making about premiums, protection, and policy termination. Thus, the HMO view of managed care is generally reflective of the insurance industry, not the health care industry. Let me repeat that: *An HMO is an insurance product, not a health care product.*

The insurance industry differs fundamentally from the health care industry, whether in the public or private sector. Dissimilar from the health care industry, insurability of managed care is a function of both the actuarial risk of a provider claim occurring as well as the underwriting relationship between revenue received from employer/member premiums and price offered to providers for risk assumed. To an HMO bearing full risk, every provider demand (cost) for the insurance company to satisfy (an accrual called a *claim*) must be minimized relative to premium revenues received from subscribers. From this perspective, every dollar spent to satisfy a claim directly reduces payer profitability and, more important, can shift the medical loss ratio (MLR) higher than its budgeted level. The MLR is the ratio of total medical losses paid for members (e.g., provided and accrued claims submitted by providers and practitioners) divided by total member revenue (e.g., premium) received (see Figures 1.2 and 1.3).

These two different views of MLR are sometimes at odds with the health care industry, in which it is widely believed that increased consumption of revenues is desirable if it leads to lives saved and comorbidities reduced. The managed care industry, especially as physicians and hospitals enter it as part of ACOs and new forms of health plans, are bringing the traditional insurance industry focus around to this more service-oriented view, especially in conjunction with the renewed focus by CMS and the NCQA to integrate managed care with PCMHs in conjunction with the PPACA.

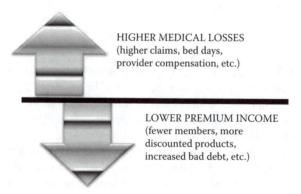

HIGHER MEDICAL LOSSES
(higher claims, bed days,
provider compensation, etc.)

LOWER PREMIUM INCOME
(fewer members, more
discounted products,
increased bad debt, etc.)

**FIGURE 1.2** Forces that worsen (i.e., keep high) medical loss ratios.

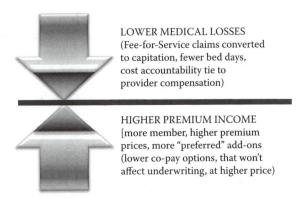

**FIGURE 1.3**   Strategies to improve (i.e., reduce) medical loss ratios.

The HMOs/ACOs and other wellness-based insurers are typically confident in predicting premium revenues on a periodic basis. For an insurer to commit to achieving a budgeted MLR, claims paid should be very close to claims reported. The variability of claims paid against claims reported is known as *incurred but not reported* (IBNR) claim accruals. Financially, IBNR represents claim accruals that have no expense offset until such claims are actually received from the authorized provider of service. In a similar perspective, higher IBNR accruals made by the insurer reduce the amount of claims that can be paid against a budgeted, stable MLR.

Figure 1.2 shows that high medical losses serve to worsen or destabilize the MLR. These claim losses can result from paid claims or accrued claims that are not paid. Obviously, IBNR is included in this category, but so are claims that are reported to the payer but remain unpaid, known as *incurred but not paid* (IBNP) accrued claims. IBNR claims age in the provider's office while waiting to be reported against an authorization accrual, while IBNP claims age in the payer's finance department waiting to actually satisfy the authorization accrual. Figure 1.2 shows that MLR can worsen irrespective of utilization, from decreases to premium revenues such as increased competition for members or their premium payments (particularly in undifferentiated managed care markets where each payer offers similar products at similar premium pricing, which is the "perfect storm" that leads to higher discounting of premium payments) and where health plans underperform or incur receivables that they cannot collect (such as with client bankruptcies), thus increasing the proportion of their premium income that is bad debt.

Figure 1.3 shows some strategies to improve MLR on both sides of the equation, that is, to both lower the numerator and increase the denominator. Specific strategies to decrease the numerator—that is, to reduce medical losses—include the following:

1. Reduce accounts payable by "franchising" members: largest integrated delivery systems given exclusivity for larger numbers of members but at reduced capitation (PMPM) rates;

2. Influence hospital providers to discount charge description master prices by at least 20%, particularly in high-outlier areas, such as bariatric surgery (where covered) and neonatal intensive care, to reduce claim expenses;

3. Impose stiff penalties on providers and practitioners who do not report authorized care provided—even from a retroactive authorization—to reduce IBNR exposure;

4. Reduce PMPM rates in more mature capitation markets to reduce claim expenses;

5. Transfer as many operations functions as possible to providers/practitioners (e.g., claims adjudication, IBNR accounting, authorization, case management, member services, and risk for excess liability insurance [so-called reinsurance] for highest-dollar and catastrophic claims) to reduce MCO operating expenses as much as possible; and

6. Encourage providers to decrease utilization (e.g., decrease inpatient lengths of stay, increase outpatient surgeries relative to inpatient surgeries, shorten maternity postpartum days for healthy mothers and infants, and reduce overall admissions for less severely acute cases) to reduce overall claims expenses.

Specific strategies to increase the denominator (which also acts to reduce the MLR ratio itself) include the following:

1. Step up HMO/ACO subscriptions for the largest employers and union benefit trusts, particularly to products that a payer can operate at least cost;

2. Convert higher-cost indemnity and so-called transitional plans (such as exclusive provider organization, point-of-service, and preferred provider organization plans) to higher-profit HMO subscriptions or convert to more cost-sensitive ACO products;

3. Diversify into more MLR-stable products (such as excess liability insurance, like so-called umbrella coverage and reinsurance);

4. Acquire competitor plans, especially those with undersubscribed Medicare risk or selected special needs plans (that combine standard Medicare risk with various forms of Medicaid risk); and

5. Advertise during "open enrollment" to compete for HMO members compliantly, particularly in undifferentiated markets, and with multiple tactics to drive different books of business (i.e., Medicare beneficiaries, brokers, self-funded plans [particularly those organized under ERISA, with each typically having its own open enrollment period], and union benefit/public employee trusts).

Unless provider and hospital incentives are aligned with payer incentives to reduce costs, Figure 1.3 demonstrates that it is highly difficult for the MLR to be predicted. Consequently, the health plans have focused much of their energy on increasing the denominator to decrease the MLR because it is the only part of the equation that they truly control once the responsibility to decrease the numerator has been outsourced to providers themselves. In so doing, health plans can act to increase the MLR denominator by increasing premium-related revenue and by subscribing additional employers (thereby adding more premium-paying members). By increasing the subscriber pool, and the premiums they pay, health plans are often able to offset increases or unpredictable behavior of losses occurring.

That is, of course, that their denominator increase strategies work up to a point. At that point, some form of critical mass occurs. An inefficient and more expensive product can grow only as far as the market is elastic enough to accommodate it and only as long as the payer makes the more inefficient plans (those with highest IBNR exposure, for example) increasingly attractive to employers to stimulate sales. The obvious problem with this strategy to stabilize MLR by selling more premiums for a broken product that cannot be fixed in terms of medical losses is that it depends on either an undifferentiated market or one in which competitors resist innovation. Once even a single competitor offers even a slightly more differentiated product (such as a zero-copay product with greater network provider selection), it is harder to maintain that stable MLR simply by selling the same product at higher cost and without any comparable innovation or enhancement.

By the mid-1980s, and again in the first decade of the 21st century, many HMOs in mature managed care markets decided to exit the business of directly managing health care providers through care-based contracting methodologies. At the governmental level, Medicare has evolved from a fee-for-service product to both a risk product (including Medicare Parts C and D) and more recently to an ACO product, whereby a fixed price was determined for each beneficiary based on a national rate that started off in the 1980s tied to regional costs-of-care differences. This fixed pricing, known as capitation, also was the basis for Medicare Part C payments to Medicare risk contracting health plans starting in the late 1990s. In addition, capitated pricing for Medicaid started in the mid-1990s, as part of waivers submitted to CMS (as part of §1915(b) of the Social Security Act) to provide wellness-based care.

The mathematical relationships in Figures 1.2 and 1.3 help to explain why care costs entered into health care contracting discussions. It also explains what actually happened when there were no more HMOs to acquire. Starting during 1997 and 1998 open enrollments, HMOs raised premium prices (thereby increasing the denominator of the MLR equation). At the same time, they began to report to CMS that the price paid to them through the Medicare risk program was insufficient to cover their care costs, during a period before national rates were set and regional differences continued to exist for certain costs (such as capital expenses and medical residency programs). In one aspect, Medicare Part C (also known as the Medicare+Choice program) was created by HCFA (Health Care Financing Administration, the former name for CMS, to equalize regional variances in price and to increase the price floor of regions with the lowest cost base.

Little of the cost and price complaints of HMOs had to do with national health care costs or the inherent inefficiencies in provider and practitioner operations under managed care. What the HMOs intended to say was that IBNR and claims management were inefficient, but they did not understand this business well enough to fix it, and the health care business is not their core business. The rationale was that efficient providers and practitioners of managed care would know how to solve the problem of high IBNR costs and might be willing to go at risk in doing so. The underlying assumption of HMOs in exiting the health care provision business in the 1990s was the realization that providers and practitioners were inherently inefficient.

The capitated relationships that ensued in many U.S. markets during the 1990s also allowed HMOs to hold back populations they did not wish to self-manage (e.g., where premium revenues are high, claim costs are low, and IBNR is predictably low). As capitated markets mature, the health plans eventually capitate all health insurance management relationships, eschewing many of the preferred provider organizations, exclusive provider organizations, and point-of-service plan organizations (see Chapter 2) that remain in a given market. The physician members of these provider organizations start seeing more capitated business and are transformed from primarily providers to primarily insurers, in juxtaposition to insurance-based providers transformed back to their core business. This core business is now collecting premiums and outsourcing care to capitated providers and practitioners.

As mentioned in this chapter, this capitation business model is not unlike a distributor who takes an administrative fee "off the top" of goods and services sold to those dealing with the larger public. Analogizing this simile to managed care, the HMO becomes a distributor, while hospitals and independent physicians become exclusive retailers of health care services. The business of hospital/physician retailers is a function of price and quality of service. The business of HMO distributors is a function of price, efficient service, and anticipating customer needs—not just price alone.

The bottom line is that the onus of managed care and legal compliance shifts from the HMO-distributor to the provider/practitioner-retailer. The provider/ practitioner is now at risk not only on price, but also on expensive claims and unmanaged IBNR. Increasingly, such providers and practitioners need to understand competitors to HMOs and to a capitated pricing methodology, all of which are covered in the remainder of this chapter. In addition, they must have a good grounding in the insurance industry operations (see Chapter 2) that they are increasingly entering through managed care relationships.

At the same time, relationships between HMOs and both providers and practitioner organizations are becoming strained. Effective services to keep members healthier and less in need of health care services compete with providers/practitioners contracted on a per unit consumption basis. HMOs went into managed care relationships with providers and practitioners because they were ill equipped to provide illness-based services to the majority of health care consumers who participate in that manner. In their contracts, HMOs introduced financial disincentives, first in case pricing and later via capitation, that were tied to the perpetuation of the illness model by participating providers and practitioners. The introduction of such financial disincentives was designed as an impetus for contracted providers and practitioners to conform to the wellness model, so that effective services are provided to keep members healthier and less in need of any health care services. This strategy of members keeping themselves, and their families, healthier is the basic strategy of HMOs and presupposes their philosophy of cost containment; in other words, costs will be reduced if members manage *themselves*, with the assistance of high-quality providers/practitioners.

The reality of managed care in America in the late 20th and early 21st centuries is almost the complete opposite of such an approach, with concerns about costs taking precedence over concerns about health. Indeed, rationing care for those who need it most (such as candidates for disease-based case management and for their at-risk children and siblings) is not only unconscionable but also evidences that the wellness model is not being upheld by contracted providers and practitioners. Managed care in an HMO organization is concerned about providing the minimum of health services needed to enhance wellness, not in spending much larger sums of money for their failure, such as when preventable trauma or foreseeable health deterioration requires expending provider/practitioner resources.

# 2 Understanding Managed Care Industry Operations

## INTRODUCTION TO THE INSURANCE INDUSTRY

The insurance industry differs fundamentally from the health care industry, especially with regard to managed care payers whose roots are in the insurance business. The health care industry is a world of providers and practitioners who provide services to their customers; these services are typically covered some 98% by insurance programs, whether of a commercial, governmental, or workers' compensation basis. Yet, few providers and practitioners truly understand the inherent nature of an industry for which almost all of their business derives.

The offering of insurance is tied to the probability of a loss occurring. A loss to an insurer is part of their accounts payable (A/P); the equivalence in the health care industry would be a valid accounts receivable (A/R) claim submitted to the insurer for payment as part of A/P. In other words, most health care A/R becomes A/P at the insurance payer level. Thus, a payer's natural inclination to reduce its expenses—even more so if the payer is publicly traded—directly results in reductions of health care provider/practitioner claims paid. In other words, insurers reducing A/P is experienced by health care providers/practitioners as higher deductions from revenue.

The following are examples of strategies health care providers/practitioners have taken in the past to reduce their own A/R by assisting the insurance industry in reducing their A/P:

- Transferring member-patients to care settings that are the least costly (e.g., less intensive) and most appropriate, thus reducing A/P by reducing A/R
- Contracting with payers for global, case-based, or front-loaded per-diem-based A/R to reduce insurance A/P by shifting and sharing risk

At the same time, the following are A/P reduction strategies geared to the A/R interests of providers/practitioners:

- Transforming variable-based contracting methodologies to fixed contracting methodologies

- Transforming fixed contracting methodologies to fully prospective or capitated A/P, thus ensuring a predictable level of profitability by shifting risk from payers to providers and practitioners
- Promising patient volumes to providers/practitioners in return for discounted pricing.
- Shifting contract payment distribution to more in-kind benefits and fewer monetary payments (see Chapter 10).

Reduction of insurance industry A/P can also include directly reducing volumes and intensities of provider/practitioner service when clinically appropriate to do so. One of the challenges of such reductions is to maintain or improve the quality of care while controlling resource consumption, a high determinant of cost reduction. It is important to note that the greatest reductions to be derived by payers from providers/practitioners lowering their consumption of health care resources is when they are given the autonomy to act responsibly—like the experts they are—rather than through micromanagement of poorly understood clinical practices that differ sharply from insurance practices.

While the following are examples of these service reductions, it should be noted that many payers will attempt to get out of the business of managing care by moving aggressively to fully prospective and capitated contracting methodologies.

- Make preventive or early care and wellness programs inexpensive or free to enrollees.
- Offer incentives to practitioners to use network providers when appropriate.
- Use precertification and incentives to reduce unnecessary or duplicate services in the interim that practitioners not only understand cost-versus-care trade-offs, but eventually go at risk for both price and enrollee health status management.
- Encourage the use of practitioner protocols (such as clinical pathways and clinical practice parameters) to establish measurable objectives in the appropriate diagnosis and treatment of medical conditions.
- Encourage the use of member lifestyle improvement contracts (LICs) to enable enrollees to improve health status through self-management incentives (see Chapter 5).
- Channel patients to providers that use fewer resources to achieve similar outcomes.
- Emphasize less-intensive or less-invasive techniques and technologies if medically or surgically appropriate.
- Incentivize providers to adopt clinical practice parameters that comply with both practitioner protocols and LICs to work together to improve value.

# UNDERSTANDING ERISA IMPLICATIONS FOR HMOS AND EMPLOYERS

The Employee Retirement Income Security Act of 1974, known more commonly as ERISA, is the legislation that governs health benefit plans of self-insured, self-funded employers in the United States. ERISA law encompasses all health benefit issues of a self-funded health insurance benefit plan, including the following:

- Health benefit plan design and all related insurance coverage,
- Competence of its administrators identified as providing plan management,
- Competence of providers/practitioners with whom it contracts,
- Grievance procedures for which covered employees and their allowed dependents might require to address its administration, and
- Responsibility for issues of professional liability.

In addition, ERISA law may preempt some state regulations. For example, ERISA preempts state laws about employee benefits but does not preempt laws regulating insurance. This apparent contradiction is still being worked out in the courts, while the laws continue to affect the administration of plan benefits. In some states, such as California and Illinois, health maintenance organizations (HMOs) can no longer hide behind ERISA law and can now be sued by their members.

Generally, patient issues fall into the general categories of responsibility for negligence and contractual responsibilities.

## RESPONSIBILITY FOR NEGLIGENCE UNDER ERISA

Judicial decisions indicate that a managed care organization (MCO) *may* be liable for the consequences of the medical management decisions and treatment authorizations it makes, as well as for the actions of network providers. Is ERISA applicable to a specific case? If it is, the MCO is not liable for damages for a member's injuries; if not, members are not bound by the limitations of ERISA on damages. This general applicability of ERISA has, so far, been unresolved by most courts and must be addressed on a case-by-case basis. Nevertheless, some states are now recognizing that ERISA can no longer be a shield behind which the lax or incompetent practitioner management of a health plan can always hide and are allowing members to litigate their insurers.

MCOs may be held responsible for adverse outcomes in several ways: administration of practice management, credentialing of network providers, and actions of employed staff/practitioners.

### Administration of Practice Management

A managed care plan may be liable if a defect in the design of its provider management program contributes to a reasonably foreseeable injury to an enrollee, even if the determination to deny a service is not challenged by the attending physician. The MCO must usually demonstrate that the decision was made in accord with documented internal procedures and generally accepted medical management practices, and that the MCO exercised reasonable care when making the determination. The result is that the utilization management programs of most MCOs are similar to establish an accepted and appropriate standard of care.

In another case, however, a court held that since an HMO cannot practice medicine, it cannot be held liable for medical negligence and must be held to ERISA standards. Yet, two other cases showed that an MCO may create the impression through its marketing materials that a physician is acting as an agent of the MCO and therefore may be liable for the physician's negligence.

## Credentialing of Network Providers

The MCO must exercise reasonable care in recruiting and supervising practitioners. For this reason, the National Commission on Quality Assurance (NCQA, the leading accreditation organization for MCOs, which is covered in more detail in Chapter 4) established accreditation standards for credential verification organizations (CVOs, directed mostly to MSOs, TPAs, and ASOs). A Missouri court found that an HMO created a foreseeable risk of harm for its members by not verifying specialty practitioner credentials.

Recent legal rulings held that hospitals that contract with unethical physicians who participate in improper criminal or civil behavior against managed care arrangements that accept federal funds (inclusive of Managed Medicaid, Medicare Risk, Medicare Part C, and Tricare/CHAMPUS [Civilian Health and Medical Program of the Uniformed Services]) are *themselves* liable for civil monetary penalties, incarceration, or exclusion from federally funded programs. This liability also extends to various hospital-specific, fraud and abuse, and antidiscrimination legislation if civil, criminal, administrative, or exclusionary penalties can also apply.

## Actions of Employed Staff/Practitioners

The MCO, like all organizations, is responsible for the actions of its employees, a legal theory known as *respondeat superior.* Staff model HMOs are thus liable for the actions of their employed physicians/staff, but the liabilities of HMOs with other models is not so clear. Despite the shield typically provided through ERISA, the independent contractor language in a typical contract could be adjudged to hold an HMO liable for a contracted physician. For example, the Kaiser HMO was liable for the malpractice of a network cardiologist because, the court held, Kaiser restricted members to a limited number of physicians, paid those physicians to perform services that the HMO was obligated to provide, and had some control over the physician's behavior—attributes of an employer/employee relationship.

## CONTRACTUAL LIABILITY ISSUES

Employers are increasingly searching for ways to avoid liability for the medical management decisions of contracting MCOs. Some groups require the MCO to indemnify or hold the group harmless against any medical management liabilities. Examples of such liabilities include

- MCOs not holding liabilities,
- Practitioners/providers liable for its own corporate malfeasance,
- Practitioners/providers holding the MCO liable for its own malpractice, and
- Providers/practitioners not asserting claims against enrollees for covered services—regardless of the payment or nonpayment of the MCO, including its insolvency.

This "hold-harmless" clause is often included in managed care contracts and is required by CMS for federally qualified HMOs (FQHMOs) and by most state regulatory agencies. The MCO is then liable for expenses and damages arising from any lawsuits.

If a plan is determined to be governed by ERISA, participants or beneficiaries can initiate civil actions to recover benefits due under the term of the plan, to enforce rights under the terms of the plan, or clarify rights to future benefits under the plan. The court may award reasonable attorney fees and costs but not compensatory or punitive damages.

## Unreasonable Benefit Determination

The administrator of the managed care plan is required to act as a fiduciary when making benefits determinations. This duty prohibits *arbitrary and capricious* behavior when making determinations, such as using undisclosed medical criteria that are more restrictive than those of other policies. Again, the courts look for *reasonable* behavior. Currently, legal fees and costs may be recovered by the member in these cases, but the scope of damages may be enlarged in future cases.

## Balance-Billing Violations of FQHMOs

Although few cases have arisen as a consequence of no-balance-billing clauses, typically part of contracts between CMS and FQHMOs, the possibility exists that an uncovered service provided may lead to a breach-of-contract suit brought by a provider against an MCO. If the dispute is held to be based on the benefit agreement itself, the case may be subject to ERISA; if it is based on the provider's contract, the case will usually be subject to the breach-of-contract laws of the respective state.

## INTRODUCTION TO MANAGED CARE UNDERWRITING

Managed care underwriting is the analysis and rating of a specific group or individual to determine the risk associated with enrolling it in a specific risk plan. Thus, the risk assessment is the primary factor in determining the premium rate for the group or individual based on risk experience. To spread underwriting risk, the managed care plan tries to enroll a broad cross-section of industries, ages, and geographical areas.

Underwriting affects the following areas of an MCO:

- Its financial performance,
- Its position and market penetration compared with competitors,
- Its ability to offer different premium rates to groups with different underwriting risks, and
- Its relationship with providers receiving capitated or risk-based payments.

An MCO needs to select risks that can be managed effectively and profitably (specific risk management and sharing techniques are covered in the following). The following factors affect underwriting decisions tied to selective risk: purchaser selection, benefit plan design, claims history, and role of MCO reinsurance.

## PURCHASER SELECTION

The methodology used to select potential purchasers, and the information considered adequate to provide a reasonably accurate price quote, are important for MCO underwriting. The criteria may include specific definitions of eligible groups (such as number of employees), and within those, qualitative or quantitative evaluations of eligible employees and dependents. Underwriting may set minimum participation requirements and maximum rate and benefit differentials, typically applied during open enrollment solicitations. Underwriting may also involve limiting coverage and effective dates, as can occur with preexisting conditions not in contravening of managed care compliance laws. Any or all of these factors can serve as selection techniques.

## BENEFIT PLAN DESIGN

The design of plan benefits is crucial to the underwriting process. For one thing, underwriting risk tends to be inversely proportional to both generous benefits and loose provider/practitioner control. An example of this inverse relationship is that high-risk groups and individuals tend to be attracted to plans with rich levels of benefits or a loosely controlled provider/practitioner network (such as through the typically open access inherent in PPO [preferred provider organization] panels). Conversely, strong utilization management will likely be a selection deterrent to those who would otherwise tend to consume high levels of care, such as victims of high-acuity chronic diseases.

## CLAIMS HISTORY

Historically, small groups that lack a sufficient claims history to make reliable inferences usually did not pass the underwriting process as readily as large employer groups. In addition, small employers with relatively higher employee sizes (such as 15 to 50, 50–100, etc.) were more likely to meet the underwriting need for sufficient claims history if one or more of the factors listed were also met. For example, a "larger" small employer opting for only a capitated, gatekeeper-directed product was more likely to satisfy the claims history factor of underwriting than a similar group opting for EPO (exclusive provider organization) or specialist self-referral within its benefit plan design.

The sufficiency of the volume of claims history may no longer be as critical a factor in the underwriting process as it once was. Most states have passed small-group reform that usually requires adjusted community rating (ACR) or excludes medical underwriting of small groups.

Large groups are usually underwritten on the basis of their history with other health plans, their financial stability, and certain participation requirements. Members of large groups, such as employees and dependents of large employers, are rarely denied coverage. HMO applicants for reinsurance are also partially underwritten on the basis of their history with other reinsurers.

## ROLE OF MCO REINSURANCE

As mentioned briefly in Chapter 1, reinsurance (e.g., excess liability risk) seeks to limit a policyholder's liability for grossly mismanaged or catastrophic claims. Depending on the mix of per member, per month (PMPM) price and stop loss to assume, some provider-/practitioner-based MCOs or MSOs may choose to purchase their own reinsurance policies, even though policies, if attainable, are much more expensive than if purchased by an HMO. Just as claims history is an important component for employers to be underwritten for managed care insurance, it is important for HMOs as well. To determine an experience rating (discussed in the rating methodologies section), typically 5 years (which is variable by reinsurer) of claims history by the HMO is required. Types of reinsurance that payers maintain include the following: aggregate reinsurance and individual reinsurance.

### Aggregate Reinsurance

Aggregate reinsurance covers claims above an underwriting threshold, particularly for a specific geography or customer (e.g., employer). The policy combines (aggregates) all claims of the same type (however defined) and indemnifies the policyholder when the aggregate value of them exceeds a specific dollar threshold. Aggregate reinsurance is a type of policy that provider-/practitioner-based MCOs will seek to receive coverage from HMOs because of the high cost for noninsurers.

### Individual Reinsurance

Individual reinsurance is similar to aggregate in its attractiveness to HMOs and provider-/practitioner-based MCOs. Individual reinsurance also applies to all claims of a particular type above a threshold, but the threshold is the difference between an underwriting threshold and the specific stop loss level selected by the providers/practitioners. The type of claimant in individual reinsurance is typically an individual policyholder, but might include employees and their covered dependents as constituting single families for which such reinsurance applies.

## INTRODUCTION TO COMMERCIALLY INSURED POPULATIONS

A *commercially insured population* refers to a specific level of managed care risk called *commercial risk*. This product is the traditional, family-type product sold by MCOs and exists in differentiation from governmental risk products that are not tied to sales volume. Two volume factors of commercial risk populations tend to affect MCO profitability from among all risk products: the "50–50 Rule" and control of commercial risk populations.

### THE "50–50 RULE"

Prior to the enactment of Part C Medicare and Part D Medicare Advantage, which came later, the Medicare risk governmental capitation product imposed on a commercial risk volume restriction was known as the "50–50 Rule". The rule required that the volume of Medicare risk-covered lives must be equal to, or less than, the volume of commercially insured population. The higher the volume of commercial risk-covered lives, the higher the volume of Medicare risk policies that can subsequently be sold. During the time that Medicare risk (Part C) premiums were tied to the average adjusted per capita cost (AAPCC) rates of the Medicare program, and not to actuarial risk or market-based prices, substantial MCO profitability was possible, sometimes with relatively minor adjustments to provider/practitioner risk contracts.

The purpose of the "50–50 Rule" is similar to a concept covered further in the chapter known as "risk banding": a strategy to ensure that providers are sufficiently capitalized for less-risky business to be indemnified for more risky business models. For the Medicare program, the purpose of the "50–50 Rule" was to ensure sufficient capitalization of provider risk pools to fund acceptable health care services for Medicare beneficiaries. Yet, this rule was predicated based on earlier studies that preceded our current managed care markets. These studies calculated that health care consumption of Medicare beneficiaries is eight times the consumption of non-Medicare patients. Sufficient risk pool capitalization (typically around 20% of fee-for-service [FFS]-based AAPCC rates) was also required by the Medicare program in selecting HMOs for participation in Medicare Risk contracts (in addition to the "50–50 Rule"), in large part based on this excess consumption theory.

One area that recognizes this change occurred when the Centers for Medicare and Medicaid Services (CMS; then HCFA) enacted Medicare Part C, which established so-called Medicare+Choice (M+C) organizations. Under M+C, Medicare HMOs and provider-sponsored organizations (PSOs such as Medicare Supplement Plans) were no longer required to comply with the "50–50 Rule," and the minimum risk pool capitalization requirement was also lowered.

In addition, regional differences in Medicare costs reported, which were influential in calculating AAPCCs, were minimized, and the minimum AAPCC rate was increased across the board. While actual Medicare Part C rates were lower than CMS promised, covered PSO populations had greater lock-in to their practitioners, given that the opportunity to disenroll with a previously chosen independent practice association (IPA) or independent medical group (IMG) is now allowed during a single open-enrollment period. This once-per-year lock-in provision differs from Medicare risk relationships that lock in for a minimum of only 30 days.

## CONTROL OF COMMERCIAL RISK POPULATIONS

MCOs historically underappreciate a commercial population's level of responsibility in improving their health status. The underwriting process presumes that commercial populations are like sheep: They are incapable of managing their own health needs, they will not be able to help themselves in accessing care—especially care that is insensitive to underwriting concerns—and will simply go wherever the shepherd directs them. Unlike other insurance products that tie premiums to past mistakes and lifestyle preferences (such as life insurance for obese smokers, automobile insurance for drivers with a history of driving under the influence/driving while intoxicated [DUI/DWI] violations, and affordable earthquake insurance anywhere inside the state of California), health insurance has previously not been tied to lifestyles of commercial populations. With Health Reform in 2011 and Health Exchanges planned for 2014, it has never been more important for payers to hold populations more accountable for their unhealthy lifestyles, their consumption of lower-cost services, and in enrollees taking more responsibility for their own health status and that of their family's. Yet, this presumption defies the way commercial populations historically access health care, long before any commercial risk underwriting began.

The reality of commercial populations' habits in accessing health care lies in health care being a "negative want." The belief by underwriters that availability of unrestricted health care, in and of itself, will make commercial populations unable to resist consuming care, by comparison, presumes that it is a "positive want." It is for this reason that the gatekeeper concept arose and was a dominant feature of commercial health plans in the 20th century. However, 21st century approaches are evaluating the success of "gatekeeper-less" plans and intranetwork self-referral options limited only by slightly higher copayments.

Yet, consumer preference studies have shown repeatedly that children or employees *choose* to go to the doctor only because they are not restricted from doing so. In reality, children "kick and scream" to avoid going to the doctor, and employees are reluctant to take personal leave time to see a physician unless they *need* care. Both of these situations suggest that access to practitioners is important when *the member* decides that it is needed, not simply because it exists. In other words, most people do not choose to start their morning with a colonoscopy simply because they can have unrestricted access to one.

At an even deeper level, practitioners and providers often presume that most members are incompetent about their health. In some respects, member responsibility recognizes that practitioners have historically had a poor track record in influencing behavior: the obese to diet, smokers to quit, and alcoholics to abstain. These lifestyle changes, which most any underwriter will readily espouse, require modifying lifestyle behaviors. Yet, modifying behavior is better accomplished with incentives for practicing the right behavior rather than disincentives for continuing the wrong behavior. Few practitioners apply this vision, as do even fewer MCOs.

This presumption of member incompetence goes to the heart of the nature of managed care. The goal of managed care is for members to take responsibility for their own, and their family's, health status. (This transformation is described in greater detail in Chapter 5.) This goal presumes that a member does not want to be in a doctor's office, regardless of copays and access restrictions that an MCO might impose based on the mistaken belief that health care is a "positive want."

## UNDERSTANDING RATING METHODOLOGIES: COMMUNITY VERSUS EXPERIENCE

The determination of the premium amount begins with the underwriting function described. In this section, information on the specific covered group—age and sex mix, industry type, employer contribution to the cost, competition, and so on—are considered using the underwriting guidelines of each HMO. If a target group "passes" the underwriting process, the rates for coverage are calculated. There are two basic methodologies: *community rating* and *experience rating*. Before selling HMO coverage, it is important to know the Department of Insurance rules of a particular state for rating differentiation among groups and for obtaining approval of new products before marketing them.

Ratings represent a reasonable calculation of future losses. Since ratings are future based, the accurate prediction of claims requires real-world situations, such as presuming that operating costs will increase. Ideally, future predictions of claims should be based on a minimum 3-year history of costs and can be predicted using a variety of regression methodologies, such as linear, multivariable, or even a simple regression. For purposes of this chapter, examples of rating methodologies use three historical years, and predictions are based on a simple ("straight-line") progression methodology.

### COMMUNITY RATINGS

Community ratings involve calculating a quoted rate based on a correlation of specific group attributes. These attribute correlations, through various procedures depicted in the following, serve to stratify the estimated risk of the population being rated. The specific stratification, taken together through formulas, results in a specific rate quote.

### Basic Community Ratings

*Basic community ratings* apply a standard rate to all groups within the community of risk being underwritten. The rating is based on the expected level of

---

**TABLE 2.1**

**Common Basic Community Rating Tier Structures**

| Tier Structure/Contract Type | | Covered |
|---|---|---|
| Single-rate composite | | Employee and all eligible dependents |
| Two-tier structure | 1 | Employee only |
| | 2 | Employee plus all eligible dependents |
| Three-tier structure | 1 | Employee only |
| | 2 | Employee plus one dependent |
| | 3 | Employee plus two or more dependents |
| Four-tier structure | 1 | Employee only |
| | 2 | Employee plus spouse |
| | 3 | Employee plus dependent children |
| | 4 | Employee plus spouse and dependent children |

---

benefit utilization of the community as a whole, not on the expected level of utilization of a specific group, according to the following procedure:

Step 1: A base revenue per enrollee requirement is calculated to determine the amount that will be needed to pay the medical and administrative expenses expected and provide a profit for the HMO.

Step 2: The revenue requirement is applied to the specific group based on the average family size, assumed contract mix, and the number of "rating tiers" quoted for the group. *Rating tiers* refer to the different rates charged based on the number and relationships of the people covered under one employee's plan, for example, single, couple, family, and so on. Most plans utilize a two- or three-tier rating. An example of a typical tiered rating coverage structure for base community ratings is shown in Table 2.1.

Using tiers effectively requires that health plans determine

- The approximate medical costs of adults and children (the medical cost standard of a child is about 45% of the medical cost of an adult);
- Average family size of the group, which may be based on the actual size of families in the employer group (if this information is available), on local demographics, or on local data from other HMOs; and
- The average number of enrollees per tier per employer (note: under the federal definition of community rating, the tier mix for an employer can be used in setting that employer's premiums).

The cost multiplier for the various tiers must also be established. In a three-tier contract, two-person and family (employee plus two or more) premiums are defined as the single premium times a multiplier, which reflects the cost differential between single and multiple coverage.

**TABLE 2.2**

**Using Basic Community Rating Tiers to Determine Premiums**

| Tier | % in Tier | Population-Based Weighting | Product: % in Tier × Weighting | Cost-Based Weighting | Product: % in Tier × Weighting |
|---|---|---|---|---|---|
| 1: Single | 25 | 1 | 25 | 1 | 25 |
| 2: Two person | 40 | 2 | 80 | 2 | 80 |
| 3: Family | 35 | 4.1 (× size) | 143.5 | 3 | 105 |
| | 100 | | 248.5 | | 210 |

Conversion Factor (Group Population:Cost) = Population Weight ÷ Cost Weight (248.5 ÷ $210) = 1.1833
Plan PMPM Revenue Target = $100
Single Premium = $100 × 1.1833 = $118.33
Two-Person Premium = $118.33 × 2 = 236.67
Family Premium = $118.33 × 3 = $355.00

Table 2.2 shows a simplified example of how basic community rating tiers can be used to calculate premiums. An HMO typically estimates that 25% of its enrollees will have single coverage, 40% will have two-person coverage, and 35% will have family coverage. Size of a "family" is typically estimated to be 4.1 people. The HMO assumes that care of two people (which may include one adult and one child or two adults) will cost twice a single person's cost. However, the family of 4.1 people will cost only three times what one adult costs because of the lower cost of children's care. Multiplying the percentage in each tier by the number of people actually estimated to be covered and dividing that by the percentage times the cost factor produces a premium.

Table 2.2 also demonstrates a weighting factor called a *conversion factor*, which is a ratio of the nature of a population weighted relative to its cost. The conversion factor times the cost PMPM yields a single premium amount, which is then weighted by coverage to produce premiums for the other tiers.

## Community Ratings by Class

The community rating by class (CRC) is a commonly used variation on basic community rating that differs from the previous procedure by adjusting "Step 1" of the basic community rating according to the specific demographics of the group or employer's industry classification (e.g., specific industry classification [SIC] codes).

In 1981, the federal government allowed FQHMOs to use the CRC methodology, which is still used today in many FQHMOs. CRC considers the unique risk characteristics of the group, compared to average risks, when establishing rates. The purpose is to align the rates more closely with the risks. Note that the actual experience of the group is not used but rather the inherent risk characteristics associated with it. Commonly used risk characteristics are age, sex, marital

**TABLE 2.3**

**Community Rating by Class: Commercial Risk Example**

| | Men | | | | Women | | |
|---|---|---|---|---|---|---|---|
| Standard Age Groups | Number in Age Group | Standard Cost Factor ($) | Number × Cost Factor | Standard Age Groups | Number in Age Group | Standard Cost Factor | Number × Cost Factor |
| Under 20 | 89 | **$0.600** | $53.40 | Under 20 | 55 | **$0.600** | $33.00 |
| 20–29 | 116 | **$0.500** | $58.00 | 20–29 | 98 | **$1.400** | $137.20 |
| 30–39 | 95 | **$0.600** | $57.00 | 30–39 | 110 | **$1.350** | $148.50 |
| 40–49 | 124 | **$0.900** | $111.60 | 40–49 | 150 | **$1.200** | $180.00 |
| 50–59 | 137 | **$1.600** | $219.20 | 50–59 | 117 | **$1.400** | $163.80 |
| 60–64 | 34 | **$2.100** | $71.40 | 60–64 | 62 | **$1.900** | $117.80 |
| Totals | 595 | | $570.60 | Totals | 592 | | $780.30 |

Total Cost Factor = Total Group Costs ($570.60 + $780.30) ÷ Total Group Members (595 + 592) = 1.138

Plan PMPM Revenue Target = $100

Projected Monthly Cost per Contract = $100 × 1.138 = $113.80

(Note that Projected CRC-Based Cost PMPM Exceeds Revenue Target)

status, and type of industry, although others, such as whether or not smoking is permitted inside the place of business, can be used.

Each risk characteristic is translated into a set numerical coefficient that weights the increased or decreased risk associated with it. The group is stratified by risk characteristics, and the factors are used to adjust the rates to meet revenue projections. **(It is extremely important to note that using CRC presupposes that these actuarial data are not only available but <u>also are accurate</u>.)** The average cost factor for the prediction of claims for a community (in effects its rating) is measured as a "cost per contract." A cost per contract divides total predicted community costs by the total number of community members.

A simplified, commercial risk example is shown in Table 2.3 using standard insurance industry age and sex factors for single members. For example, single men between 30 and 40, being relatively healthy, are assigned a cost factor of 0.6. In this case, there are 95 of them in that group; when multiplied against the PMPM revenue target of $100, the projected liability for this group of men would be $5,700. Women between the ages of 30 and 40, however, have a cost factor of 1.35 because of their higher utilization of maternity benefits. In this case, the 110 group members multiplied against the $100 target projects a liability for this group of women of $14,850. The total cost per contract for this community (with a $100 PMPM revenue target) would be $113.80, which indicates that the PMPM revenue target of $100 is too low. If the $100 PMPM target can vary by no more than 10%, for example, $113.80 would be too high; as an alternative strategy, the cost-per-contract factor can be

## TABLE 2.4
## Community Rating by Class Formula

[(A Segment Members × A Factor) + (B Segment Members × B Factor)] × PMPM Revenue Target =
  Projected Monthly Cost per Contract

**WHERE:**

**A Segment = Men by Age Grouping**

**B Segment = Women by Age Grouping**

reduced to 1.06 if the community excludes 60- to 64-year-olds. Table 2.4 illustrates this example in equation form. (For Medicare risk models, the standard cost factors for men and women over the age of 64 are 2.20 and 2.80, respectively.)

### EXPERIENCE RATING METHODOLOGIES

With experience rating, the other common rating methodology, the rate of the group is based wholly or partially on the medical claims experience of that group. The increase in costs for the contract period is projected using a trend factor. Obviously, actual experience statistics—claims expense data—are necessary for experience rating and are difficult to obtain for groups with which the HMO has had limited experience. In some states, the amount of increase in premiums is limited to prevent buying new accounts and then dramatically increasing premiums.

An experience rating is a multivariate progression model, as the actual experiences with claims, costs, and utilization of the group become the prediction variables. Experience rating can produce more competitive rates (see "Contracting: Part 2 discussion within Chapter 10) and can reduce the variability in profits from group to group. However, there are some cautions to keep in mind: Experience rating requires up-to-date and accurate data, it takes time and expertise to administer, it is not appropriate for all groups, and it may involve divulging certain proprietary data to the purchaser, to which the MCO might object.

An experience rating is based on the assumption that the behavior of a group in the past is an accurate predictor of its behavior in the future. Answer these questions in considering any experience rating:

- How many years of trend history can be analyzed?
- How large is the employer group (the larger the group, the more credible the data)?
- What portion of the group is enrolled in this one plan?
- Have large, unexpected claims skewed the data (a measurement of kurtosis) and distorted the experience of the group?
- How stable is the group? Minimal changes in enrollment and benefits from year to year make for more reliable data.

Usually, many years of experience are used for projections, although the most recent years carry the most credibility. Large claims may be removed from

**TABLE 2.5**

**Experience Rating Example Optimally (Based on 3 Years of Data)**

|  | Year 3 (12 Mo.) | Year 2 (12 Mo.) | Year 1 (12 Mo.) |
|---|---|---|---|
| Paid claims PMPM | $78 | $65 | $52 |
| Incurred claims PMPM | $95 | $79 | $63 |
| Pooling charge PMPM | $9 | $8 | $7 |
| Pooled claims | ($17) | ($10) | ($3) |
| Actual claims | $87 | $77 | $67 |
| Plan average | $90 | $75 | $60 |
| Experience ratio | 0.97 | 1.03 | 1.12 |
| Credibility factor of PrevYr | **90%** | **10%** | |

Plan PMPM Revenue Target = $100 (includes markup)
Rate = $100 × [(0.97 × 0.90) + (1.03 × 0.10)] = $97.60
*Note:* All amounts rounded.

consideration to minimize their impact on the data, but in those cases, the large-dollar claims are replaced with a "pooling charge" that represents the average large claims costs for the plan. This pooling charge is then charged to all groups to ensure that premium revenues will cover their potential charges.

In the science of probability, the reliability of a prediction is measured by its coefficient of variance. In creating ratings, the coefficient of variance is known as a "credibility factor." The insurance industry standard for credibility factors is to assume 90% reliability in using the costs of the immediately prior 12 months and 10% for previous cost experience. The cost-per-contract factor multiplies the projected experience ratio of plan actual costs to plan average costs by the respective credibility ratio of the cost prediction reliability of the previous year.

A simplified example of how experience rating works is demonstrated in Table 2.5. The example provided in Table 2.5 also shows another characteristic of experience: incurred-but-not-paid (IBNP) claims. Since all paid claims are reported, IBNP claims can be used to approximate Incurred-But-Not-Reported (IBNR) claims, which reflect the potential for overaccruals, in that accrued liabilities for authorized care by providers/practitioners will not be fully reported to the health plan.

IBNR's effect on health plan financial management is if the debit can't be credited against actual care provided (to ensure that care provided will not exceed its accurals for authorized expenses). In this example, IBNR varies from $11PMPM in Year 1 to $17 PMPM by Year 3, predicated primarily on poor provider compliance with encounter reporting. Based on a $100 PMPM revenue target, all of the projected revenue markup for the plan will likely be consumed by IBNR liabilities. For this reason, IBNR management (or shifting IBNR risk to integrated delivery networks [IDNs] or management service organizations [MSOs]) is crucial for keeping reported claims as close as possible to incurred claims.

Rates must be quoted before the contract is signed and members enrolled—or, in general, some 3 to 4 months before the effective date of the plan (8 months for some government agencies). Since rates are normally guaranteed for 1 year, these rates will be, practically speaking, in effect for 16 to 18 months. Clearly, the underwriting function and the budgeting function must be working hand in hand to ensure accurate trend projections in medical care expenses.

### Experience-Based Community Ratings

One common experienced-based community rating is called the ACR, also called a group-specific community rating, and is similar to the CRC. ACR is a hybrid of both community rating and experience rating. It can be calculated two different ways. One is by using the experience ratios and credibility factors used in experience rating, along with the cost-per-claim factor developed in CRC, in the equation shown in Table 2.6. The other version of ACR is based on utilization data, with an example shown in Table 2.7. The utilization data show HMO industry standards of how cost experiences are weighted to derive an experience ratio. The standard is that ambulatory services (office visits) will reflect 50% of the cost, inpatient services 40%, and prescription services (which are driven by either hospitalization or outpatient care) only 10% of the total cost experience in any single year. In this example, the ACR-based rate is near 20% higher than the target PMPM rate, meaning that the target needs to be increased by 19.7% just to break even for the group's contract.

## UNDERSTANDING AND PREDICTING MEDICAL LOSSES

Health insurers dependent on minimal or stable medical loss ratios (MLRs) have largely been unable to predict reported medical losses (e.g., claims) and accrued medical losses, such as IBNR claims, reliably. Addressing static or decreasing MLR by managing claims (reducing the numerator of the ratio—the dollar effect of all medical losses) is problematic.

Managing claims to impact MLR is problematic because the nature of provider/practitioner operations is poorly understood by most insurers. For example, insurers are typically unable to reserve losses accurately, in part, due to provider and practitioner lags in submitting claims that create IBNR. Another reason is that the preauthorization through gatekeepers can be medically unresponsive to

---

**TABLE 2.6**

**Adjusted Community Rating Formula**

PMPM Revenue Target × {(Credibility Factor + Experience Factor) + [(1 − Credibility Factor) × CRC Factor]} = **ACR-Based Contract Rate**

---

**TABLE 2.7**

**Adjusted Community Rating Example**

| | Estimated Future Year | Current Year | Past Year |
|---|---|---|---|
| **Inpatient Days per Month** | | | |
| Group inpatient days | 335 | 345 | 355 |
| Plan mean inpatient days | 315 | 320 | 325 |
| Ratio (group days to plan mean) | 1.07 | 1.08 | 1.09 |
| HMO industry standard weighting | 40% | 40% | 40% |
| **Office Visits per Month** | | | |
| Group office visits | 3,350 | 3,225 | 3,100 |
| Plan mean office visits | 3,000 | 3,000 | 3,000 |
| Ratio (group visits to plan mean) | 1.13 | 1.08 | 1.03 |
| HMO industry standard weighting | 50% | 50% | 50% |
| **Prescriptions per Month** | | | |
| Group prescriptions | 4,800 | 4,900 | 5,000 |
| Plan mean prescriptions | 4,900 | 4,800 | 4,700 |
| Ratio (group scrip divided by plan mean) | 0.98 | 1.02 | 1.06 |
| HMO industry standard weighting | 10% | 10% | 10% |
| Average ratio | 1.09 | 1.06 | 1.06 |
| Credibility factor of previous year | **90%** | **10%** | |

Plan PMPM Revenue Target = $100

ACR-Based Contract Rate = $100 \times [(1.09 \times 0.90) + (1.06 \times 0.10)] = \$119.70$

acute, chronic, or catastrophically ill members; such service lags increase the risk of member dissatisfaction and potential litigation. For these reasons, the dollar effect of medical losses has been difficult for insurers to manage to reduce the numerator of the MLR ratio.

Consequently, the HMO insurers have focused much of their energy on the other way to decrease the MLR: increase the denominator by adding more premium-paying members to offset increases or unpredictable behavior of losses occurring (or accrued to be occurring). The game plan HMOs devised actually grabbed the headlines through much of the 1990s:

1. Acquire more HMOs, the bigger the better;
2. Use aggressive marketing tactics to enroll more medium- and large-size employers whose employees could become premium-paying members;

3. Diversify into other products for which MLR is more stable, with the denominator representing a combination of stable and relatively unstable risk; and
4. Use image advertising to get increasingly larger groups of employees during "open enrollment" periods (typically in autumn) to switch to its HMO product.

This mathematical relationship helps to explain why care costs entered into health care contracting discussions. It also explains what actually happened when there were no more HMOs to acquire. Starting during 1997 and 1998 open enrollments, HMOs raised premium prices (thereby increasing the denominator of the MLR equation), but in so doing, HMOs became targets during the first decade of the new millennium, resulting in specific restrictions to such practices (including MLR minimums on 2010's PPACA. At the same time, HMOs inappropriately started complaining to DHHS that Medicare rates were too low even though Medicare Past C established capitated pricing (which normalized regional variances of AAPCC rates) to CMS that the price paid to them through AAPCC rates was insufficient. The common scenario is that many MSOs and HMOs began to leave the health care industry, leaving nonpayer MCOs to manage care that no one else had been able to manage effectively.

## INTRODUCTION TO ACTUARIAL MATHEMATICS

Actuarial mathematics involves calculating the minimum premium price that an MCO can offer that suitably addresses all known risk factors. The ratings and tiered pricing previously discussed are important in these calculations. A key aspect of actuarial mathematics involves estimating the probabilities of a loss occurring and estimating known costs associated with those losses.

Analyzing cost data is one part of an actuarial analysis. An actuarial cost model incorporates utilization, cost per unit, and claims cost assumptions. These data can make it possible to compare two completely different plans to show their relative cost effectiveness.

One approach is to summarize competing plans in terms of a single plan (benefit design), preferably a typical one. The values of copayments, deductibles, and benefit limitations are calculated and added back to the cost of the plan to determine a total cost for comparison purposes. Efficiency is also measured by actuarially based costs to show comparative value based on rates.

Cost data are also extensively used in actuarial analysis when an MCO is developing new products. For example, let us assume that CarePlus HMO is planning to develop a product for a new market segment based on a specific SIC code.

The actuary cannot use conventional approaches to estimate the anticipated utilization and cost but must consider when, where, and why the services will be used. Thus, the targeted market must be segmented into those that will use the managed care plan all of the time, most of the time, some of the time, and never.

---

**TABLE 2.8**
**Sources of HMO Revenue**

✓    Premiums
✓    Recovery of insurance benefits
✓    Coordination of benefits

Adminisrative fees charged in provider network contracts.

---

Within these categories are differing demographic distributions: different ages and sexes, people with varying health statuses, and families of varying sizes. Demographic characteristics are key indicators of actual utilization and cost, so cost projections will vary with different demographic groups. Of course, the competition will affect enrollment as well.

Pricing models for proposed services can be developed, similar to the cost analyses previously presented, given certain assumptions.

## PREMIUM AND PRODUCT ISSUES

Premium is one of the traditional revenue sources of HMOs (see Table 2.8). Premium is the end result of the actuarial process that, through underwriting, determines the per-plan-pricing by tier to offer to the customers of the MCO.

### PAYER PREMIUM REVENUES

Premiums, the amount paid by a purchaser in exchange for the provision and administration of medical benefits, represent the predominant revenue source of an MCO. Again, premiums are established and paid in advance of the period for which health care services are to be provided or accrued and generally cannot be changed during the contract period. Premiums are paid regardless of whether any actual or accrued services are provided.

Premiums are reported as revenue in the month in which the covered members are entitled to (or accrued to) receive health care services. Premiums collected in advance are reported as deferred income. Incremental premium revenue sources include cost increases charged to current customers as well as developing, marketing, and selling new premium products, or add-on benefits of existing products, to both current and new customers.

### PAYER NONOPERATING REVENUE SOURCES

Interest income from cash and investments can provide another source of revenue. Since premiums are billed and collected in advance of services, and contracts with providers generally allow a reasonable period for payment of claims

(30 days), interest income can be substantial if premiums are collected promptly. Interest and investment income are recorded as revenue.

## EMPLOYER BENEFIT PLAN DESIGN

Managed care plans are ultimately designed to meet consumer demand for health care value that is a balance of price, access, choice, and cost. Plans control costs through utilization management, select networks of providers, negotiated prices, risk sharing and incentive compensation, and benefit plan designs that direct beneficiaries to use their provider network.

Designing the benefit plans to be offered to members must leverage the provider network of the plan in such a way that it meets the consumers' (members') demand for a wide range of covered services at a market competitive price. Many health plans accomplish this range of price per range of features by establishing a single core benefit plan that typically includes hospitalization, primary care services, specialty physician services, and lab work. Certain benefits are mandated to be included in a comprehensive plan design by federal or state governments (e.g., coverage for mammography, minimum maternity length of stay). Health plans then offer additional benefits through policy riders that are purchased as an "add-on" benefit as specified in the employer group contract (Table 2.9).

Add-on premium products are also offered, especially for managed Medicare clients. These aftermarket products for Medicare clients might require monthly premium payments (or as additional copayments imposed under certain Medicare Advantage plans or supplement), especially for zero-copayment options, additional prescription drug coverage, access to clinical pharmacology services to help manage pharmaceutical use, PPO-type panels for dentists, and negotiated discounted fee-for-service (DFFS) pricing for alternative medicine providers (e.g., acupuncturists) and community wellness resources (e.g., fitness centers). Many employers and a growing number of health plans include cash rebates for measurable lifestyle improvements attained as well as enrollee-risk-based products tying more generous coverage to compliance with personalized health status improvement objectives.

### TABLE 2.9
### Common MCO Premium-Based Riders

- Mental health
- Chemical dependency
- Pharmacy
- Vision
- Dental
- Infertility

## COST-SHARING IMPACTS ON PRODUCT DESIGN

MCOs design benefit plans to encourage members to alter their behavior in using and accessing health care services. First, health plans seek to shift members' patterns of accessing primary health care services from an "as needed" basis (illness model) to preventive care (wellness model). The motivation for the MCO to help enrollees progress to the wellness model is clear: Acute care is far more expensive than primary care services. In addition, acute care carries less "bang for the buck" since it is episodic in nature and less geared to enhancing long-term health status.

Second, health plans seek to prevent members from accessing services the member does not need. Although cost saving is sought, the primary driver of this is the quality of care to the member. Everyone has heard of patients who underwent a hysterectomy on the advice of a physician when an alternate, less-invasive (and less-costly) procedure may have been available. Unfortunately, there are also some health plans that incorrectly deny services to members in the pursuit of profits.

The gatekeeper model, coupled with cost-sharing mechanisms, help to accomplish the shift in member health care decisions. Health plans design benefit plans to include various cost-sharing mechanisms to influence the members' decisions regarding if, when, where, and how to seek medical care. Examples of cost-sharing mechanisms include the following: deductible mechanisms, share-of-cost payments, out-of-pocket maximums, and incentives and disincentives.

### Deductible Mechanisms

Deductibles are flat dollar amounts, generally $100 and up, paid by the enrollee before benefits are paid or for reaching a certain level of risk at which deductibles are imposed before care is covered (such as "prescription doughnut holes" prevalent in Medicare Part D and most commercial plans in which a "health fund" is established for the lowest level of risk before prescription drugs are again covered). The financial effect of a deductible is literally that: to establish a fee mechanism deducted from the covered charges. Other cost sharing is calculated after the deductible has been met. A range of deductibles might exist for tiered products. Using the typical two-tier premium-pricing model, for example, a DFFS-based premium product (such as PPO-type panels of dentists instead of negotiated discounts of 20% off any dentist's billed charges) might have separate deductibles per covered individual and per family.

Some deductibles are set "per confinement," which means that a flat dollar amount is paid by the enrollee for each hospital admission, including ambulatory surgery.

### Share-of-Cost Payments

Coinsurance is one type of share-of-cost payment. Coinsurance is the percentage of covered charges paid by a DFFS-based benefit plan, such as indemnity, PPO, and some allied health practitioner (AHP) products. Coinsurance typically ranges from 70% to 80%. Remaining charges are paid by the individual, up to a specified maximum.

Copayment, a different share-of-cost structure, is typically a minimal share-of-cost feature typical of exclusive provider organization (EPO), point of service (POS), and HMO products. Copayments are typically fixed dollar amounts paid directly to the practitioner at place of service. In commercial risk products, copayments of $10 to $15 are typical and apply to covered pharmaceuticals as well. As far as pharmaceuticals, most all MCOs today drive more copayment revenues to contracted vendors by limiting prescriptions to 30-day supplies (each refill means another copayment) and limiting practitioners to six refills per "scrip" (each scrip typically requiring another office visit and hence another copayment).

For managed Medicare products (Medicare Parts C and D), for which consumer preferences are tied to capitation rates, copayments for pharmaceuticals and office visits typically range from $10 to $15 (with $0 copayments available on add-on premium products). Most Medicare Advantage plans establish a $50 (or higher) mandatory copay for emergency room (ER) visits that do not result in inpatient admissions.

Percent of pay is a third share-of-cost structure in which employees' out-of-pocket costs (such as for add-on premium contribution, deductible, coinsurance, or out-of-pocket maximums) are fixed as percentages of a respective employee's salary. This structure ensures that total out-of-pocket expenses will never deviate from a set percentage of an employee's salary.

## Out-of-Pocket Maximums

An out-of-pocket maximum is the dollar limit (usually in the thousands of dollars) set on the total amount of covered charges that will be paid by the beneficiary. Generally, after a certain total has been reached, cost sharing ends, and the services are covered at 100%. The utility of this mix between out-of-pocket maximum costs and shifted responsibility above the maximum has to do with stop-loss and reinsurance, covered in greater depth further in this chapter.

By comparison, coverage maximums may have different annual or lifetime maxima. These longer-term maximums impose a fixed limit on the benefits paid over a 12-month or lifetime period. For example, many long-term care insurance plans (which are typically add-on Medicare products) assume liability only after Medicare's 100-day lifetime maximum benefit has been exhausted. In addition, dental and mental health benefits are frequently capped on the basis of annual or lifetime coverage.

## Incentives and Disincentives

Financial disincentives to enrollees are important aspects of cost-sharing relationships that are critical to premium setting as part of the actuarial interest in ensuring that losses will not be generated that are inappropriate to assumed medical loss predictions. One enrollee disincentive is a penalty provision that reduces benefits when key plan safeguards are ignored. Examples of such violations include required second opinions and preauthorizations.

Financial incentives represent the opposite structure. Incentives are perhaps more critical than disincentives since they are instruments of positive change in the cost-sharing behavior of enrollees. Incentives increase benefits for correct behavior, such as preadmission testing, health status improvements, or complying with childhood immunization schedules.

Health plans must use caution in structuring cost-sharing mechanisms such as setting coinsurance or deductible levels. Plan designs that push too much claim liability back onto the members will not sell well in the marketplace, but too little economic responsibility on the part of the members will not yield the institution the proper care-setting goals that are important to the health plan. In addition, cost-sharing mechanisms that are highly complex may not be well understood by the members, which can adversely affect profitability, public relations, and member retention.

## Health Plan Enrollment

Once the employer has added one or more MCO products to its benefits roster, the hands-on part of product promotion begins for a completely different customer. The marketing process starts over with assessing the employee market and its characteristics and the competition within the employer's benefits plan.

Again, the marketing department of the MCO will analyze the employee base: their ages, education, economic level, position in the organization, home, and work location. There will be market segments: young employees interested in obstetrics and well-baby care, new parents interested in pediatric and immunization benefits, and middle-aged employees looking for health status improvement benefits as they approach retirement age. Messages to these segments will present the price, benefits, process, and accessibility of the plan in the strongest possible ways.

Even after the employee is enrolled, two additional revenue drivers occur. The first driver is to identify whether the outcomes of product promotion attracted the market segments assumed by underwriting to be obtained. Sometimes, the wrong types of employees subscribe to a product that was promoted to the right types of employers. Sometimes, it is possible to move higher-risk employees to different products that can absorb such risk, but the price will necessarily change (due to actuarial mathematics described) unless the grouping is large enough and diverse enough to minimize price changes.

Another follow-up revenue driver is retaining low-utilizing employees while discouraging high-utilizing ones, especially if they are part of EPO or POS products. Enrollee retention occurs through effective communications and service. In short, retention is a job of the entire MCO.

The impact of cost-sharing mechanisms must also integrate well with how the provider network is contracted. Most health plans prohibit balance billing by network providers, so the health plan must be certain both the members and providers know how to handle high-deductible plan designs.

## COST DATA TO PREDICT LOSSES

A key strategy by which MCOs operate is in measuring the interrelationship between benefit design offered and plan costs assumed. Certain loosely restricted plans might have a negative correlation with predicted costs. For example, the allowed use by members of nonnetwork or nonplan practitioners must be considered in terms of manageable costs. This example also factors into utilization management, as nonnetwork physicians will likely not be bound by the same utilization management constraints as capitated practitioners who are part of the health plan.

## COMMUNITY UTILIZATION AND SERVICE INTENSITIES

The anticipated utilization and costs for the targeted group are estimated using composite utilization rates based on the demographics of a target group.

## IMPACT OF UTILIZATION MANAGEMENT

Utilization management may reduce inpatient services, for example, through reducing length of stay and channeling some inpatient procedures to outpatient facilities.

## EFFECTIVENESS OF HEALTH CARE MANAGEMENT

This analysis is concerned with the impact of the proposed delivery system, namely, the degree to which health (and health care) is managed. This factor analysis includes provider payment arrangements, provider cooperation with utilization management activities, and both the provider incentives to manage well and the provider disincentives that accrue when health is poorly managed.

## PROBABILITY MATRIX OF PREDICTED USE

Another cost-based analysis is the distribution of the targeted group by the extent to which they will use the system, on a continuum from "for all conditions" to "never." In situations in which employees are choosing between a traditional indemnity plan and an HMO, higher levels of employee cost sharing in the indemnity plan will produce much higher participation in the HMO. (The opposite is also true, of course.)

Once developed, costs of proposed products are translated into revenue targets, and from there—through ratings—to premiums. The competitiveness of the price and the product design will determine the success of the new product.

## OPERATIONAL LOSS SOURCES

Even the best-designed benefit plan and the most highly targeted premium features can be compromised by provider/practitioner behavior and MCO operations inefficiencies. Sources of loss include higher-than-predicted claims arising from practitioner-based management, from institutional-based claims representing higher-than-predicted courses of treatment and acuity of care, as well as from IBNR claims. These sources of loss are discussed more specifically in Chapter 6.

The internal operations of an MCO might also account for the source of some loss. However, the greatest source of inefficiency occurs when the MCO has to micromanage a provider or practitioner, including adjudication, provider profiling, and incentive setting, as well as imposing financial disincentives on practitioners. MCO efficiency is enhanced if it can outsource these tangential services, preferably via capitated pricing, to TPAs, MSOs, or ASOs that have greater skill sets in these areas and can operate more efficiently than the payer can. Sometimes, these administrative services that can be the source of additional MCO losses can be assumed by an IDN headquarters or by an IMG; additional capitation can be offered IMGs and IDNs above capitation received for service delivery through a simple contract rider.

Without regard to quality of care, care outcomes, and health status management, minimizing loss sources, and the amounts of such loss, is relatively easy. The challenge of managed care is to maintain or improve the quality of MCO outputs while controlling the cost of inputs. The best solution to take into account all sources of loss is to engage in managed care strategic planning (MCSP).

## MCO OPERATIONAL ELEMENTS TO MINIMIZE LOSSES

The successful managed care system will usually include the following elements:

- A defined benefits package
- A medical director experienced in resolving cross-provider management issues
- The ability to negotiate and contract with hospitals, physicians, pharmacies, and other providers
- A management information system that provides
  - Financial tracking on an accrual basis
  - Current enrollee eligibility, premium collection, and paid claims history
  - Encounter, referral, procedure, and hospital reporting
  - Coordination-of-benefits (COB) tracking
- A quality assurance (QA) program that includes
  - Provider credentialing
  - Performance monitoring
  - Follow-up and corrective action
- A utilization management program that includes
  - Prospective review and authorization
  - Concurrent daily review
  - Retrospective review of all providers' performance
- An enrollee and patient grievance program that includes
  - Reporting
  - Recording
  - Corrective action and follow-up

## PAYER–PROVIDER RISK RELATIONSHIPS

A key operational component of MCOs borrows from the commonly held belief of the origins of managed care (see Chapter 1) that the desire by payers to outsource the provision of care resulted from an organizational change of mission. In managed care, risk relationships were created once the HMO industry declared it was in the business of *arranging for* the provision of health services and no longer in the business of providing care themselves, whether as part of a staff model or FFS-based delivery model (as was one time typical with governmental payers). In this way, and through capitated managed care (Table 2.10), payers and providers fundamentally changed the way they interacted.

The first change was contractual. Providers frequently mistake managed care contracts they sign as reflective of a provider's operation, instead of the payer's frame of reference in which it was created. The difference in the basic relationship is fundamental since payers exist to provide insurance by minimizing losses (in this case, to pay claims), while providers exist to increase them by submitting claims. For PPO-based claims, the payer reprices claims that providers submit and impose larger service discounts. The larger PPO discounts, relative to indemnity insurance based solely on the usual customary or reasonable rate (UCR, which is itself a discount of "full-retail" service fees), amount to discounts of discounts. While payers have negotiated these rate reductions with providers, the bottom line is that payers are still at risk on the basis of business they do not control: actual and accrued claims submitted by providers for care consumed by the insured.

Payers' requirements of utilization review (UR) were intended to introduce the minimization of use that is part of actuarial mathematics and product ratings. Instead, providers treat UR the same way CMS requires it: on a retrospective basis, similar to QA. Both QA and UR measure how efficiently and effectively care was consumed from the standpoint of generally accepted medical and

---

**TABLE 2.10**

**Provider Risk Relationships: Fee for Service (FFS) versus Capitation**

| Relationship Feature | FFS | Capitation |
|---|---|---|
| Services | Services generate revenue | The cost of providing services is expenses charged against revenue. |
| Revenue | Based on services provided: more is better | Based on plan enrollment, quantity of services is irrelevant. |
| To increase revenue | Provide more services or charge more | Revenue is only increased by enrolling additional covered lives or increasing premiums. |
| Patient care | Provide patient services as care is needed | Provide early treatment and wellness programs to reduce total cost of care. |

nursing standards. These processes inherent in FFS have fallen far short of providers changing their claims submission behavior on a real-time basis. Since there is only so much elasticity of premium price in given markets, especially if premium is tied to employee salaries, there is only so much that payers can do to protect their MLRs. And, since the financial resources of MCOs are so integrally tied to a budgeted MLR, the only other solutions are to grow premium to make the loss of control easier to bear or to transform the risk relationship so that the payer is not at risk for losses it has never been able to control. One solution that payers have adopted is to outsource the responsibility of managing care directly to providers through capitation.

Many managed care plans are capitated; that is, providers or groups of providers (such as IPAs, IMGs, or physician-hospital organizations [PHOs]), are prepaid a set amount of money based on the per capita enrollment of the plan, historically expressed as a contractually set amount PMPM. This simple change *completely* transforms the risk relationships on which providers traditionally depend, again as depicted in Table 2.10.

Under capitation, provider revenue is now fixed to the number of covered lives within a given geography rather than variable to the services provided. This shift is fundamental in and of itself. PMPM is paid by HMOs according to a static MLR that itself is not the basis of the operations of a provider. The only way for the MLR attributed to a PMPM price to be sufficient is if the provider conforms to an MLR in practice management. Since provision of services to generate claims is the antithesis of withholding services to reduce claims, success at capitation is not simply reducing all services. Rather, successful capitated providers must become quasi-MCOs to know which services to reduce and which services to provide, it is hoped tipping the scales on the side of reducing risk by reducing overall costs.

This change in perspective is what distinguishes most MCOs from traditional health care providers. It is important to keep in mind, however, that many providers are in transition—and may be for some time to come. Some of their business will be capitated and some FFS. This state of transition will affect the relationships of MCOs with these providers, from contracts to incentives to claims processing.

## STOP-LOSS AND PMPM RELATIONSHIPS

One aspect of the actuarial and underwriting processes that create capitated pricing is the result of an assumed matrix of service use probabilities. The process of cost sharing also factors into these matrices, which presupposes a fundamental nature of capitated pricing. A PMPM price is offered to providers at a specific level of stop-loss relative to underwriting requirements.

A *stop-loss* is the limit of out-of-pocket liability that a capitated practitioner expects to pay for any per member risk relationship. PMPM price is directly proportional to the level of stop-loss assumed; the higher the stop-loss assumed, the higher the PMPM price that can be offered because the practitioner is willing to accept risk that is closer to the underwriting threshold. The difference between an underwriting threshold, known as the *attachment point*, and the level of stop-loss assumed is known as *reinsurance*.

## UNDERWRITING AND REINSURANCE RELATIONSHIPS

Stop-loss and reinsurance, in contrast to the direct proportional relationship between stop-loss and PMPM, are inversely proportional. Thus, the higher the stop-loss assumed, the lower the attachment point (and hence the need for a lower reinsurance policy required to satisfy the underwriting threshold). The lower the underthreshold reinsurance, the less dilution of PMPM price that is necessary, as shown in Table 2.11.

A common underwriting threshold is the assumption of $1.0 million of practitioner liability through capitated pricing. If a practitioner assumes all $1.0 million as a single stop-loss, then the HMO is responsible for all catastrophic care costing in excess of $1.0 million, a relatively insignificant probability from an actuarial standpoint (except for members at greater risk for catastrophic conditions, such as professional skydivers and motorcyclists). One reinsurance policy pays for any care below the threshold, to the limits of stop-loss assumed, while a second reinsurance policy pays for any care above the $1.0 million threshold commonly assumed in capitated relationships.

---

### TABLE 2.11
### PMPM Pricing by Stop-Loss and "Underthreshold" Liability

Assumed underwriting threshold = $1,000,000
Assumed full-risk practitioner capitation = $50 PMPM
Assumed under-threshold reinsurance = $1.25 PMPM per $100,000 liability

| Practitioner Stop-Loss | PMPM with Reinsurance | PMPM without Reinsurance |
|---|---|---|
| $1,000,000 | $50.00 | $50.00 |
| $900,000 | $48.75 | $49.75 |
| $800,000 | $47.50 | $49.50 |
| $700,000 | $46.25 | $49.25 |
| $600,000 | $45.00 | $49.00 |
| $500,000 | $43.75 | $48.75 |
| $400,000 | $42.50 | $48.50 |
| $300,000 | $41.25 | $48.25 |
| $200,000 | $40.00 | $48.00 |
| $100,000 | $38.75 | $47.75 |
| <$100,000 | $37.50 | $47.50 |

---

HMOs or self-funded ERISA plans often self-insure for liability in excess of the underwriting threshold or can leverage economies of scale to obtain very low rates for obtaining an overthreshold reinsurance policy from another carrier.

The relationship between PMPM pricing and stop-loss gets more complex based on a matrix of reinsurance responsibilities. For example, an HMO may maintain "over-and-under" excess liability insurance, which covers both the over-threshold portion (relatively inexpensive) as well as the underthreshold portion, which becomes more expensive the lower the stop-loss assumed.

Another variable in this matrix is who assumes the "under" reinsurance relative to a given underwriting threshold, typically $1.0 million. If the HMO assumes over-and-under reinsurance, the practitioner will receive less capitation than if he or she bought his or her own underthreshold reinsurance. Table 2.11 displays this matrix relationship; the variability of PMPM paid, based on an underreinsurance rate of $1.25 PMPM per $100,000 liability, ranges from $1 to $10 PMPM less if the HMO bears this responsibility. Multiplied by a population of 25,000, this difference could mean as much as a quarter-million dollars _less per month._

It should be clear from Table 2.11 that the premium cost of underthreshold reinsurance is inversely proportional to the amount of stop-loss a provider/practitioner is willing to assume. What this relationship means is that the lower the PMPM paid per successively lower stop-loss liability results in a successively higher reinsurance premium. Yet, a payer has a reasonable expectation that a low stop-loss is not going to be assumed, _in part_ because of the increased premium burden of paying for higher reinsurance. (The other part of this expectation is explained further here.)

How expensive can stop-loss premium really be for a company that is in the insurance business? It is certainly less expensive, in part due to economies of scale, for an excess liability insurer to be insured than for a practitioner or provider to be insured. In addition, even when the provider/practitioner bears the responsibility for obtaining underthreshold reinsurance (see the "PMPM Without Reinsurance" column in Table 2.11), the payer still makes some money in reduced PMPM costs.

Let us also consider the reinsurance business itself. For the most part, reinsurers of health care excess liability know little about the health care industry. For all intents and purposes, a reinsurer has traditionally acted as a "giant checkbook." Claims submitted above a stop-loss or above an underwriting threshold are simply paid.

Reinsurers have not participated in case management or in any loss avoidance efforts. They have rare interactions with HMOs, other than at a premium policy level, and have even rarer interactions with Medicare PSOs and self-funded ERISA plans to reduce the amount of claims that result in reinsurance coverage.

Their relationships with most practitioners and providers has been close to none. This is another behavior that led to contraction and mergers/acquisitions in the HMO industry after capitating essentially all of their covered lives: They ignored the growing trend by employers (first the largest, then the midlevel market) to engage in direct contracting with practitioners/providers by establishing ERISA plans. As direct contracting increases and as HMOs are increasingly being bypassed in employer contracting, the reinsurance industry also loses its only link to the practitioner/provider community unless it becomes more involved.

So, what does the difference in PMPM prices offered, as illustrated in Table 2.11, really mean? Is the difference simply a pass-through of the cost of obtaining reinsurance? When the question is asked this simply, the most reasonable answer should be simple as well. Insurance companies are businesses. The PMPM offered is no different from the price offered for a product or service of any business; the price includes a markup above the cost of obtaining incremental reinsurance.

## OTHER INTERRELATIONSHIPS

As seen in the preceding section, the incremental reinsurance premium expense, large or small, was given as part of the explanation of why payers assume that practitioners/providers will opt for higher, rather than lower, stop-loss. The answer points to an intangible relationship between the stop-loss level a practitioner is willing to assume and the likelihood such a provider will even receive a capitation contract at all.

The true interrelationship to evaluate here is more squarely a problem of the practitioner/provider. A practitioner/provider accepting lower stop-loss is clearly inexperienced in bearing capitated risk. For starters, why does PMPM decrease in the rightmost column of Table 2.11, as the onus for reinsurance is not the payer's? The best reason is that a practitioner/provider purchasing reinsurance has a sufficient size of capitation business to minimize cost. Never mind that the reinsurance industry is far less critical of practitioner/provider quality and claims history than are HMOs. The point is that a practitioner/provider unwilling to accept higher stop-loss could logically be assumed to have

- Little trust in its ability to accept capitated risk,
- A capitation mix of less than 20% of total revenues (the midpoint of a "stage 2" managed care market) within a highly capitated market (stage 3 or stage 4), and thus
- An operation more susceptible to fluctuations in variable revenue.

Because of these factors, practitioners/providers assuming lower stop-loss levels than their competitors raise questions in the minds of provider liaison staff of HMOs, MCOs, and MSOs. If a practitioner or provider has such a low reliance on capitated revenues, the practioner or provider will continue to budget revenue and expense on a variable basis, looking at capitation as an anomaly. By contrast, practitioners/providers with more than 75% capitation budget their revenue and expense on a fixed basis and consider noncapitated revenue (e.g., DFFS) as the anomaly. Finally, low-penetration practitioners/providers typically lack the economies of scale necessary to bear risk for better service outcomes at lower capitation rates.

One final interrelationship bears mention in the study of health care finance. A missing piece of the discussion so far is that capitation is paid to all practitioners and providers according to the assumption of a specific stop-loss. Who determines when the stop-loss level has been reached and at what point a reinsurance claim needs to be initiated? For this reason, capitated providers/practitioners must submit encounter data that include the costs of care consumed. The easiest means of capturing this information is through the claims management process (discussed separately here), even though they will not be used for reimbursement. Any occurrence when a provider or practitioner does not submit a claim results in an increase in IBNR (see more detailed discussion further in the chapter).

## RISK BANDING AND PROVIDER RISK-SHARING ARRANGEMENTS

Frequently, "withhold" pools are established in a capitated market to provide incentives for efficient care and a means of managed care risk sharing. These withholds refer to holding back a percentage of bimonthly earnings distributions to fund efficient care incentives, to pay out-of-pocket costs for contracting specialists not subcapitated, and to fund fully a suitable risk pool that meets payer and regulator requirements to offset shortfalls of monthly capitation revenues available to pay monthly practice expenses. For example, many new IMGs will demand a 10% to 20% withhold of normal distributions for a minimum of 6 months to ensure proper risk pool capitalization. For each IMG practitioner earning the $120,000 per year average, the effect of a 10% withhold would be a one-time risk pool contribution of $6,000, amortized over the first 6 months of practice.

The core of risk banding is the strategy that payers or providers want practitioners to succeed rather than set them up to fail. Failure is easy to accomplish with capitation, especially if many of the practitioners have little prior experience medically managing capitated lives. Failure is even easier if new groups bear high-acuity risk and need guidance from the capitating payer to succeed. This reality gives payers incentives to risk band as well.

Risk bands—also known as "risk corridors"—place the payer or the provider responsible for a portion of overutilization of capitated resources over a defined period of time, rather than risk pools failing within the first year or practitioners motivated to extricate themselves from practices that are continuously underfunded and require additional withholds to stave off bankruptcy. Risk banding can be with either an open cap, meaning that any overage relying on risk banding has no upper limit of provider responsibility (and can be expensive), or a closed cap, for which the band is the limit of overage liability (with any overage above the cap being the responsibility of the practitioner or a third party, such as a reinsurer). One risk-banding relationship is depicted in Table 2.12. Another risk-banding relationship was discussed in conjunction with the 50–50 rule.

In Table 2.12, the risk-banding provider paid $2.25 million to the IMG in excess of capitation revenue that the medical group received. By contrast, the group

## TABLE 2.12

### Example of a 4-Year Payer-IMG 25% Risk Band

**Assumptions:**
- **20 physicians each paid $10,000 per month ($120,000 per year)**
- **20% risk pool withholding of monthly distribution, first 12 months**
- **Yearly revenues = $4.8 million (4,000 Medicare Lives at $100 PMPM)**

| Fiscal Year End (FYE) Period Ending | Risk Pool End Balance Amount ($) | Capitation-Based Expenses ($) | Underage/ (Overage) at $4.8 Million Revenue/Year ($) | % of Payer Overage Risk | Payer Opportunity Cost ($) | Practitioner Contribution ($) |
|---|---|---|---|---|---|---|
| 1st 6 Months | 240,000 | 3.6 million | (1.2 million) | 100 | 1,200,000 | 0 |
| Balance at 1st FYE | 480,000 | 2.8 million | (400,000) | 100 | 400,000 | 0 |
| 2nd FYE | 480,000 | 5.4 million | (600,000) | 75 | 450,000 | 150,000 |
| 3rd FYE | 330,000 | 5.1 million | (300,000) | 50 | 150,000 | 150,000 |
| 4th FYE | 180,000 | 4.9 million | (100,000) | 25 | 25,000 | 75,000 |
| 5th FYE | 105,000 | 4.825 million | (25,000) | 0 | 0 | 25,000 |
| 6th FYE | 80,000 | 4.75 million | 50,000 | 0 | 0 | Add $50,000 to risk pool |

contributed $400,000 (15%) toward the overage of capitation-based expenses to revenues received. The onus of the IMG for paying overages out of risk pool funds did not start until the second year and then on a 25% graduated basis. In addition, the use of this contractual relationship ensured that operational efficiencies in the fifth year were almost enough to cover capitation revenues, with full breakeven early in the sixth year. The beginning of the seventh year would see a risk pool balance of $130,000, with at least $50,000 annual balance increases if cost savings continued to be maintained, if not improved via economies of scale.

While the example provided is expensive to the provider, it does point out a key benefit to risk banding. Consider the alternative to this risk-banding scenario had the hospital simply "washed its hands" of this IMG that had little skill in managing capitated business. With no risk pool capitalization going into the first month of the contract, the IMG generated $400,000 of capitated revenues against $600,000 of capitation-related expense, leaving a $200,000 shortfall. Even with the 20% withhold imposed in the first month, of $40,000, the IMG would have been $160,000 in the red within 1 month. In fact, by the first distribution check the group would have had to withhold an additional 20% of earnings just to cover the shortfall, leaving a remainder of $3,000 per physician applied to employment taxes just on the first paycheck.

Under such circumstances, few groups would have existed after only 15 days. Even if the group continued into the seventh month, when capitation-related expenses shrank by 17%, there was still an average $67,000 shortfall, which would have required an additional 42% withhold (only $2,325 net of withholds per paycheck then subject to employment taxes) for each of six more months. Even for the most determined, an IMG without risk banding would have been insolvent well within its first year.

However, the death of this IMG is not the end of this example. What if it became known that the hospital stood by and watched its most promising managed care physician group progress rapidly to bankruptcy, without doing anything (such as risk banding) to prevent this progression? If the media were told of this loss, what would be the opinion of the hospital according to the rest of its medical staff as well as its market area? Is the protection of this IMG worth $2.25 million to this provider? Considering that the hospital would likely lose sizable managed care revenues (if not revenues from other sources as well) from among all of its practitioners, most hospitals would consider risk banding to be a bargain, even at $2.25 million.

## PAYER–PROVIDER FINANCIAL RELATIONSHIPS

The managed care relationships between payers and providers are not limited to matters of risk. Some significant financial relationships need to be discussed.

### COST SHARING

Copayments are key determinants of cost sharing, as they affect consumption behavior and will have a positive impact on cost control. The degree to which cost sharing, such as copayments, influences payer losses can be seen in Table 2.13 as representing over $5.00 PMPM.

While copayments do have a positive impact on reducing costs, Table 2.13 tells only part of the tale. The key statistic in this chart is the effect copayments have not only on unit costs, but also on utilization. Copayments reduce projected annual office visits by members from 3.5 to 3.0, a 14% reduction. However, who

**TABLE 2.13**
**Effect of Copayments on Cost**

|  | With Copayment | Without Copayment |
|---|---|---|
| Cost of average office visit | $48 | $48 |
| Copayment | $10 | $0 |
| Final cost | $38 | $48 |
| Projected visits PMPY | 3.0 | 3.5 |
| Cost per year | $114 | $168 |
| Cost PMPM | $9.50 | $14.00 |

benefits from this reduction? From an insurance industry standpoint, this reduction is beneficial, as the primary objective is to reduce losses and maintain a static MLR. However, at the practitioner level, this objective works only for populations who do not need to be in a physician's office, such as for a population that is known to be otherwise healthy. Populations known to be unhealthy, such as those known (e.g., via encounter data) to have a chronic disease requiring acute or medical management, may require an *increase* in visits and care consumption, at least over a short period of time.

## REINSURANCE RECOVERIES

Most states require HMOs to maintain insurance coverage, called reinsurance or stop-loss insurance. Stop-loss insurance is also needed for self-insured ERISA plans offering managed care to employees. This coverage insures against losses incurred in honoring what are usually called catastrophic claims. A *catastrophic claim* is defined as one (not a combination of claims for the same individual) that exceeds the underwriting threshold (e.g., $1 million), meaning it is an extremely high-cost claim.

Reinsurance operates like a standard medical insurance policy. There is usually a deductible based on a fixed amount per member per year, which is the amount of medical benefits expense that the HMO must pay before the insurance applies. Once the deductible is met, costs are shared on a coinsurance basis up to some limit. The HMO is charged a premium based on the deductible, the coinsurance level, number of enrollees, and experience with the HMO. Reinsurance premiums are considered medical benefits expenses.

Once the deductible has been met in a particular year, the HMO receives reimbursement for claims, called a *recovery*, from the reinsurer (usually after COB liabilities are determined, discussed separately herein). The HMO records the claims as medical benefits expense since it pays them. It records the recovery from the reinsurer as revenue or a contraexpense to claims. Recoveries should only be recorded when they have been determined on the basis of benefits provided and charged until the reinsurer has verified the actual amount. However, accrual of reinsurance recoverables based on calculations defined in reinsurance contracts is typically recorded prior to verification of actual amounts by the reinsurer.

## COB RELATIONSHIPS

COB, defined in conjunction with third-party administration in Chapter 1, is another source for reducing HMO medical costs. Like in basic A/R management, COB refers to the situation in which an enrollee is also covered by another medical program, often through a family member's employer. Once recorded in the system, COB data are integrated into the claims-processing work flow. Claims adjudicators can also be alert to COB clues, such as amounts already paid toward charges or certain diagnoses, like dialysis treatment. Accidental injury claims may be covered under workers' compensation or automobile insurance policies; these cases are covered by state law.

If a subrogation clause is included in the member's schedule of benefits, it gives the plan the right to recover damages received by the enrollee from a third party responsible for the injury in order to cover medical expenses incurred. When a COB situation arises, there are two aptly named approaches to take: pursue and pay and pay and pursue.

## "Pursue-and-Pay" COB Method

Under the pursue-and-pay COB method, the HMO investigates the other coverage and determines the liabilities of each carrier before paying. If the HMO is the primary carrier, it pays the claim just as it would if there were no other coverage. When the HMO is the secondary payer, it may avoid payment of a portion of the claim.

## "Pay-and-Pursue" COB Method

Under the pay-and-pursue COB method, the HMO pays each claim as though it were the primary payer and then seeks to be reimbursed by the other carrier. If the HMO is the primary payer, the other carrier owes it nothing. If the HMO is secondary, the primary carrier reimburses it for the amount of the primary liability.

Most managed care contracts require that benefits be coordinated with these other plans to avoid duplication and overpaying. Identification of these other benefits is often disclosed on health insurance applications as well as when enrollees first see their primary care practitioners (PCPs) and when they present themselves for care at the facility of a contracted or noncontracted provider.

## CAPITATION ADJUSTMENTS BASED ON PERCENTAGE OF PREMIUM REVENUE

Capitation adjustments are based on percentages of premium revenue rather than actuarial changes over time, success indicators (such as health status adaptation over time; see discussion for a more complete explanation), or risk pool overaccruals. Percentage of premium adjustments represents one attempt to satisfy critics of MCOs that they receive too much profit and can step provider/practitioner payments when tied to premium revenue received. This methodology requires not only that payments are tied in some way to revenue but also, more importantly, that HMOs disclose and report their revenue.

Disclosing and reporting HMO revenue at all is generally not favored by the payer community. For one reason, HMO plans are not only profitable but also their profits are typically used to cover operating losses in other health insurance option products, most specifically indemnity and PPO business. In addition, most state insurance agencies require a statement of revenues without the need to disclose revenue by product line; as such, many HMOs will try to avoid a payment methodology that fixes payments to their success in selling premium.

Tying provider/practitioner payments to revenue is to be avoided for two other reasons as well. First, disclosure of HMO revenues could create exposure for non-HMO lines of business that may be operating at a loss or without sufficient capitalization to cover anticipated losses, perhaps below FQHMO or state licensing agency requirements. Second, all payers would readily agree that changes in premium directly related to HMO advertising should not have to be shared by providers who contribute nothing to that effort. Why entitle them to increased capitation for which they were not responsible or did not bear the risk for associated promotion costs?

In addition, tying capitation to monthly fluctuations in revenue makes PMPM less fixed for providers/practitioners by *simulating* an FFS mentality that works against their success. Such practices will avoid budgeting on PMPM, as monthly fluctuations in both members and capitation rate will change substantially each month, particularly if competing products of other MCOs take market share away. With such competition, moreover, the provider/practitioner will be penalized when less revenue is received, versus a "straight" capitation that pays an annual, set PMPM each month regardless of revenue fluctuations. For these reasons, the tying of PMPM to premium revenue is best suited to immature capitation markets and not to communities where MCOs must battle competitors monthly to retain their market share of members in every single product they sell.

## CLAIMS MANAGEMENT AND PROCESSING

Claims management varies in complexity, generally according to the following factors:

- How many plans and types of plans are being handled?
- How many types of payment and contracts (capitation, per diems, discounts) are involved, and how variable is their processing?
- Are all claims (e.g., in network and out of network) handled the same way?
- How much work is actually done by the computer system and how much by the claims adjudicator?
- How many claims will a single episode of care produce?
- Who submits the claim?
- How are specific benefits like prescription drugs handled?

Keeping tabs on claims management directly affects the MLR and hence the very existence and profitability of an MCO. Standard weekly reports cover the quantity of work in process, quality issues, and bottom-line effects. Work in process issues may cover the following:

- Production reports: department production quantities, individual production quantities, progress toward goals, improvements, and resolution rates
- Turnaround time reports: age of oldest claim on hand and percentage of claims resolved within 14, 30, 60, 90 days, and so on
- Backlog reports: number of weeks of work on hand, number of reports pending (both in the system and not yet entered)

Quality reports might include percentage of accuracy rates, percentage of claims with customer complaints, number of claims adjusted.

Financial reports include

- Budget reports, such as cost per claim by product and claims per 1,000 enrollees and
- Revenue/savings reports, with the results of COB, recovery, medical review statistics, and audit activities.

Claims processing is the means by which MCOs gauge probable losses to which the MLR is applied. Eligibility, coverage, authorization, and payment terms converge in this one function. It also affects the ability of the MCO to attract and retain members, negotiate successfully with providers, and achieve the cost containment necessary to keep premiums in line with the market and achieve desired bottom lines.

Claims payment information is generally prepared by the provider but may be submitted by the provider or the patient, whoever is being reimbursed. The accuracy and completeness of claims data are vital to a true picture of the operation of the MCO. The payer has, in the past, required only the data necessary for payment. Now, data needs have expanded to encompass the appropriateness and quality of care as well as the care patterns and changing needs of the covered population.

The increased utility and pervasiveness of affordable computer technology has led to increased electronic submission and payment of claims. However, many of the processes are similar to those still used to process paper claims.

The claims-processing department itself is generally divided into production and support personnel. Production is what moves the claim from the mail room to the final storage area. Support staff coordinate issues with other departments and outside entities.

The information required for claims processing (Table 2.14) includes patient or enrollee ID, patient age and sex, provider ID (and referring provider ID if appropriate), date of service, type of service, type of diagnosis/major diagnostic category, procedure code, primary diagnosis code, secondary diagnosis code, other diagnosis codes as necessary (as many as five may be needed under DRGs [diagnosis-related groups] for hospital reimbursement), DRG classification, episode of care identifier, cost center uniform billing (UB) code for hospitalization.

A key element of enrollee data related to claims processing is information on COB, that is, information about any other health plan or carrier that may share liability for health care expenses via a spouse's coverage or the like. Enrollees themselves have to provide this information, and some MCOs will not enroll an enrollee unless COB data are encoded at enrollment.

In the past, secondary payers may have covered all expenses not covered by the primary payer, in effect providing the patient with 100% coverage and nullifying the copayment incentives of the primary carrier. However, secondary payers are increasingly limiting their payments to their own maximums. This restores some of the ability of the primary payer to motivate enrollees through copayment and other benefit design features. With the relatively high cost of health insurance, the

---

**TABLE 2.14**

**Information Required for Claims Processing**

- Patient or enrollee ID, age, and sex
- Provider ID
- Referring provider ID
- Date of service
- Type of service
- Type of diagnosis/major diagnostic category
- Procedure code
- Primary, secondary, and other diagnosis codes
- DRG classification
- Episode of care identifier
- Revenue center (UB-04) code for hospitalization
- Coordination of benefits (COB) information

---

likelihood of multiple policies in a family has been falling. As such, the extent of COB as a whole has been declining except for workers' compensation, auto accidents, and working aged.

The claims payment process is closely tied to the authorization process and involves reviewing much of the same information: eligibility, provider relationship, and medical appropriateness. Claims data should be screened in terms of treatment, provider, and finances. "Screening software" (used for editing key data fields) is now used for automating some of these reviews.

Treatment screening issues include

- Applicability to patient's age, sex, and medical history
- Number of treatments compared to maximum acceptable
- Appropriateness for diagnosis
- Whether conditions of coverage were met
- Likelihood of COB for the treatment or diagnosis

Provider screening may include

- Participation of provider in network
- Qualifications of physician to perform a procedure
- Appropriate referrals, including history of abuse

Financial screening may include

- Charge for the service and reimbursable amount
- Applicable fee schedule or discount or determination of whether the provider is capitated

- Amount withheld for risk-sharing pool
- Fulfillment of requirements for copayments or deductibles, such as authorizations

New needs for data, and the questions raised about the quality of those data, have helped to create some new "gray areas" in claims processing. For example, a provider may question diagnosis and treatment reports that seem to show over-treatment of patients and point out that the commonly used codes do not indicate the severity of an illness. Conversely, payers may charge providers with "code creep": submitting claims with procedure codes that refer to more costly proce-dures than the ones that were actually performed or treating associated proce-dures (activities performed in one surgical operation, for example) as if they were independently performed.

## CLAIMS ADJUDICATION

The processing of a claim begins with its arrival at the MCO. Its first experi-ences are mundane but important. Opening, date stamping, counting, and sorting claims are not exciting activities, but controlling and organizing the paper earlier makes downstream tasks easier. An organization may choose to microfilm or electronically image claims as they are received to guard against future loss.

Next, claims are sorted and batched for the claims adjudicators, first by type of plan and product: HMO, PPO, POS. A simple way to skip this step is to assign separate post office boxes or suite numbers to the different products or plans so they arrive sorted. However, invariably some manual sorting will still be neces-sary. The next level of sorting is by type of claim: PCP, radiology, prescription drug, referral specialist, and so on. The claims in each category are sorted by provider and finally are bundled and assigned, in date order, to an adjudicator.

The next stop for the claim is the claims adjudicator, who enters the claim into the system. He or she identifies claims that are missing data, corresponding authorization, and the like and routes them to the appropriate person for follow-up. A "clean" claim goes on with the process and finally ends its career in storage while the corresponding check—or denial letter—is mailed or, increasingly (and eventually more typically), transmitted to the provider's bank account via elec-tronic funds transfer (EFT).

The claim might not stay in the file drawer for long, however. The support staff of a typical claims department includes a quality reviewer, who will review claims for compliance with policies and procedures as well as compliance with benefits. The department may also include a nurse reviewer, who will review sur-gery claims, physical therapy claims, and those for which inappropriate treatment may have been involved. The claims liaison function will deal with claims involv-ing errors, complaints, and other problems.

When COB data are integrated into the claims-processing work flow, claims adjudicators can also be alert to COB clues, such as amounts already paid toward charges or certain diagnoses (e.g., dialysis treatment). Accidental injury claims may be covered under workers' compensation or automobile insurance policies; these cases are covered by state law.

If a subrogation clause is included in the member's schedule of benefits, it gives the plan the right to recover damages received by the enrollee from a third party responsible for the injury in order to cover medical expenses incurred.

## REFERRAL MANAGEMENT

Managing referrals generated by the provider network of an MCO is a key component of minimizing and managing IBNR. Because of this correlation to IBNR, many MCOs try to shift the responsibility for managing referrals to providers and their integrated networks or MSOs, as practitioners can more appropriately manage other practitioners. And, subcapitation (see much greater mathematical discussions that follow) can be a vehicle by which practitioners can minimize referral portals (such as referral to specialists only within the same IMG or IPA) to reduce out-of-network referrals.

### PROVIDER AUTHORIZATIONS

The use of service authorization is one of the defining characteristics of an MCO and is a key element of managing care. Its link to the claims-processing system makes authorization a part of internal control as well.

One of the major areas in which provider information and enrollee information are used together is authorization. HMOs and EPOs generally require authorization for specialty services. PPOs may require authorizations for inpatient and some outpatient services. The requirements for prior authorization are steadily loosening as members with the muscle of state legislation are seeking more direct access to specialists (e.g., many states now mandate that women have direct access to OB/GYNs [obstetricians/gynecologists]).

Prior authorization enables the MCO to gather information in advance and identify potential problems. One of these is potentially catastrophic cases, which, if identified early, can be taken under case management. Usually a function of the UR department, case management seeks to improve the continuity and quality of care as well as control costs in these situations. It involves such activities as special agreements with and referrals to tertiary care facilities, specialists, home health care, and durable medical equipment (DME) providers. Early identification of these higher-cost cases can serve as an aid in setting claim reserves. (An introduction to IBNR can be found in a separate section.) Prior authorization also helps track these high-cost cases.

Prior authorization also provides a means of studying referral patterns, such as inappropriate referral relationships and physicians who under- or overrefer. Prior authorization records initial diagnoses at the beginning of the case. Combined, these records make it possible to profile providers for appropriate diagnoses and, by comparing the outcomes of similar diagnoses, create quality profiles of providers.

Authorization serves several purposes:

- It enables the medical management staff of an organization to review a case for medical necessity.
- It channels care to the most appropriate setting or provider.
- It provides timely information to the case management system and the concurrent review utilization management system.
- It enables the finance department to estimate the monthly accruals for medical expenses.

Authorization may be as simple as precertification in a PPO or as complex as requiring authorization for anything other than primary care services in an HMO. Defining the authorization system of an MCO means defining the following:

- Services that require authorization
- Who can authorize services
- What timing requirements exist for authorizations
- Categories of authorization

Primary care services never require authorization; hospitalization (except emergencies) always does. In between is the gray area. The tightest controls require all services not provided by the PCP to have authorization, including referrals to specialists. PPOs typically only require authorization for elective hospitalizations and select other procedures. The more services that require authorization, the greater the potential for managing utilization. Examples of utilization management techniques can be found in Table 2.15.

There will be cases for which the service cannot be authorized in advance, primarily emergencies or out-of-town crises. Most authorization plans provide for authorization to be granted after the fact in these cases if a review shows medical necessity.

Even if the system defines the PCP as the source of authorizations, it must go a little further. For example, if a patient is authorized to see a specialist, can that specialist authorize further services, such as another referral or surgery? In some cases, the specialist might obtain authorizations from the medical management staff of the MCO instead of going back to the PCP.

A few areas of health care are general exceptions to the rules. One is mental health or chemical dependency care, often treated entirely differently from the rest of the plan because of its unique services. Other exceptions are high-cost, controversial, or experimental treatments, which may require authorization from the medical director, especially if the MCO has contracts with specific providers for those procedures (e.g., transplants, infertility cases, etc.).

There are six general categories of authorization: (1) prospective, (2) concurrent, (3) retrospective, (4) pended, (5) denied, and (6) subordinate.

**TABLE 2.15**

**Utilization Management Techniques**

| | | |
|---|---|---|
| Prospective | Referrals | Primary care physician or "gatekeeper" coordinates, manages, and authorizes all services for the patient. |
| | Precertification or authorization | Requires determination that the proposed medical service is appropriate for the patient. Used with both inpatient and outpatient procedures. |
| | Second surgical opinion | An opinion from a practitioner other than the specialist making the recommendation about the appropriateness of a proposed treatment. |
| Concurrent | Concurrent length-of-stay review | Evaluation during the patient's hospitalization, covering appropriateness of admission, timeliness of care, and need for continued stay. Also used for emergencies in which prior authorization was not possible. |
| | Discharge planning | Evaluation of patient's continued need for hospitalization and provision for services after discharge. |
| | Case management | Process for identifying potentially high-cost cases and developing and implementing less-costly and more appropriate care. |
| Retrospective | Pattern analysis | An analysis of practice patterns intended to target individual case reviews and identify potential problems. |
| | Medical record review | Review of medical record data to determine appropriateness of treatment (also for concurrent review). |
| | Appropriateness review | Claims are reviewed against standards of care and a determination made about payment. |
| | Procedures code review | Claims are reviewed for correct coding by providers using code review software. Claims are recoded or suspended. |
| | Bill audits | Claims are reviewed for billing, payment errors, and appropriateness for related service to identify duplicate claims and high-cost services. |
| | Retrospective claim review | Statistical review of paid claims to identify providers or patients with anomalous utilization patterns. |
| | Identification of fraudulent bills submitted by providers | Identification of fraudulent bills submitted by providers. |

## Prospective Authorizations

Prospective authorization, often called precertification or preauthorization, is authorization issued before the service is provided. This should, in theory, be your most common type of authorization. It enables care to be directed to the appropriate provider or facility, offers the opportunity for review by the medical management staff, and provides you with current utilization information for financial reporting.

Referral authorization and the gatekeeper concept are the front lines of utilization management. In most gatekeeper managed care plans, a patient must have a referral from a PCP for any service other than standard primary care or emergency services. The function of the gatekeeper, usually the PCP, is to coordinate, manage, and authorize all of the services for his or her patients. By controlling referrals and authorizations, the gatekeeper controls costs and utilization. Unfortunately, the term *gatekeeper* implies one who is attempting to limit patients from receiving care and so should probably be avoided.

Precertification or prospective authorization, the most common utilization management technique, requires that certain services be assessed and approved to help ensure that the procedure or service is medically necessary and a covered service. It is almost always required for hospitalization and often for outpatient procedures and expensive diagnostic tests.

There are four basic reasons for prospective authorization:

1. To bring the case into the utilization management system so that concurrent review, retrospective review, and if necessary, large case management processes can take place.
2. To make sure that care is delivered in the appropriate setting: for example, at a network hospital rather than a nonnetwork hospital or in an outpatient facility rather than in a hospital.
3. To provide data for financial accruals of medical expense liabilities. A well-run utilization management system will capture information on over 90% of cases, including potentially high-cost cases, enabling the finance department to react appropriately. Precertification is not possible in emergencies, so authorization takes place while or after the emergency is handled.
4. To ensure that authorization remains a method of internal control, as discussed near the end of Chapter 6.

Second opinions are a utilization management technique of long standing, again with the purpose of reviewing medical necessity and exploring less-expensive or less-invasive options for treatment. However, at times this utilization management technique may cost more than it saves.

## CONCURRENT AUTHORIZATIONS

Concurrent authorization is issued at the time the service is provided, generally for some urgent service (although it can also be for services scheduled but not authorized prospectively). Concurrent authorization does provide utilization information for financial reporting, but it limits the ability of the MCO to manage the utilization of resources as well as the medical management staff's ability to intervene.

The key to concurrent review is the utilization management nurse. This person is usually on the staff of the MCO (or could be contracted or delegated) and is responsible for on-site facilitation of utilization management. The utilization management nurse's job is information gathering. The information must be accurate and timely and must include at least admission date, diagnosis, type of service (surgery, maternity), type and timing of procedures planned, admitting physician, consultants, anticipated discharge date, and discharge planning necessary.

In some MCOs, this information is gathered by telephone; in others, it is gathered in person. Telephone "rounding," or information gathering, works well in areas where facilities are too widely spread to make in-person rounding practical, when a hospital will not allow in-person rounding, or when utilization is not closely managed and the utilization management staff is looking for anomalous data only.

In-person hospital rounding, if practical, provides the most timely and accurate information, including information available only through personal observation. Key items observed might include potential quality problems, information necessary for discharge planning (such as the need for durable equipment) that may not have been communicated earlier, and even practice behavior that needs correction to control costs. Examples would include extending a patient's stay solely for the scheduling convenience of the hospital (e.g., cannot schedule a test on a weekend) or a physician's scheduling convenience (e.g., out of town for the weekend, no coverage). Personal rounding is also an indirect marketing tool, helping to raise customer satisfaction levels simply through personal contact with patients and their families.

Some hospitals with strong, active utilization management departments of their own will discourage in-person rounding by the utilization management nurse of the MCO. A hospital utilization management department may not provide all the information needed in terms of quality and cost control and may not allow any member satisfaction reviewing to take place.

Most MCOs have one utilization management nurse for each 8,000 to 12,000 enrollees, depending on the extent of the on-site duties the person personally fulfills. A utilization management nurse who collects most data over the phone can handle more cases.

Concurrent utilization management takes place during a hospitalization. The first technique, length-of-stay review, reviews the case and assigns a maximum or target length of stay for the patient, based on the *International Classification of Diseases, Ninth Revision, Clinical Modification* (*ICD-9-CM*) code or diagnostic code. Any stay beyond the assigned maximum will not be covered (assuming the

MCO is not paying on a DRG or other case rate method). In addition to length-of-stay review, the utilization management nurse may review the case against other established treatment criteria.

Discharge planning should start before the patient even gets to the hospital. In addition to the expected discharge date, planning includes the expected outcome of the treatment or procedure and special requirements, such as equipment needed on discharge. The purpose is to plan ahead so that discharge is both smooth for the patient and less expensive for the MCO. For example, ordering needed equipment in time means that the patient will not be spending (expensive) time in the hospital waiting for it. Part of discharge planning is making sure that the patient and his or her family know what to expect in terms of timing and the condition of the patient.

## RETROSPECTIVE AUTHORIZATIONS

*Retrospective authorization* is authorization after the fact. It is intended to apply to emergency cases in which prospective authorizations are impossible—a car accident or heart attack. In practice, retrospective authorizations are just as often caused by provider carelessness, procrastination, or lack of physician cooperation and may not be even identified as retrospective.

Utilization management does not end when the patient is discharged; it then becomes retrospective review. Because it takes place after services have been provided, retrospective review focuses on ensuring that claims are processed properly or studying patterns of utilization.

Claims-processing-related reviews involve ensuring that the claim itself is correct: codes are correct, data are complete, and so on. In most cases, this screening is done by computer—claims are compared to norms and questionable claims identified.

Other forms of retrospective review focus on patterns of care: analyzing utilization data as a whole to look for desired (or undesired) patterns of treatment, outcomes, costs, and lengths of stay. This type of retrospective review enables the management of an MCO to focus on potential problems, evaluate network participants and reward good performance, as well as provide useful feedback to providers. Giving providers utilization profiles, comparing their levels of utilization to comparable providers in their area, has been shown to reduce utilization by those providers.

## PENDED AUTHORIZATIONS

Pended authorizations are essentially "on hold" pending medical or administrative review. Large numbers of pended claims means there is a problem with the system.

## DENIED AUTHORIZATIONS

A denied authorization for a service means that it will not be issued. It should not be confused with a claim denied for payment.

### SUBORDINATE ("SUB-") AUTHORIZATIONS

A subordinate (or "sub-") authorization means that one authorization is used for a number of related services; for example, one authorization may cover a referral to a specialist plus tests ordered by the specialist or all the related activities of one hospitalization. This type of authorization offers the opportunity to subvert the system through "linking," which violates the division-of-responsibility rule of an internal control system. *Linking* refers to paying claims for unauthorized services by linking them to authorized services through subauthorizations. In our specialist example, the visit to the specialist may have been authorized but not the tests. The claims processor may create subauthorizations to link unauthorized tests— and their costs—to the authorized visit when internal controls are suboptimal.

The types of authorization issued should be tracked so that problem areas can be identified and corrected. Indeed, precertification information integrates with a wide variety of clinical and financial areas. If, for example, a preauthorization is skipped in favor of concurrent or retrospective authorization, there will be serious effects on the accuracy of financial data. As such, sound systems of retrospective authorization are important for both loss prevention and proper internal control. For example, only the medical director or utilization management staff can initiate retrospective authorizations; prospective authorizations are not to be issued after services are provided; or concurrent authorizations may not be issued more than one business day after the service is provided.

The authorization process also interfaces with both adjudication and the overall claims-processing function. In effect, authorization acts as a purchase order, and the concept of segregation of responsibilities means that claims clerks should not be issuing authorizations.

The bottom line for gatekeeper models (not loosely managed PPOs or AHPs) is that claims for anything but primary care services should not be paid without an authorization unless they are specifically included or excluded by policy. For more discussion of internal control of MCOs, please see Chapter 6.

## PAYER DEVELOPMENT OF PROVIDER PANELS

Payer-provider relationships change over time in managed care relationships, in part due to changes in provider dynamics, in part due to payer dynamics, and in part due to general business realities. In immature managed care markets, creating IPAs, for example, is substantially easier than creating IMGs. (In fact, a hospital-created IPA can be created legally well within 48 hours, as the bulk of compliance laws require only that equal access to IPA membership be offered.)

The ease of creating an IPA in an immature managed care market—or even the creation of panels of providers or practitioners (which is even easier than creating IPAs)—points to a different problem: Payers have no means to control losses when providers/practitioners are organized as PPO/AHP panels or IPAs. PPOs, for example, rely on enrollees' inherent protection of their own wallets to change consumption behavior. However, payers whose enrollees continue to pay the price for the freedom afforded them must ultimately leave a market that is impervious to premium escalation.

In another example, immature IPAs involved in capitation contracts compensate their panel members on the basis of intensities of service performed. Examples of such service intensities, which act to weight a practitioner's claim to the pool of capitation funds available (net of their PMPM contracts and the covered lives for which risk is borne), include resource-based relative value scale (RBRVS), relative value units (RVUs), and units of the College of American Pathologists (CAP units). A similar set of methodologies based on weighting a practitioner's compensation on a pro-rata basis can be found on page 78. To practitioners, any of these methodologies typically results in a deduction from what they would estimate their claim to be worth. The bottom line is that change is not necessary because practitioners continue to view their consumption of health care resources as reimbursable (regardless of how discounted) and because they bear little actual risk (that the capitation contract created) other than a deeper claim payment discount. The direct relationship between consumption and earnings is allowed to remain intact.

The problem in the development of these panels, moreover, is that capitation is not reimbursement. Payers have little leverage over practitioner behavior through capitation.

## OUTCOMES REPORTING

Outcomes reporting represents the next major evolution of managed care contracting in the most mature capitation markets. MCOs accredited by the NCQA (see Chapter 4) are increasingly being held accountable for selected outcome indicators, such as appropriate immunizations for children, mammograms for women at risk for developing breast cancer, and ophthalmological retinopathy examinations to prevent blindness among at-risk diabetics (particularly those with poor glucose control). These indicators exist under the current version of the Healthcare Effectiveness Data and Information Set (HEDIS; see Chapter 4).

Reporting of outcomes was a capability that payers have always desired from practitioners and providers and that fueled much of the moves by HMOs to capitation-based pricing. The original intent of capitating practitioners was to minimize A/P and MLR exposure (e.g., variability of IBNR) for HMOs and bring health insurance more in line with automobile insurance, casualty insurance, and every other insurance product that ties premium to policyholder experience. This incongruity is different from experience ratings, as these ratings are based on the experiences of a class of employers in order to derive a premium price. With the exception of "preexisting conditions," there is little tie between premium paid and an individual member's health status, even though capitation was supposed to bridge this gap.

Complicating this discontinuity is the fact that few, if any, health plans have actually obtained outcomes data in any form. This complication exists, in large part, because of the reasonable mistrust between payers and practitioners. A logical fear of practitioners is that outcomes will be used to reduce capitation and that those who are poorer performing risk expulsion from a network, therefore constituting a sentence of death for a practice.

At the same time, the HMO industry bears part of the responsibility for its lack of access to outcomes data. Providing outcomes data could have been a fiat, in other words, one of the first conditions for receiving capitation. In reality, though, the managed care industry never could have predicted that HEDIS requirements of NCQA accreditation were going to evolve such that outcomes data for specific disease states would be needed. And, considering that they were not required at the outset, this practitioner reaction is a natural phenomenon in the field of change management and should not be considered a deterrent to obtaining these valuable data.

One of the best uses of these data is to establish managed care industry guidelines for specific interventions highly correlated with specific outcomes, rather than adjudicating costs and places of care. Such data would have completely transformed the clinical practice of medicine and could have been available over a decade ago.

## ADVANCED STUDIES IN CAPITATED MANAGED CARE

In Chapter 1, substantial detail was provided about the basics of capitation and the challenges to practitioners/providers and their service-based MCOs in actually managing capitation after a contract is signed. Please remember that traditional definitions of capitation were focused on the contract because capitation is an insurance industry product, and the signing of the contract to outsource a particular product was the endpoint of that involvement. That point of an executed contract is that the insurance industry is out of the field of health care management and is more firmly back in the premium sales roots of the industry. That same point, moreover, is also the exact moment when practitioners and providers need to "step up to the plate" and manage the business for which they are now contracted, even if they *choose* to define their role simply as performing a contract compliance role. The *fact* is that, by signing a capitation contract, a provider or practitioner is *at risk* for the consumptive behavior and direct outcomes of such behavior by a given population of individuals, for which the provider cannot identify by name. While the practitioner typically knows the members' names (as well as their social security numbers, addresses, and dates of birth), he or she is given almost no wherewithal to actually manage this population of faceless names.

This section is addressed from this very different perspective. How can the wellness model be implemented, especially where it did not previously exist? Does every one of 2,000 covered lives, for example, need to be treated as patients, knowing that every expenditure and every second of a practitioner's time spent is coming out of a ridiculously low capitation payment? Is it even possible to provide quality care with such low PMPM payments? On what is PMPM based that the prices could be so low?

## Per Member, per Month

Many managed care plans and risk-bearing practitioner organizations are capitated; that is, providers or groups of providers/practitioners (IPA, PHO, IDS, etc.) are prepaid a set amount of money based on enrollment in the plan, usually expressed as a contractually set dollar amount PMPM. This simple change turns around all the traditional health care financial management relationships and most every health care finance publication. Table 2.16 points out such changes for both payer and provider/practitioner organizations.

Under capitation, services provided become an expense, not a source of revenue, so the new goal is to reduce unnecessary or inappropriate services. The underlying theory is to place emphasis on keeping people well (wellness programs, preventive medicine, early detection of problems). Unfortunately, this theory applies only when the population is otherwise healthy; for example, no otherwise-healthy child should require seeing a pediatric nephrologist. The

**TABLE 2.16**

**Operation Impacts of Discounted FFS and PMPM**

|  | DFFS | PMPM |
|---|---|---|
| Services | Services generate revenue; the more acute the service, the greater the revenue | The cost of providing services is an expense charged against revenue; such a model is exactly the opposite of how most every segment of the health care industry defines its business. |
| Revenue | Based on services provided: more is better | Based on plan enrollment, quantity of services is irrelevant; capitated providers and practitioners have not reengineered their business to handle fixed revenue, and most vendors do not have a clue how to generate their sales (revenues) for capitated health care clients. |
| To increase revenue | Provide more services or charge more | Revenue is increased only by enrolling more covered lives, increasing premiums, or selling aftermarket premium products. |
| Patient care | Provide patient services as care is needed | Stratify covered lives into HEDIS/The Joint Commission disease states ("chronic"). Manage chronics using disease management model (see Chapter 9). Define all other lives as "nonchronic" and provide traditional gatekeeping using EPSDT (early and periodic screening, diagnosis, and treatment), and phone/Internet management to increase accountability while reducing total costs of care. |

problem is that populations are sold via PMPM or homogeneously as a single-risk population. Thus, the underlying theory of PMPM is that every member in the group is essentially similar to everyone else.

Everyone knows such a premise of homogeneity is far from the truth. On an epidemiological basis, we know that more than half of the U.S. population is clinically obese, which itself poses significant health concerns, including comorbidities such as heart disease and diabetes mellitus. It is a far stretch to say that even morbidly obese Americans should be considered healthy and sold as part of a larger population that is sold to gatekeepers. The sale by capitation contract is merely a convenience for the seller (the MCO) and is not intended to constitute an optimal care strategy. To be sure, if there were an optimal care strategy, it makes no sense for an MCO to incur a fixed obligation (through capitation) if it could have managed these members by itself. The contract is clearly to outsource this business, and practitioners need to recognize that their perspective is now forever changed.

How drastically does the perspective change? First, it should now be clear that covered lives are not sold in the same way they are to be managed; in fact, managing these people on the basis of withholding high-cost care did not work at all. Not only did loss prevention not work in managed care, the efforts resulted in multimillion-dollar jury awards and state and federal legislators rushing to pass laws enabling members to sue their MCOs. Since much of the health care industry has *never* understood capitated managed care from the standpoint of managing care, it stands to reason that health care would try to replicate the same exact mistakes and unmanageable risk rather than take the tougher path of making sense of capitation in a realm other than an insurance-based world.

This change in perspective is what distinguishes most MCOs from traditional health care providers. It is important to keep in mind, however, that many providers are in transition—and may be for some time to come. Some of their business will be capitated and some FFS. This state of transition will affect relationships with these providers, from contracts to incentives, to claims processing, and to referrals.

In the mid-1990s, Medicare risk HMOs began to complain to CMS about the disparate AAPCC rates in certain high-volume/low-cost regions like Dade County (Miami), Broward County (Fort Lauderdale), as well as Hillsborough and Pinellas Counties (Tampa-St. Petersburg) in Florida. Little of the cost and price complaints, all of which are nonmedical factors, had to do with national health care costs or the inherent inefficiencies in hospital operations. What the HMOs intended to say was that IBNR and claims management were inefficient, but they did not know why. What HMOs did say was that the inherent nature of doctors and hospitals themselves were inefficient.

Through capitation, MCOs are also able to sell populations they do not wish to self-manage (e.g., where premium revenues are high, claim costs are low, and IBNR is predictably low). As capitated markets mature, the health plans eventually capitate all health insurance management relationships, eschewing much of the PPO and PSO business that remains in a given market. The practitioners themselves start seeing more capitated business but lack the training to practice the "art" of managed care medicine (Table 2.17), choosing the failed strategy of

**TABLE 2.17**

**Dimensions of the "Art" of Managed Care Medicine**

| | FFS Mentality | PMPM Mentality |
|---|---|---|
| Patient care | Patients come to the office, and they/their insurers are billed for services rendered. | Practitioner calls patients on the phone or via password-restricted Intranet, and monitors their health; problem areas handled in office. |
| Hospitalization | Practitioner bills more the longer patient stays; no incentive to evaluate alternative delivery sites. Position is at odds with hospital desire to get patients discharged faster and with better outcomes. | Practitioner shares hospital desire to get patients discharged sooner, while staying compliant with The Joint Commission performance measures (see Figure 41) and hospital UM policies. |
| Lab tests | Practitioner practices defensive medicine, ordering any test (such as a Chem-12) that will allow for an exhaustive definitive diagnosis. | Practitioners take more detailed histories that pinpoint which specific concern lab tests are to address (e.g., a BUN/creatinine alone, not a Chem-12 that includes BUN/creatinine at a much higher [wasted] expense). |

acting primarily as insurers and becoming overfixated on reducing costs. Using this art form, diagnostics themselves are specific to the suspected condition, not inclusive within more comprehensive (and more expensive) tests (see Table 2.17).

PMPM also creates an even stranger bedfellow than practitioners imitating insurers. Through outsourcing via PMPM payment, the MCO is also in a new, poorly understood line of business as long as it continues to collect premium payments and write PMPM checks to contracted practitioners and providers.

This capitation business model is not unlike a distributor who takes an administrative fee "off the top" of goods and services sold to those dealing with the larger public. Analogizing this simile to managed care, the HMO becomes a distributor, while practitioners and providers become exclusive retailers of health care services. Under capitation, this exclusive retailing enterprise of practitioners and providers becomes a function of price and quality of service. The new *distribution* business of HMOs is poorly understood by the insurance industry; success in the distribution business is a function of price, efficient service, and anticipating customer needs—not just price alone. MCOs continuing to differentiate on PMPM alone may well be committing slow suicide in this new distribution realm. It is against this backdrop that HMOs started to be viewed as "overhead" in contractual relationships with large purchasers of managed care. This led first to limited direct employer contracting by providers, then by the employers themselves forming their own health plans under the broad protections of ERISA, sometimes contracting with HMOs and other times not. Again, the HMOs, and their industry as a whole, mostly "did it to themselves." It is quite clear that this trend will not be an isolated case but will create new competitors for PMPM pricing.

The bottom line of PMPM pricing is that the provider and practitioner are now at risk not only on price but also on expensive claims and unmanaged IBNR. In addition, they must adhere to ever-changing compliance laws at the federal level. Equally problematic is that some compliance areas, such as providing evidence of medical necessity for Medicare patients and adhering to Medicare's 72-hour rule, are beyond the capabilities of older billing software that practitioners have in their offices and beyond the capabilities of some of the newer software as well. Practitioners bear the onus of knowing to ask such specific questions about information systems products. (An in-depth discussion of information systems issues is presented in Chapter 7.)

The harm of being noncompliant in these PMPM contracts is also profound. Compliance law allows HMOs and hospitals to incentivize capitated physicians to reduce costs and IBNR. Yet, hospitals rewarding their noncapitated physicians for the same behavior are criminally noncompliant and subject to civil monetary policy (CMP) and possible exclusion from federal programs. The law allows HMOs to recommend to providers ways to reduce laboratory costs. Yet, hospitals that implement these recommendations and automate their billing software accordingly through a process known as *down-coding* (Chapter 8) could be subject to substantial civil and criminal penalties under the federal False Claims Act of 1863 (31 USC §§ 3729-3733), also known as Lincoln's Law. FCA violations are incurred when illegally down-coded claims are submitted to any federal agency to be paid.

## FULL-RISK CAPITATION

*Full-risk capitation* means any and all provider or practitioner services consumed by a given population of capitated enrollees, whether such services are consumed by members of the capitated entity or by those outside it. In the case of "full medical risk," such services include patient care done in a physician's office, in an urgent care center or clinic, in an institution (other than provider charges exclusive of professional fees), or in any and all other medical or nonmedical settings (such as a chiropractor's office, if chiropractic services are part of the payer's stated coverage).

An early-1990s price commonly paid in Southern California for full-risk medical capitation was approximately $40 PMPM. As that market began to compress, the prices started to fall. Because of the reality that full-risk capitation is increasingly less reflective of practice expense and increasingly more reflective of greater profitability requirements, practitioners also need to change the way they do business under full-risk capitation. Practitioners receiving full-risk medical capitation are therefore disincentivized to refer to higher-cost specialists at all. In addition, the practitioners are incentivized to create as many subcapitated relationships as possible to avoid having to pay many specialists on a DFFS basis. This strategy puts capitated practitioners at risk for full-retail or slightly below-retail charges.

Full-risk institutional capitation involves providing for all nonmedical care rendered within the institutions of the MCO *or in other institutions not part of the MCO*. For example, the care for a capitated enrollee who requires inpatient psychiatric care would be the responsibility of the MCO provider receiving institutional capitation for nonmedical services, whether or not such an institution is part of the MCO; in this example, if care is rendered within a psychiatric hospital not part of the MCO, the bill for any and all institutional services is sent to the MCO. Thus, MCOs retain more capitation dollar based on their breadth and depth of affiliations and on their ability to enter into case rates—or, ideally, subcapitation—with external institutional providers on which the MCO must depend.

The financial impetus for HMOs to enter into full-capitation arrangements, both medical and institutional, is to reduce their administrative expenses and break down their infrastructure. In the days when HMOs were paying on FFS or DFFS, their infrastructure and infrastructure-related expenses were tremendous. Since the HMO was reimbursing providers on the basis of billed claims, the organizations required tremendous infrastructures to handle thousands of claims every day (e.g., storage, mail rooms, delivery personnel, trash management, computers, claims personnel, claims adjudication personnel, UR nurses [or subcontracts for such services], postage costs, etc.) to do a type of job that they had little experience doing themselves.

When HMOs contracted with each pairing of professional service organization (for full-risk medical) with health service organization (for full-risk institutional), the HMO cut its infrastructure down from tens of thousands of claims each month paid to all providers to 24 checks a year: 12 checks to the capitated practitioner organization and 12 checks to the capitated provider organization. In addition, the plan was able to bundle other fixed costs with a full-risk capitation. Examples of such bundled costs included reinsurance, authorization, subrogation, adjudication, or HEDIS statistical reporting. This change in contracting has freed HMOs to do what they do best: sell premium.

## GLOBAL CAPITATION

A newer contracting trend in very mature capitation markets like Southern California is to cut the infrastructure back from 24 checks per year for two integrated providers to 12 checks per year to a single, "superprovider." This trend, unimaginatively called "full-risk capitation" is different from full-risk medical capitation and from full-risk institutional capitation. The term *full-risk capitation* (albeit sometimes confused with the lesser forms of capitation) is given to very large practitioner organizations, typically also contracted as Medicare+Choice PSOs, with sufficient depth and breadth of coverage (controlling at least 100,000 covered lives) at an amount equal to the full-risk medical capitation plus somewhere between 50% and 75% of the standard full-risk institutional capitation rate. This pricing is based on an assumption of a benefit from economies of scale and the reduced need to duplicate each other's services to manage capitated business.

In the early 1990s, full-risk medical and institutional services (also known as "global risk") was initially priced at about the $60–$70 PMPM level. The current pricing trend of increasing premium prices is in response to six consecutive years of heavy premium discounting during open enrollment periods, especially in Southern California. Since MCOs have limited price elasticity (meaning that they are unable to do conventional "cost shifting" by increasing premium prices), the largest employers in a given market—those most aggrieved by premium increases—have an incentive to purchase health services directly from the super practitioner organizations and cut out the "middleman," namely, the MCO.

## GATEKEEPING AND PRIMARY CARE CAPITATION

Like subcapitation (see the discussion in a separate section that follows), gatekeeping capitation is one of the types of capitation that results for parceling risk into smaller pieces to facilitate contracting. PCPs that are "gatekeepers for hire," as the theory goes, are better able to leverage economies of scale in practicing gatekeeping than is a single full-risk entity that provides a plethora of services that include gatekeeping.

For example, in early 2000, gatekeeper capitation was less than $5 PMPM in Southern California but over $35 in New York City, an area that still has little capitation. While New York City has higher costs of living than Greater Los Angeles, the costs are not seven times higher. Indeed, this huge discrepancy for relatively the same actuarial risk is proof that mature-market full-risk capitation bears little resemblance to the actuarial and underwriting processes that first created PMPM.

This price differential reflects the higher costs of living in the early 2000 decade relative to the early 1990 decade and is slightly reflective of the cost differential between New York City (five boroughs) and Greater Los Angeles (five counties). And, since general costs probably explain the variance in full medical risk capitation prices in February 2000, they also show that mature-market, full-risk capitation is more reflective of what the market will bear than on core insurance pricing practices resulting from market segmentation, benefit plan design, actuarial mathematics, underwriting, and empirical determinations of premium pricing and PMPM offered.

## CONTACT AND SPECIALTY CARE CAPITATION

Contact capitation, most typically done in IPA settings, involves a more equitable distribution of capitation or subcapitation (see the next section and Chapter 1) than acuity-based formulas that benefit overconsumers of health care resources. In contact capitation, the weighting criterion is the volume of similar-acuity members seen rather than the relative acuity of each one. Please bear in mind that contact capitation does not involve a PMPM and is not actuarially derived; in fact, it is just a simple weighting, not much different mathematically from a Z-score. Contact capitation therefore lends itself to subcapitated specialists or to specialty care capitation within a larger organizational structure, such as a medical foundation, a clinic without walls, or a physician-hospital organization (PHO).

## SUBCAPITATION MODELING

One of the strategies that medical providers employ to reduce their need to ration, regardless of their risk strategy, is to enter into subcapitation arrangements with specialists. As discussed in Chapter 1, *subcapitation* is a parceling of risk from among a larger risk basis of a different practitioner or provider organization. The subcapitated entity then provides the appropriate level of care for the same overall population connected to the larger risk basis.

Using 5,000 covered lives against a $40 monthly rate for full-risk medical capitation, for example, obstetrical care could be subcapitated for $1.85 PMPM. The impact of this subcapitated rate is that a full-risk medical group could indemnify itself from routine obstetrical care that 5,000 individuals might demand for $9,250 per month (within contracted corridors of liability that are reflective of the reinsurance contract that the capitated seller might have negotiated with the MCO). By comparison, DFFS pricing of an obstetrician might be $1,000 for a vaginal delivery versus $3,000 for a cesarian delivery. Therefore, subcapitation is an important component of the field of capitation.

For practitioners believing in a "risk-is-good" contracting strategy, subcapitation is motivated less by profiteering and more by seeking those who can provide value added to full-risk providers, enhancing the way in which they practice and the way they deliver high quality per capitation dollar received. By contrast, practitioners believing in a "risk-is-bad" contracting strategy enter into subcapitation contracts motivated more by price with the intent to try to subcapitate the same parcel of risk to someone else. Both subcapitation motivations, good risk and bad risk, are equally legitimate forces in maturing capitation markets. And, given that there is no price parity yet among commercial risk practitioners, the bad risk contracting strategy continues to flourish even in the most mature capitation markets, such as in Southern California.

The CMS requirement that 50% of FQHMO-paid capitation must be accrued to a risk pool is a highly variable expense, especially if out-of-network providers submit bills to the capitated physicians for services rendered, whether paid via FFS, DFFS, or some form of "per case" contract. Given this reality, subcapitation could be used to reduce the exposure such physicians could have from such consumption-based contracting by making the risk pool less variable and, therefore, more "fixed." As a general rule, then, subcapitation is a strategy that medical providers utilize to make their risk pools less variable. The more subcapitation that they can negotiate with specialists, the less consumption-based exposure they face. The goal for bad risk players is to approach 100% subcapitation to specialists for risk pooling; the goal for good risk players is to have as much specialty care done within the group or within a defined network, with whatever out-of-network specialty care done on as close as possible to a 100% subcapitated basis (negotiated on a combination of price, patient care performance, and clinical outcomes—a *value* basis). An aggregated average of subcapitation, reflecting both good risk and bad risk provider strategies, is approximately 50% of total risk pool allocation.

From a different viewpoint, moreover, there is a greater good that bad risk contracting creates in the managed care marketplace. Such types of subcapitation act to accelerate the polarization of available practitioners in a given market to adopt one of the two risk strategies and to enter such markets with purposeful intentions. In other words, forcing subcapitation down to the lowest acceptable price (which has yet to be reached, surprisingly enough) forces practitioners to perform some form of strategic and market planning, critical processes that few practitioners do (but most every provider and PHO do) today.

There is also a legal consequence in many subcapitation arrangements. A curious aspect of subcapitation, especially "gatekeeper subcap," is that some MCOs choose to be oblivious to the practice if practitioners do not specifically disclose all such relationships. In fact, because of the strong market forces that incentivize practitioners/providers to have subcapitated relationships with other ones, this form of contracting is truly the backbone of capitated managed care relationships. This "plausible deniability" of MCOs is exacerbated by the fact that few capitation contracts specifically prevent assigning risk to providers/practitioners with whom the payer organization does not have a direct relationship. A denial of the existence of undisclosed subcapitation by an MCO is not, in and of itself, evidence that the payer is unaware of its proliferation; moreover, such a denial likely violates the spirit of a capitation contract that does not specifically prevent the practice.

Another legal consequence has yet to present itself widely in early 21st century America. Since the public has such little understanding of capitation, especially in the general mass media, and since many MCOs claim to be unaware of subcapitation influences of their own capitation contracts, how is the existence of subcapitation told to members for whom their care has been sold to other practitioners? In other words, how are members channeled to subcapitated practitioners they did not directly choose? So far, most practitioners have created excuses rather than open a "Pandora's box" of potential liability for member litigation. One common excuse is, "I'm sorry, but Dr. X has a 12-week backlog for seeing new patients, but Dr. Y is seeing some of Dr. X's patients, and I could get you in to see Dr. Y tomorrow morning if that's okay."

## TERTIARY CAPITATION

Tertiary capitation is often a misnomer for specialized, high-acuity hospital services that are quaternary (no longer tertiary) in nature for which a capitated indemnification is sold for an entire population. The contribution margin that providers in capitated, and increasingly subcapitated, arrangements receive is less completely linked to profit because of the need to pay noncapitated institutional fees. Again, tertiary capitation represents neither a PMPM nor an actuarially sound price-setting mechanism.

For example, a single bone marrow transplant (BMT), which can easily cost a capitated provider $0.25 million for one leukemia patient, easily wipes out an entire year's risk pool. Yet, a tertiary capitation price of $0.20 PMPM ($2.40

PMPY, per member per year or simply PMPM × 12) to insulate a provider from the cost of BMT, when multiplied against a population of as much as 1.0 million lives, would cost $240,000 to indemnify a million for *less* money than the DFFS cost of one member undergoing the procedure in any single year. In addition, because such risk is quaternary, geographic proximity need not be a factor in negotiating for such tertiary capitation.

As providers are successful in subcapitating more of their institutional risk to others, and subcontracting institutions become more receptive and adept at accepting subcapitated secondary and "tertiary" institutional risk from MCOs or other capitating hospitals, hospital risk pool earnings will increase and might yield incremental earnings to practitioner interests inherent in such accrual funds.

## NONINDEXED CAPITATION

Nonindexed capitation equates to a flat-fee basis for accepting specific risk for an entire population of covered lives, more typically held by another practitioner organization. Of course, the provider's administrative costs (no more than a "cut" off the top of the pool of funds made available to the subcapitating provider) are included before any nonindexed capitation is offered. Whereas "traditional" capitation derives price as the product of a PMPM and a volume of covered lives, nonindexed capitation sets a fixed price for any and all covered lives who require a specific type of care. In other words, nonindexed capitation exists in the most mature of capitation markets and is sold for a single, budgeted monthly or annual price. The single fee is paid even in the absence of members, whereas indexed capitation paid to practitioners fluctuates monthly based on the updated number of members.

Nonindexed capitation is even riskier than "traditional" capitation, especially in the mature managed care markets in which it proliferates. There is some equanimity proportional capitation, for which a practitioner receives incremental capitation for incremental covered lives. Nonindexed capitation, by contrast, is inversely proportional since the value of the nonindexed capitation paid to a practitioner decreases as the number of covered lives increases.

# UNDERSTANDING OF "OPERATIONAL" CAPITATION FOR THE HEALTH CARE INDUSTRY

As discussed in Chapter 1, capitation has traditionally been defined as the PMPM payment itself and has remained undefined once the contract is signed. For care to be managed, providers need information about the inherent health of individuals, against which the management of care can be "benchmarked" against the ideal state and against the state of the beneficiary from the time of original assessment. In short, managing care should be no different from other forms of classical management: evaluating operational and financial data, maximizing the benefit of actions against their cost or their expected financial or operational "return," gauging how efficiently resources are mobilized for expected returns, and so on. Classical management deals with controlling and changing known organizational structures and behaviors, improving the level of control for previously unknown or poorly known processes and organizations, motivating workers to provide maximum output for minimum needed inputs, and both controlling organizational costs and maximizing financial returns. The underlying necessity in such managerial processes is knowledge and the wisdom to use such knowledge appropriately.

Capitation itself is poorly defined in the health care industry. What is clearly defined, however, is the method by which capitation contracts are negotiated. The sum of money might be indexed in various ways to make it seem less fixed (e.g., adjusting for population-based demographics such as age, sex, and socioeconomic status). The provider accepting capitation might be a specialty or PCP, or coordinated organizations of such physicians, who accepts less than total health care risk for a given population to make the enterprise seem less risky; of course, such physicians are paid less money for accepting less population risk. Regardless of the variations, the core contracting principle is still the same: Capitation involves providers/practitioners accepting risk on a population basis, and it is hoped armed with some appropriate information.

The level of knowledge that health care providers require to manage care, just like the field of information management (see Chapter 7), starts with the search for factoids. In the case of "managed care," the search for factoids presumes that the manager requires a level of knowledge about the individual that is yet unknown. Yet, the efficiency in collecting factoids is dependent on the ability of managers to engage in fact-finding. For example, the butterfly catcher needs binoculars to find the butterflies, a butterfly net in which to capture them, and specimen jars to retain the butterfly after it has been caught. In capitated managed care, the fact-finding financial manager requires a different set of tools, as shown in Table 2.18.

This level of inquiry into a search for factoids is not yet occurring in a surprisingly large number of provider/practitioner organizations. Curiously, many otherwise-competent and well-trained financial managers do not even recognize that they lack the basic information to manage appropriately. For example, the "Pareto principle," a standard business management theory, states that 80% of a group's statistical variance around an average is explained by 20% of its cause; which 20% of the population should be targeted to reduce 80% of expense variance? When only the PMPM is believed to be important for managed care, and not the processes that are important to make the PMPM profitable, how can any management occur?

These perhaps-rhetorical questions are not to suggest that payers are largely to blame for contracting with unknowledgeable provider/practitioner organizations. The blame rests *squarely* with the provider/practitioner, at least for the following three reasons:

**TABLE 2.18**

**Financial Manager Skill Set to Operationalize Capitation**

- Keep an open mind and gather any factoid you can to help explain the unknown.
- Search out individuals with knowledge of facts and factoids that, in the possession of other learned individuals on your staff, could become meaningful data by which to manage your operation for a given volume of covered lives.
- Create an environment that can properly record factoids whenever and wherever they are encountered, which can be properly captured as data.
- Obtain the knowledge of computerized database management and data modeling techniques to retain data captured, to create an environment to create information from such data, and to adapt this information into meaningful intelligence.
- Do not be afraid of outcomes, no matter how badly they reflect on practitioners. It is far easier to downplay outcomes for which no cause has yet been determined than to explain why the quest for the truth about outcomes was never undertaken.
- Be vigilant in attempting to quantify, in a measurable way, the cost and operational ramifications of strategic, marketing, contracting, and channeling decisions to enable proper budgeting and variance reporting.

- MCOs cannot be held accountable for providers/practitioners with no strategic business plan, no marketing plan that addresses the entrance into the capitation marketplace, and no conceptual notion of how much capitation to accept (and at what stop-loss, at what high/low price, and for what carve outs, if any), and no idea how to be profitable in this line of business.
- MCOs cannot be held responsible for providers/practitioners who have no idea whether they want good risk or bad risk capitation and leave themselves entirely at the whim of capitating and subcapitating entities that could easily take advantage of—and ultimately destroy—them.
- Providers/practitioners bear general responsibility for their own actions, notwithstanding how they relate to their covered members (see Chapter 5), even if their limited view of capitation has no place for consideration of members and their interests. (MCOs have a right to expect the highest level of quality for their capitation payments, regardless of a practitioner's price for assuming risk.)

Let us consider an operational situation that is not so blind. Say that Harry Jones is the administrator of an IMG that has been contracted to provide quality, cost-effective health care to a particular population offered by a health plan. Harry knows from the managed care contract of the IMG what its financial obligations are and the capitated price it will receive as an indemnification of such obligations. He also understands how little the health plan will do from the moment the contract is signed and how the IMG accepts a greater level of responsibility up to certain dollar thresholds for each member of the managed care population that it will be serving. While the IMG knows that it will be financially responsible for this population, and the consequences of such financial responsibility both on the upside and the downside, it would be provided no tools to manage this population within such financial constraints. Indeed, Harry knows next to nothing about this population for whom the IMG has significant financial responsibility. What he does know is that medical records exist only for the subset of a larger population who have consumed health care services (whether in a doctor's office, in another ambulatory setting, or as an inpatient). Even worse, the IMG has no computerized data, except perhaps for billing and collections information that records only the level of information needed to receive money for a billed claim.

This example represents horrible operational management in any industry and in any business sector. The IMG would not know which members of the population are current or behind on immunizations (including tetanus boosters), which members are most at risk for preventable medical conditions, which members are most at risk for unpreventable medical conditions (for which the IMG has significant exposure), and which members of the population are healthy enough that they likely will not require any health care at all. In short, Harry's group is "set up" to be surprised and to be injured financially from such surprises. As such, he has no means to manage the population of lives covered by the IMG, to plan how to manage this population better, or how to assess what level of financial losses that this population will create for his group.

When capitation is defined as the PMPM, and not as the actual managerial processes to expend less expense PMPM against capitated revenue received with improved or unchanged outcomes, rationing is the inevitable result. When rationing is a priority, outcomes are not. And, in late 1999, when Illinois and California—and a few other states—passed legislation to allow members to sue their MCOs, the price of ignoring outcomes in deference to PMPM is indeed a risky proposal, probably too risky for practitioners in such states to continue to perpetuate.

So, Harry's grand strategy for his IMG would be to institute enterprise-level rationing. Strategies would include shortening hours of operation, eliminating weekend and holiday hours of service, reducing operating expenses (including staffing), reducing capital expenditures, as well as cutting back on PBX (private branch exchange, switchboard) expenses by installing voice mail. It is not surprising to hear voice mail in so many medical groups and IPAs that have signed managed care contracts, particularly capitated ones.

The operational focus of the group will change as well. Harry might therefore consider any member contact to be a negative contact, especially if allowing such contact would have a certain negative financial consequence and only an uncertain negative quality consequence. Taking this approach to the ultimate level (hypothetically speaking, and not to suggest that this strategy exists to a widespread degree), one might install voice mail with the express intent of discouraging employees from returning all but the most urgent member phone calls (since the call was placed to initiate a consumption of health care service and not returning the call would eliminate a less-than-clearly appropriate consumptive contact).

Such "one-way" software often features user-*un*friendly menus that discourage all but the most tenacious member from leaving a message in the first place. In short, the group would have financial disincentives for consumptive behaviors on the part of the population for whom it is financially responsible, but no means to distinguish between truly appropriate and inappropriate consumptive behavior. In other words, Harry is inadvertently challenged and operationally straightjacketed to manage the population in a quality-conscious manner, if at all, at the same time that the group is financially disincentivized for each incident of health care consumptive actions. As the chief manager for this group, Harry would be left to manage only what he could manage, even though the act of doing so is nothing short of rationing. The rationing actions of the group therefore represent all that it is able to do and do not represent a malicious intent to cheat its members or to downgrade the level of quality and value that they might derive from the practitioners. In other words, the group is predestined to manage by ineptitude. Ineptitude, in any industry, is not an optimal managerial solution, and ineptly managed enterprises should not be expected to remain in business, certainly not for the duration of the capitation contract.

It should be no surprise that a substantial and increasing number of practitioner organizations and MSOs in the 1990s sought bankruptcy protection to indemnify or otherwise protect their organizations from the effects of their rationing operational and financial mismanagement and contractual noncompliances. When their contracted providers and/or enrolled members sue, the practitioner, provider, and MCO are equally named in litigation subpoenas.

## CONCLUSION

This chapter is indeed voluminous, but it is hoped for good reason. As of this point, the typical financial manager with a basic understanding of managed care should be left with lots of questions: How are providers/practitioners supposed to manage their operations if not by rationing and given that operations indeed does have a place in understanding capitation? How do providers/practitioners change their operations to accommodate covered lives paid for through capitation? The answers to these questions can be found in Chapter 3.

# 3 Managed Care Provider and Practitioner Operations

## INTRODUCTION

With the enactment of Part C of Title 18 (Medicare) of the Social Security Act via the 1997 Balanced Budget Act, and later as results of the Medicare Modernization Act and the enactment of Medicare Advantage, both CMS (Centers for Medicare and Medicaid Services) and HCFA (Health Care Financing Administration) before it initially permitted traditional provider and practitioner operations to join together in compliant ways to direct contract as Medicare professional (or provider) service organizations (PSOs) and more recently as accountable care organizations (ACOs) in conjunction with the Patient Protection and Affordable Care Act (PPACA) of 2010. These PSOs had to adopt certain aspects of traditional managed care organization (MCO) structures to operate in compliance with CMS requirements under Part C. This chapter describes some of the more common MCO organizational structures and functions that successful provider- or practitioner-based operations typically adopt.

## THE BOARD OF DIRECTORS

Most managed care plans, excluding those that are subsidiaries of larger companies or lines of business within an insurance company, have a board of directors that is responsible for the governance of the operation.

All health maintenance organizations (HMOs) are legally required to have boards, with the specific requirements determined by the laws and regulations of each state. Some states require member representation on the board, even that up to a third of the board members be enrollees in the plan. However, many national HMO companies use the same corporate officers as the board for each locally incorporated HMO, with local representation as required. In this case, clearly, the management of the organization controls the company rather than the board.

The composition of the board will vary depending on whether the plan is for profit or not for profit. In the former case, representatives of the owners or shareholders may hold the majority of seats. In the latter, there may be more community representation. Whether the board contains outside directors rather than plan officers depends on company bylaws and local history. The existence of

---

**TABLE 3.1**
**Responsibilities of the Board**

- Fiduciary
- Legal
- Policy
- Quality
- CEO

---

external board members can be an element considered in the awarding of government-related contracts (Medicare risk, Trocare/CHAMPUS [Civilian Health and Medical Program of the Uniformed Services], etc.). Provider-sponsored plans will generally have provider-dominated boards and must be careful of antitrust implications.

The function of the board is governance: overseeing the plan and maintaining final responsibility for it. The board gives final approval to the corporate bylaws, which govern the basic power and control the structure of the plan and the board itself. The responsibilities of the board fall into five general areas: fiduciary matters, legal affairs, policy, quality, and hiring and review of the chief executive officer (CEO) (see Table 3.1.)

The fiduciary responsibility of the board in an operating plan is its most important. It includes general oversight of the profitability or reserve status of the plan as well as oversight and approval of such significant fiscal events as a major acquisition. If the plan is for profit, the board protects the interests of the owners—the stockholders—and is responsible for the accuracy of financial statements provided to them.

The board of directors has legal responsibilities as well. These may include reviewing reports and signing documents, such as the quarterly financial report to the state regulatory agency, reviewing investment portfolio composition and performance or any acquisition documents.

Another common role of a board is setting and approving policy, ranging from overall policies like the use of a gatekeeper in the plan to reviewing organizational plans and structures. The board itself may set a policy indicating the policies for which it must approve changes and additions. An important role of the board of directors of an MCO is the supervision of the quality of care of a plan in general and its quality management program in particular. This responsibility may be handled by a board committee (discussed further in this chapter). And, of course, the board of an independent MCO is responsible for hiring the CEO, who reports to the board, and reviewing his or her performance. The board may also be involved in developing the CEO's compensation package.

## BOARD COMMITTEES

Depending on the size of the board of directors and how active it is, it may form committees to "specialize" in making certain decisions and recommendations. Typical committees may include

- Executive committee
- Finance committee
  - Approve budgets
    - Set and approve spending authority
    - Review and approve sources of outside funding
  - Review financial results
  - Review annual audit
- Member advisory committee
  - Review benefit plan changes
  - Oversee appeals and grievances
- Compensation committee
  - Issue general compensation guidelines
  - Approve and issue stock options
  - Set CEO's compensation
- Quality management committee
  - Review quality improvement program
  - Review reports on findings and activities
  - Oversee medical advisory subcommittee
    - Provide feedback to medical director and plan staff
- Compliance committee
  - Oversee compliance program
- Address alleged compliance or fraud incidents

# MCO MANAGERS

Each MCO may have its own titles and definitions for key staff members, depending on myriad factors: the type of plan and its legal organization, its product line, its relationships to other businesses, and the people involved. However, certain general roles need to be filled, and these are as described in Figure 3.1.

## CHIEF EXECUTIVE OFFICER

The top individual in an MCO may be called a CEO, an executive director, a plan manager, a general manager—it depends on whether the organization is a subsidiary of another, freestanding, and so on. Whatever the title, the CEO in an independent MCO is responsible for all operational aspects of the organization, general administrative functions, and public affairs (large national organizations may have other structures). The officers and senior MCO managers report to this position; the CEO reports to the board.

## Sample Managed Care Organization

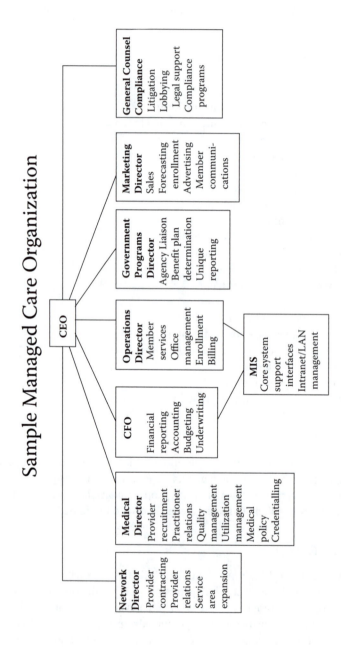

**FIGURE 3.1** Sample managed care organization. EDI, electronic data interchange; LAN, local-area network; MIS, management information system.

## MEDICAL DIRECTOR

The medical director is a board-certified physician usually responsible for quality management, medical management, and medical policy and usually reports to the CEO (or to the board). The medical director may be a full-time staff person or part time. As the MCO grows, it may well start adding physicians as associate medical directors. The associate medical director's duties may be a functionally or geographically assigned slice of the medical director function. That is, the associate medical director may be responsible for one functional area, such as utilization management appeals. Or, he or she may be assigned to all the medical director functions at one site or in one geographic region. The medical director typically chairs various subcommittees, which often contain physicians from the community. Examples of common committees include the credentials committee, the pharmacy committee, the medical advisory committee, and the independent second opinion advisory panel.

## NETWORK DIRECTOR

Network composition and contracts are the backbone of all managed care operations. The network director is responsible for ensuring sufficient size and quality of contracted providers to attract and service members. Negotiation of acceptable provider prices that will allow for market-driven premiums and profitability goals of the plan is a constant balance that network directors seek.

## CHIEF FINANCIAL OFFICER

The chief financial officer (CFO), also reporting to the CEO, is responsible for all financial and accounting activities, including reporting, accounting, underwriting, and budgeting. MIS (management information systems, see Chapter 7) may report to the CFO or to the operations director.

## OPERATIONS DIRECTOR

The operations director is found primarily in large plans in which a division of responsibilities is indicated. This person, who generally reports to the CEO, may be responsible for claims, MIS, billing on enrollment services, and office management.

## MARKETING DIRECTOR

The marketing director brings in the business. He or she is generally in charge of sales and forecasting enrollment numbers. Marketing also handles advertising and member communications and creates and directs new MCO product lines as well as aftermarket and add-on premium products and sales. The marketing director also will negotiate vendor discount arrangements to retain market shares in senior risk products (such as hearing aid and eyeglass negotiated discounts with local businesses and national chains, e.g., services of Sears and other major department stores).

## GENERAL COUNSEL/COMPLIANCE

Large plans generally require in-house counsel and compliance professionals to help manage the legal and compliance risk of the plan. Medium-size plans might have a part-time attorney in this position until enrollment supports the employment of a full-time in-house counsel.

## PAYER BENEFIT DETERMINATION

In Chapter 2, the concept of the creation of a customer-sensitive benefit plan design was presented, as well as an overview of the impacts of certain financial elements in the control and noncontrol of certain plan design features. In this section, certain economic and regulatory forces at the payer level also come to bear on benefit plan design, which ultimately affect the ability of an MCO to offer provider- and practitioner-sensitive plan options and products. These factors include the core services most commonly comprising a comprehensive MCO product (for which competition among health plans is less intense than for supplemental services that are more specifically niched), the economics by which an actuarially based medical loss ratio (MLR) is balanced by plan marketability and sales, sufficiency of risk pool accruals within regulatory limitations (including incurred but not reported [IBNR] exposure), availability of specialty products that address local and regional needs plus opportunities to resell customers on new MCO products, as well as meeting the qualifications of the Federally Qualified HMO (FQHMO) Act to differentiate among smaller payer organizations and become qualified to offer contracts to nationally distributed employers as well as to state and federal governmental agencies.

### MCO SERVICES

A comprehensive HMO plan will cover

- Physician services, including inpatient and outpatient coverage
- Outpatient prescription drugs
- Ancillary services, such as laboratory tests and X-rays
- Inpatient hospital stays
- Emergency services, including out-of-town emergencies
- Skilled nursing facility or convalescent care
- Mental health and chemical dependency treatment

Some HMOs also offer senior care, dental and vision care, behavioral health coverage, and Medicare Advantage products geared to Medicare beneficiaries or special needs populations for separate coverage. These, plus mental health and chemical dependency treatment, may be subcontracted to specialty HMOs (discussed in the next section). In reality, however, there is a close interrelationship between mental health and physical illness that likely will be missed if behavioral health assessment is viewed only as a specialty service. For example, many state Medicaid managed care programs that require practitioners to adhere to the EPSDT (early and periodic screening, diagnosis, and treatment) model require inclusion of behavioral health assessments. In this manner, the thinking of the private sector about primary and specialty care is long behind the enlightenment of the public sector.

## MCO ECONOMICS

The success of an MCO depends on its ability to balance the often-contradictory needs of providers, patients, purchasers, and other stakeholders. The plan must pay providers enough to attract the best quality but must offer attractive premiums to cost-conscious purchasers. Patients want the widest possible choice of physician, but smaller networks offer more opportunities for cost control.

As mentioned in Chapter 1, MCOs take full risk of covering their costs with the premiums collected from purchasers. The percentage of premium revenue that goes to medical costs, called the MRL, is a key measurement of the financial health of a plan: It quantifies how much is available to cover administrative costs—mostly fixed costs—and provide profits. The financial health of an HMO depends on achieving a favorable MLR by controlling medical costs and charging appropriate premiums. Specifically, Chapter 1 suggested a variety of strategies to make the MLR more predictable, less variable, and stable enough to keep provider and practitioner costs under greater control.

## SPECIALTY HMOS

A specialty HMO takes the MCO model into specialty fields. Dental, mental health, and vision plans are the most popular. They can be separate plans or add-ons to medical plans, which are typically insurance riders that can pay for certain specialty care providers out of the medical risk underwriting. In mature managed care markets, specialty independent practice associations (IPAs) form to become specialized members of an integrated delivery network paid via subcapitation of full-risk practitioner panels.

Some states require MCOs to offer a broad range of health services; in these states, specialty HMOs are not possible. HMOs contracting as part of managed Medicare are required to provide access to a full array of services.

## FEDERAL QUALIFICATION ELIGIBILITY BY OFFICE FOR MANAGED CARE

Federal qualifications and eligibility are the stamp of approval of the federal government: the federal certification process for MCOs. They ensure that certain elements are in place and configured appropriately. In addition to HMOs and Medicare Advantage plans, the federal government approves competitive medical plans (the forerunners of Medicare PSOs and ACOs), which, while provider or practitioner based, were treated exactly like HMOs (e.g., capitalization, risk pools, 50–50, and relatively low average adjusted per capita cost [AAPCC] rates). Most CMPs that existed, for certain federal or state funding, have reorganized under Medicare Parts C or D and likely within certain states as part of their respective health care exchanges.

Qualification and eligibility are strictly voluntary and involve some advantages and disadvantages that we discuss in this chapter. To become qualified as an HMO, the plan must submit an application to the Office for Managed Care (OMC). The OMC is part of the CMS of the U.S. Department of Health and Human Services (DHHS).

The applications and the reviews that are part of the process ensure that the HMO meets federal compliance standards for its health care delivery system, its financial viability, its marketing, and its legal and organizational status. Table 3.2 shows the key areas for structural and compliance review of HMOs. It should be noted that complete compliance regulations of HMOs, ACOs, and Medicare

---

**TABLE 3.2**

**OMC's HMO Areas of Structural and Compliance Review**

| | |
|---|---|
| Financial viability | Performance |
| | Budget assumptions |
| | Cost and revenue projections |
| | Capitalization |
| Health care delivery | Availability, accessibility, and continuity of health services |
| | Quality assurance |
| | Utilization controls |
| | Physician risk arrangements |
| | Management information systems |
| | Feedback to physicians |
| | Evidence of physician willingness to service Medicare population |
| Marketing | Enrollment projections and assumptions |
| | Strategy Marketing materials |
| | Minimum 5,000 commercial members (1,500 rural) |
| | 50% Medicare or Medicaid (which increases to 75% in certain states), 50% commercial membership |
| Legal | Organized under state law |
| | Insolvency arrangements |
| | Provider agreements |
| | Subscriber agreements |
| | Board oversight (HMOs) |
| | Management ability to control operations |
| | Staff capability |

Advantage plans are voluminous and noncompliance could subject federal contractors to potential violations of any or all of the following:

- False Claims Act of 1863 (31 USC §§ 3729–3731), carrying both criminal and civil enforcement as well as treble damages for punitive costs,
- False Statements or Representations [42 USC §§ 1320a-7a(a)],
- Antireferral statutes [42 USC § 1395nn (Stark I and II)],
- Exclusion from Medicare, Medicaid, and Tricare if officers are officers criminally convicted or as part of a sentencing guideline [42 USC 1320a-7],
- Anti-Kickback Provision [42 USC §§ 1320a-7b(b)],
- Emergency Medical Treatment and Active Labor Act (EMTALA, 42 USC § 1395dd).

It should be noted that exclusion from federal and state health programs can accrue to an HMO if the violated statute includes a provision for CMP under violations of both "False Statements and Representations" and EMTALA; moreover, specific federal sentencing guidelines exist for CMP. One such guideline is exclusion from federal and state programs; a health plan's exclusion just from Medicare would be disastrous for almost all but highly niched specialty HMOs.

### Application Process for FQHMO Qualification

The qualification process for HMOs is described in Title XIII of the Public Service Health Act (also known as the HMO Act) and summarized in Table 3.3. Specific regulations and requirements are found at Section 42 of the *Code of Federal Regulations* Part 417 (42 CFR 417.00 through 417.180). The eligibility standards for CMPs are mandated in Section 1876 of the Tax Equity and Fiscal Responsibility Act (TEFRA) and the regulations at Section 42 of the *Code of*

---

**TABLE 3.3**

**Distinguishing HMO Qualification from CMP Eligibility Requirements**

HMO

- No longer required to use community rating; can use experience rating for larger groups depending on your local regulations
- Comprehensive benefit requirements
- Few limitations regarding time or cost of benefits
- Up to 10% of services may be provided outside the HMO (self-referral)

CMP

- May be community or experience rated
- More flexibility in benefits design
- May limit benefits regarding time and cost
- Services must be "primarily" (at least 51%) provided through the CMP

*Federal Regulations* Part 417 (42 CFR 417.400 through 417.810. Table 3.3 shows the major differences between the requirements for HMOs and CMPs.

HMOs can apply for federal qualification only or can apply for a Medicare contract at the same time. The same dual-purpose applications can be used for federal qualification of a regional component of an HMO, which may be established so that separate community rates can be used in each component. For CMPs, application for eligibility and a Medicare contract are combined because the two are inseparable: CMP status is only for the purpose of Medicare contracting. To expand the service area already qualified or eligible, the HMO or CMP must complete another application.

Once the application is completed and sent to OMC, it goes to the Office of Operations, a unit of OMC responsible for qualification and eligibility determinations, Medicare contracting, and monitoring Medicare contacts. First, the application is reviewed for completeness, and the MCO is either informed about missing information or is told approximately when to expect a site visit. Next, the application is intensively reviewed by specialists in Medicare, finance, and health services delivery. If the MCO passes this review, the site visit is the next step.

## Site Visit Prior to FQHMO Qualification

In the site visit, a team of specialists meets with managers and discusses and reviews the financial, Medicare, health care delivery, and legal systems of the organization. The team may also request additional information. After the site visit, members of the team report on their findings and recommend approval or disapproval. A final consolidated report is reviewed by OMC senior staff. The MCO will receive one of the following verdicts: approval, intent to deny (applicant has 60 days to correct problems before being disapproved), or disapproval.

## FQHMO Postqualification Process

Once approved, HMO qualification applicants must sign and return an assurance stating that the HMO meets and will continue to meet the applicable requirements. Once this is complete, the HMO is qualified, with one of the following designations:

- *Operational*: The HMO is organized and operates in accordance with regulations to provide basic and supplemental services to its enrollees.
- *Preoperational*: The HMO has no enrollees and is not yet operating but will be qualified when it does. It must become operational within 60 days after signing the assurance.
- *Transitional*: The HMO is operational and has enrollees but does not offer the qualified commercial benefits requirement. This requirement is to be met as contracts with employers are renewed.

After an HMO or CMP has been qualified or found eligible, coordinators in the regional offices of CMS will monitor it to ensure continued compliance and conduct site visits regularly once a Medicare contract has been awarded. Payments for Medicare enrollees were previously established by CMS based on average areas per capita costs, with more standardized rates (in most areas, higher rates) for Medicare+Choice organizations and now complete capitation for Medicare Advantage plans. Initially, ACO providers were to be compensated through existing fee-for-service mechanisms, even while the ACO organizations themselves would be capitated for accountable care.

## MCO MARKETING AND PRODUCT DEVELOPMENT

Managed care payers exist in competitive markets that require competent marketing and creation of service-based products that employers, union benefit trusts, and self-funded plans will likely purchase in a given market. Without marketing, the financial manager of an MCO will have few finances to manage since developing, marketing, and selling products people will purchase is altogether the key to add business. While not intended to duplicate the entire fields of marketing, sales, and product development, the products offered by an MCO and the ways in which they are promoted and sold obviously have an effect on finances. The strategic decision level of marketing is where the financial manager needs to be involved.

The key to successful marketing—and a successful business for that matter—is to start with the complete intelligence about potential markets for products. (Conversely, the unsuccessful approach to marketing is to start with a product and promote it through the most economical mailing house.) The key concept in marketing strategy is the realization that MCO products are sold *twice*: first to the employer (or similar organization, such as an ERISA [Employee Retirement Income Security Act of 1974] plan) and then to the individual employees, who have a variety of competing plans from which to choose. It is important to note that the final consumer, in actuality, has only one or two competing plans from which to choose. In the most mature capitation markets (e.g., capitation comprising over 50% of all insurance plans), MCO plans do not typically compete with PPO (preferred provider organization), indemnity, or group insurance based on discounted fee for service (DFFS).

MCOs have different customers from which to derive revenue. Hence, it is unlikely that one MCO can offer a single product that will appeal to all of the differing needs of different customers.

### MARKET SEGMENTATION STRATEGIES

The methodology for designing different product features to drive revenues for different customers is called *market segmentation*. The purpose of segmenting the market is to arrive at a specific market demographic profile with similar needs, buying patterns, and competitive situations. There are any number of ways to segment a large market. For example, segmentation can occur by

- Market size
- Geography (i.e., local, regional)

- Organizational proprietary status
- Industry (i.e., manufacturing, service)

The ideal segment is easily defined, of sufficient size, economically healthy, and with few competitors. Deciding which market segment to pursue is a strategic decision on the part of the MCO and involves questions like the following:

- Is this segment large enough to produce profitably?
- Is it one for which we can develop a competitive product?
- Is it one that fits in with the rest of the strategies of our organization?

## DEFINING DESIRABLE MARKET SEGMENTS

Once the target customers have been defined and segmented, market research is needed to verify if the targeted premium market correlates well with the desired segmentation strategies. The purpose of market research is to define the market numerically in terms of its size and potential and to discover how the purchasing decision works: which factors influence premium purchases, which competitors exist in the targeted market, and which of the competitors design premium products for the same market segments. In other words, develop market intelligence to compete effectively for premium-based segments and preempt competing premium products, if possible.

Different premium market segments have different sales drivers. For example, large employers are interested in price, service, and quality, while smaller employers are interested primarily in price. National firms will want a national provider network, while manufacturers might want a workers' compensation component. Factors in the purchasing decision can be summarized as follows:

**Price:** How much will the premium cost? (As mentioned, price may be the *sole* purchasing factor for a small-business customer.)

**Features and Benefits:** What are the features offered for the premium price, and are features tied effectively to the desired market segment? In other words, do the features meet the needs of the employer and its employees?

**Service and Satisfaction:** What do other employer customers say about the premium product they purchased? Do they receive complaints from their employee members, and what do they say about the MCO? Do they receive good services, and are they happy with the plan to which they subscribed? How often do things go wrong, and how well are they fixed?

**Convenience:** Are plan providers and practitioners located in areas convenient to where employees live and work?

**Reputability:** Do the premium plan and the contracted provider/ practitioner network of the MCO have a positive reputation in the community?

## Strategic Product-Positioning Drivers

Another consideration of payer revenue drivers is how well the premium product is positioned for a specific market segment. Each decision maker in purchasing a premium product will react differently according to how the product is marketed. The decision maker can vary from the human resources manager, the benefits manager (who is typically a subordinate of the human resources manager), the CFO or CEO (or his or her spouse), and so on.

The premium product-positioning strategy depends on the size and nature of the organization. The union or school board usually has a voice. And remember, many employers buy their health plans through brokers, agents, TPAs (third-party administrator), or work closely with other consultants, so the decision maker is sometimes outside the organization entirely.

Competitors certainly vary for each market segment of a premium product. This level of market intelligence is in the realm of the marketing and sales departments of an MCO. Their analyses include analyzing the factors and developing strategies to promote the strengths of the product effectively and in a way that preempts or "one-ups" a popular competing product.

These strategies are tested primarily in consumer focus groups, in which alternative benefit plan designs and premium prices are rated by potential and previous customers in terms of how likely they are to purchase the feature/price package of a given product. While focus group participants are rating these products, their verbal and nonverbal reactions are typically videotaped (for later review) and observed through one-way glass, primarily for senior managers and consultants to gauge overall group reactions in real time. Real-time observation also lets the facilitator alter presentation style and fine-tune the product mix once the focus group ends. (Transcripts, reports, and videotape copies can introduce a lag time of as much as 1 month.)

## Distribution Channel Drivers of Effective Product Placement

Distribution channels vary between markets and even by market segment. There are four principal distribution channels:

1. Consultants
2. Brokers
3. Direct sales markets (e.g., Internet)
4. Collective "purchasing groups"

Direct selling to employer groups occurs in markets or segments deemed underserved by brokers and consultants. Both consultants and brokers provide advice to employers in selecting new benefit plans. Consultants are usually paid by the employer on a project basis for their advice. A broker, however, receives a commission, normally a percentage of the premium. The goal of the employer is to have an unbiased third party present complete options from which the employer can choose. This presentation is tied to focus group findings of which products should be offered to which employers at what price range.

When an employer works with a broker or consultant, the real decision maker may be unclear. It is best to treat everyone involved as a decision maker and not attempt to bypass any party. Maintaining positive, long-standing relationships with consultants and brokers is a critical success factor for the marketing department.

Direct selling to employers may be done by licensed in-house sales staff or licensed agents. Many states require agents to be appointed by the MCO and to have that appointment registered with a state agency.

## REVENUE DRIVERS BASED ON REQUESTS FOR PROPOSAL AND REQUESTS FOR INFORMATION

Requests for Proposal (RFPs) and Requests for Information (RFIs) are two very important, but often overlooked, revenue drivers for MCOs. Both require good networking between MCOs and their customers and must tap the measured high-quality aspects of their plan providers and practitioners. MCOs effective in responding to these proposals must have clear and high-quality participation with appropriate accrediting organizations (see Chapter 4).

### REQUEST FOR PROPOSAL

An RFP is sometimes issued by an employer looking for a new managed care provider, or by the employer's broker or consultant, to solicit bids. It is a formal methodology used to document the needs and requirements for a project and used frequently when multiple bids are desired or received. Receiving an RFP depends on the relationship that the sales staff of an MCO has built with employers, brokers, and consultants and offers an opportunity to enhance that relationship and further drive premium revenues.

An RFP will ask for financial data and for information about experience, proposed benefits, claims, and quality measures. It will generally also ask why the plan of an MCO is best for this employer. When responding to an RFP, it is important to provide the information requested completely and clearly and to present your information in terms of the needs and priorities of the employer. However, information requests vary widely from one RFP to another. This results in the RFP process being burdensome for many plans. Proposals received by the employer—or typically a consultant—are reviewed, and certain plans are invited to provide oral presentations or site visits, which are the last step to securing a sale of a premium product.

### REQUEST FOR INFORMATION

An RFI sometimes precedes an RFP. The RFI may be as simple as a community rate and its supporting demographics or as complex as requesting extensive company information, enrollment data, profitability information, and more. Those who "pass" the RFI process will receive an RFP. Sometimes, desirable products gleaned from the RFI will serve as the benchmark for RFP consideration; this situation is ideal if the product of an MCO is already known to preempt its competitors and to surpass their most popular products. In this way, much of the uncertainty associated with bidding RFPs can be eliminated through careful and complete market research and product positioning through desirable distribution channels.

## PAYER AND PRACTITIONER/PROVIDER SERVICES

The purpose of this section is to highlight payer operations that have an impact on the operations of providers and practitioners. These operations include payer and provider/practitioner managed care contracting and outsourcing of certain operations.

### CONTRACTING

Contracting is the primary relationship between payers and providers/practitioners. Clearly, the key to successful managed care contracting is setting the amount that will make both the physician and the MCO happy. The first step in primary care capitation is to define what primary care is. A standard list might include inpatient visits, office visits, minor office surgery, routine lab studies, injections and immunizations, physicals, preventive services, and infant care. There are numerous gray areas, including certain tests and other surgery, that will need careful consideration. The definition of primary care is not an idle exercise. It forms the basis of the costing that will lead you to the capitation amount.

As shown in Table 3.4, there are two costing methodologies for developing per member, per month (PMPM) contracts: fee-for-service (FFS) and budgetary or cost (B/C) methods. Pertinent examples that include medical costing data and processes are shown in Table 3.5. To calculate costs based on demand estimates instead of utilization, the budgetary or cost methodology is preferred. To calculate costs PMPM using the fee-for-service methodology, both average service charges and utilization estimates are necessary. The capitation rate is set once the PMPM costs are derived, using either methodology.

The capitation rate will approximate the PMPM cost, with some additional factors added to the mix. These factors can include member age/sex mix and the effects of cost-sharing and geographic variances in consuming health care

---

**TABLE 3.4**

**PMPM Costing Using Fee-for-Service (FFS) and Budgetary or Cost (B/C) Methodologies**

$$\text{PMPM Cost Method} = \frac{\text{FTEs per 1,000 Enrollees} \times \text{Average Annual Compensation}}{1,000 \text{ Enrollees} \times 12 \text{ Months}}$$

$$\text{PMPM Fee-for-Service Method} = \frac{\text{Volume of Service Utilization} \times \text{Average Cost per Unit}}{12 \text{ Months}}$$

## TABLE 3.5
## Examples of PMPM Costing Using Both FFS and B/C Methodologies

### Standard Industry Assumptions

1. 0.75 physician budgeted FTEs per 1,000 enrollees (3 FT practitioners per every 4,000 lives)

2. Average compensation is $180,000

3. Average *cost* per visit is $5

4. 3–3.5 PCP office visits per year

### Primary Care Physician Cost Using Budgetary or Cost Methodology

0.75 FTEs required per 1,000 members per year

Average total compensation is $180,000 per year

$$\frac{0.75 \text{ PCP FTEs} \times \$180,000 \text{ per year}}{1,000 \text{ Enrollees} \times 12 \text{ Months}} = \$11.25 \text{ PCP Labor Cost PMPM}$$

### Medical Supply (Used During a Visit) Cost Using Fee-for-Service Methodology

Demand is three visits per member per year

Average cost per visit is $5

$$\frac{3 \text{ Visits} \times \$5 \text{ per Visit}}{12 \text{ Months}} = \$1.75 \text{ PMPM}$$

services. Payments in most capitation systems vary with the age and sex mix of the enrollees to accommodate their differences in utilization. For example, infants under 18 months have a high utilization rate. The rate drops for 1- to 2-year-olds and drops again after age 2. After age 18 and up to age 45, utilization by women will be higher than utilization by men because of childbearing, and so on. If these considerations seem familiar, it is because they are similar to the age and sex factors described in Table 2.3.

Other factors that may be considered in setting capitation payments include some of the other rating factors, such as the type of industry involved, geographic concentration, service volume, and membership size. Utilization rates vary by location, both nationwide and regionally, and need to be considered.

The capitation rate may also be adjusted for business reasons. For example, an HMO may pay a higher capitation to providers who are not part of the network of any other HMO (commonly referred to as exclusivity). Conversely, the capitation paid to providers/practitioners under a point-of-service (PSP) plan typically receive 35% less PMPM due to the higher actuarial risk associated with members having no restrictions for going out of group or out of network; the business decision in this product line means that part of the 35% withheld is used to fund a separate risk pool for out-of-network DFFS reimbursement. The rate may also exclude certain benefits or services called "carve-outs" or include certain services (such as mental health screening, which would otherwise be included in a higher-cost carve-out) called "carve-ins."

## CARVE-OUTS VERSUS CARVE-INS

Carve-outs are specific benefits or services that are administered separately from the rest of the managed care plan and which may be managed by other third parties. They usually include such elements as mental health (above basic behavioral health screening that is part of EPSDT-based managed care) and substance abuse services, vision, dental care, prescription drugs, and so on. These normally covered services are carved out of the capitation payment and reimbursed on a fee schedule or are subcapitated. Subcapitation, as seen in Chapters 1 and 2, represents an unbundling of risk, similar to a carve-out, that is sold to providers and practitioners on a PMPM basis.

To keep carve-outs from undermining the cost control system of capitation, they should apply only to services that are not subject to discretionary utilization and where guidelines for use are fairly clear cut. This includes, for example, such services as immunizations and dental checkups but not office-based lab tests.

Whereas a carve-out is a strategy to encourage providers to be able to negotiate for a particular book of business, a carve-in is a strategy to do the same thing for health plans themselves. A perfect example of a carve-in is primary medical eye care, which is indemnified by a payer either under a vision risk plan or as a vision rider for a medical risk plan, even though neither such contracting strategy will provide actual medical eye care that can help diagnose both systemic and nonsystemic medical conditions (not necessarily ones involving vision) that are more effectively and cost-efficiently detected via an eye exam. The ability of a specialty IPA to offer primary medical eye care to a health plan via a carve-in contract allows the health plan to improve its marketability to its own brokers and customers without the need to "reinvent the wheel" at substantial additional time and expense.

## OUTSOURCING

In Chapters 1 and 2, the concept of capitation was presented as a vehicle for payer outsourcing, as well as specific issues presented for consideration of "optimal" capitation. In this section, the rationale is not limited to payers.

Outsourcing is a realistic operational consideration available to providers/practitioners. For all the reasons presented to this point, outsourcing has advantages and disadvantages. Certainly, a key advantage is to leverage economies of scale and experience for other entities to manage a specific aspect of operations more cost effectively and cost efficiently. By the same token, a provider or practitioner can reasonably predict operation costs by scope of operation and specific contract, preferably on some form of fixed pricing with incentive to keep costs as low as possible.

Certainly, disadvantages have to be weighed as well. Practitioners/providers lose day-to-day control of one or more specific operations. In addition, payers may be reluctant to contract with a provider/practitioner organization that outsources substantial aspects of its operation. The reluctance is that since there is no level of comfort to manage substantial operations, there is naturally even less comfort by the payer. Finally, outsourcing key aspects of operations, particularly those related to high-expense potentials—like IBNR and authorizations—coupled with low stop-loss levels is a "kiss of death" if dependent on payer contracting.

## STRATEGIES TO MANAGE PROVIDER/PRACTITIONER COSTS

The PMPM costing methodologies presented in Tables 3.4 and 3.5 evidence the necessity of quality, accurate utilization or operations data; these are necessities for capitation rates or fee discounts to be set optimally. Inaccurate utilization data will cause inaccuracies "downstream," resulting in multiple MCO problems.

The risk sharing built into or added to these payment systems is also closely based on utilization. Only through high-quality data can an MCO or a provider have any idea how much risk is being assumed in any given situation. In particular, utilization management data are vital to case management and controlling catastrophic costs. For example, most reinsurance companies require advance notice of a potentially high-cost case; this requirement could not be met if utilization management data were inaccurate or suspect. Hence, utilization data are clearly a vital part of assessing and rewarding the providers and practitioners within the network. This process may include both provider profiling and a reward system.

### PRACTITIONER PROFILING

*Practitioner profiling* refers to the collection and analysis of information, primarily utilization information, to develop profiles of individual practitioners. The purposes of profiling include

(a) Providing feedback to providers to help them modify behavior
(b) Determining the focus of utilization management efforts
(c) Identifying specialists to whom certain cases will be sent
(d) Scanning for potential fraud and abuse
(e) Identifying providers or practitioners who should be added to, or removed from, the network
(f) Providing information for incentive compensation systems
(g) Performing economic modeling

Profiling too often focuses on individual actions of specific practitioners. For example, such focuses tend to compare the behavior of a particular practitioner to some norm, with the attendant difficulty of defining the norm. The focus of practitioner profiling is often inpatient care, at least partially because the case and the related physician are readily identifiable, and the information is accessible from the hospital. A more accurate picture may be gained by profiling in terms of episodes of care.

## EPISODES-OF-CARE PROFILING

Episodes-of-care profiling tries to examine practitioner behavior from the point of view of outcomes and total health care resources consumed, including those not directly billed or delivered by any practitioner. For example, an episode of care based on a medical evaluation of an obstetric case will look at prenatal, antepartum, and postpartum care (not always detail billed), use of diagnostics, and so on, not just at length of stay or cesarean rate. In other words, an episode-of-care perspective evaluates practitioners based on what happens to patients they serve.

The difficulty of profiling on the basis of episodes of care is that responsibility for care can be difficult to define, as can the episode of care itself. For example, once diagnosed, the care of a diabetic can last a lifetime. This difficulty is exactly why capitated disease management is a better management strategy for controlling the variable costs of diabetes mellitus over the longer-term duration of the disease rather than cross-sectional consumption of individual services that typify care episodes.

## INCENTIVE COMPENSATION DATA

As discussed in Chapter 2, some incentives are built into pricing structures, and are not truly under the control of the MCO. Other incentives, like bonuses and withhold pool payouts, are additions to the basic payment system of the MCO. These additional payments normally reward behavior that the MCO prefers, which may be other than cost control. Utilization management data and other information more directed to quality issues may be used as the basis for paying incentives. There are behaviors that are important to the MCO that do not necessarily result in a direct, short-term economic reward to the practitioner, such as member satisfaction.

For example, payouts from a withhold pool may be based partially on meeting referral targets, on appropriate hospital utilization, and on authorization compliance. For this simplified example, let us assume the three bases are equally important; that is, 33% of the payout is tied to each. The system might be set up on a point basis, with 33 points available in each category. Referrals will be measured in terms of number of referrals or referral costs PMPY (per member per year). Hospital utilization may be measured by days per thousand per year, admission rate, or average length of stay. Compliance with authorization requirements is measured as a percentage of cases properly authorized. The individual physician's behavior patterns are measured against a standard of preferred behavior for each category, either prospectively (performance goals) or retrospectively (measured against peers). The number of points a practitioner receives for each category is based on the percentage of the time that the behavior measured corresponds to the norms. If this behavior occurs 90% of the time, the practitioner gets 90% of 33 points, or 29.7 points. Point totals below a certain level may disqualify a practitioner from the program entirely; payouts are then allocated on the basis of each practitioner's points.

## PAYER/PROVIDER BUDGETING AND FINANCIAL/RESOURCE ESTIMATION

The process of budgeting for medical and administrative expenses is the cornerstone of health care financial management for MCOs. The costing of clinical processes (by both fee-for-service and budgetary/cost methodologies) and controlling provider/practitioner management of those costs were presented in the previous two sections. This section reviews these processes from the standpoint of the reported costs of the MCO. Chapter 6 details MCO management approaches for cases reported—referring primarily to utilization management and case management—as well as both costing resulting from utilization management and management strategies for IBNR costs.

### MCO Budgeting

Like any business, the purpose of MCO budgeting is to bring in anticipated revenue in excess of anticipated costs. The catch, of course, is knowing and being able to predict costs with reasonable accuracy. Through capitation, the MCO budgets on a fixed basis, with the possible exception of incurring reinsurance liability for grossly unmanaged or catastrophic care that exceeds the underwriting threshold. A payer's costs are either medical or administrative, as discussed in detail previously in this chapter.

### Analyses of Administrative Costs

For an HMO, administrative costs cover all of the expenses incurred in administering enrollees' medical benefits. Administrative costs are generally grouped into five categories: administration, sales and marketing, medical management, occupancy, and other expenses (see Chapter 6).

### Analyses of Capitated Medical Service Costs

Careful analysis of the cost of capitated medical services is essential to the financial health of the MCO because of its basis to the capitation rate. The capitation rate must be both appropriate for the levels of utilization expected and translatable into competitive premium prices.

The first step in an overall cost analysis is to define the plan to be costed, including covered services and copayment requirements. This overall analysis reveals cost information that needs to be determined, most typically for a commercial risk population (additional requirements exist for managed Medicare populations).

Commercial risk costs are based on two variables: frequency of health service utilization per member per year and average cost per unit of service, as shown in Table 3.4 above.

## ANALYSES OF FEE-FOR-SERVICE PRACTITIONER COSTS

A fee schedule along with a summary of the activities for a year at a medical group form a good basis for projecting the costs of all services and the utilization of ancillary services. The summary should include number of services and charges by standard RVU or current procedural terminology (CPT) code, physician specialty, and payer type. These data can be used to create a summary of average charges for each specialty and type of service. Breaking out utilization and cost data by specialty is important since number of visits, laboratory services, and other physician services can vary substantially by specialty.

A sample of patient utilization and charges may be analyzed as described in the following. However, often the only area-specific utilization information for physician services is available from other managed care plans. When using these data, it is important to understand the organization/model of the HMO and the practice patterns of the physicians to evaluate its relevance. A simplified example of such a fee-for-service costing approach is shown in Table 3.6.

**TABLE 3.6**
**Simplified Example of Fee-for-Service Costing (Non-POS)**

| Covered Service | Industry Standard | Average Charge | Cost PMPM |
|---|---|---|---|
| **Utilization PMPY** | | | |
| Primary care services | | | |
| Office visits | **3.50** | $ 48.00 | $14.00 |
| Consultations | **0.10** | $110.00 | $.92 |
| Laboratory | **3.50** | $20.00 | $5.83 |
| Miscellaneous procedures | **1.40** | $30.00 | $3.50 |
| | | | $24.25 |
| | | | |
| Inpatient hospitalization | | | |
| In area, in network | **0.25** | $1,000.00 | $20.83 |
| In area, out of network | **0.05** | $2,000.00 | $8.25 |
| Out of area | **0.02** | $2,000.00 | $3.33 |
| | | | $32.41 |
| Outpatient surgery | **0.08** | $1,500.00 | $10.00 |
| Total cost per member per month | | | **$66.66** |

## OFFICE VISIT FREQUENCY

Office visit frequencies are often estimated using industry norms but should be used with caution. First, the industry norms used should reflect a market similar to the one being estimated. Second, industry data are often misinterpreted. Some industry data reflect only physician-related encounters, leaving out the nurse practitioners, physician assistants, and other physician extenders used by many medical groups. There are many types of physician encounters, such as physical therapy, office surgery, and immunizations. The data used should be understood before estimating industry norms.

## NONNETWORK AND REFERRAL SERVICES DATA

Information on utilization and charges for specialists and nonnetwork providers can be based on national statistics in *Series 13 of Vital and Health Statistics,* published by the National Center for Health Statistics (NCHS), or on other managed care industry data. Costs for physician referrals are generally based on the experience of other managed care plans; therefore, adjustments should be made to account for the fee schedules of the physicians used. Utilization is also generally estimated using industry experience.

## HOSPITAL INPATIENT UTILIZATION/PAYMENT DATA

Hospital inpatient utilization and payment data needed for a cost analysis includes admission rate, length of stay, bed days per thousand population, and average charges per day by type of admission. Sources from which to obtain these data include

- *Blue Cross/Blue Shield; other insurers; union benefit trusts; and self-funded ERISA plans,* by seeking large local employers. (If such data are available, pay attention to well-baby nursery days included in overall bed days, as well as whether costs are shown at gross or at net.)
- *Annual statements filed by HMOs and health insurance companies* requested by state insurance departments.
- *State health department studies,* which are useful if separate statistics are generated for over-65 and under-65 groups; otherwise, the higher utilization by the population 65 and older will skew these statistics higher.
- *American Hospital Association (AHA) studies,* such as its published utilization statistics by state (which can usually be adjusted to exclude the population aged 65 and older) as well as its annual *Guide to Hospitals,* which includes limited utilization statistics.
- *Practitioner organizations and clinics* (inpatient and outpatient utilization can be generated from clinic records for a random sampling of patients; as a caveat, be aware that a statistically valid, random

sampling should include at least 1,000 individuals, with an age/sex mix approximating the community's under-65 age population).

- *Hospitals* may have the *Professional Activity Study* (PAS) published by the Commission on Professional and Hospital Activities (CPHA), *Medicare Cost Reports*, and other AHA-published information.
- *Professional associations, like the Healthcare Financial Management Association* (HFMA), which publishes data trends, as well as its "Industry Scan" and "Updata" regulatory changes in its monthly journal, *hfm*; managed care statistics as part of its "Fax-It" service; and up-to-date regulatory changes on its Web site (http://www.hfma.org).
- *Actuaries and utilization management companies (like Milliman).*

Inpatient hospital utilization data should be examined for the following:

- The age and sex mix of the targeted enrollment population
- The types of employer groups studied and targeted for sales
- The comprehensiveness of benefits, especially maternity
- The utilization controls to be implemented

A breakdown of per diem charges and charges for ancillary services can be found in Schedule D of the annual *Medicare Cost Reports*. This source, as well as any hospital per diem charge data, should be combined with inflation estimates when costs are projected. (Hospital charge data should always be considered in light of the population it covers compared with the population targeted, with adjustments made as necessary.)

Managed care plans often emphasize shorter lengths of hospital stays. It is important to note that shorter stays will increase the average charge per day by as much as 10% since most charges are incurred in the first few days of hospitalization, especially in surgical cases. Inpatient data should not be used for outpatient cost estimates. Hospitals generally do not have average cost and utilization data available for all procedures, but a sample of about 50 typical procedures should give base cost information.

Cost data are also used extensively in actuarial analyses for new product development. For example, let us assume that HealthyCare HMO is planning to develop a product for a new market segment based on industrial classification.

The actuary cannot use conventional approaches to estimate the anticipated utilization and cost but must consider when, where, and why the services will be used. Thus, the targeted market must be segmented into those who will use the managed care plan all of the time, most of the time, some of the time, and never. Within these categories are differing demographic distributions, that is, different ages and sexes, people with varying health statuses, and families of varying sizes. Demographic characteristics are key indicators of actual utilization and cost, so cost projections will vary with different demographic groups. Of course, the competition will affect enrollment as well.

Pricing models for proposed services can be developed, similar to the cost analyses we looked at, given certain information on which to base assumptions:

1. *Community utilization norms and costs per service*: The anticipated utilization and costs for the targeted group are estimated using composite utilization rates based on the demographics of the targeted group.
2. *Utilization management* (see Chapter 6): Utilization management may reduce inpatient services by reducing length of stay and substituting outpatient for some inpatient procedures.
3. *Impact of the proposed delivery system*: Degree to which health care is managed, including provider payment arrangements, including incentives, as well as provider cooperation with utilization management activities.
4. *Continuum of care availability*: Distribution of the targeted group by the extent they will use the system, on a continuum from "for all conditions" to "never"; if employees choose between traditional indemnity and MCO plans, higher levels of employee cost sharing in the indemnity plan will produce much higher participation in the HMO. (The opposite is also true, of course.)
5. *Plan features and benefits*: Features of the particular product plan must be evaluated on their effects on costs, such as level of copayments (see Chapter 2, Table 2.13), access to specialty practitioners, as well as accessibility to nonnetwork providers.

Once developed, costs of proposed products are translated into revenue targets and from there, via rating, to premiums. The competitiveness of the price and the product design will determine the success of the new product.

## COMPARATIVE MARKET DATA

Both the experience of an MCO and the experience of other MCOs in the same or a similar area should be reviewed in cost determinations. Comparing data from other organizations enables MCOs to evaluate changes that they may need to make to be or stay competitive.

Managed care industry data can be found in the *HMO Industry Profile*, published by the American Association of Health Plans (AAHP). State departments of health may also publish utilization and cost data for state-regulated MCOs. These data can be used in establishing inpatient and office visit target encounter rates, comparing lab and radiology ordering patterns, and reviewing referral experience of other plans. For these data to be considered usable for comparative purposes, the data for a plan should encompass at least 5,000 enrollees for at least 1 year.

Hospitalization rates of entire geographies can be derived from patient origin by zip code data that many states provide or make available through public-private consortia. These data are valuable for building an experience rate of historical hospitalization patterns within certain geographies (e.g., a specific market trade area encompassing a range of zip codes). If patient origin data by DRG (diagnosis-related group) or by major diagnosis code (MDC) are also available by zip code, service-specific use rates can be constructed to stratify disease state populations and cost MCO products by specific comorbidities.

Four key areas of cost analysis represent a significant portion of the controllable core medical costs of an MCO:

- Office visit frequency
- Physician payments, ordering patterns, and costs of ancillary services
- Inpatient hospital utilization rates
- Inpatient hospital payments

## CONCLUSION

This chapter attempted to portray accurately the balance that exists in managed care among payers, providers, and practitioners. The availability of accurate and appropriate data is key to the successes of all three roles; without the ability to cost and develop utilization forecasts for experience or adjusted community ratings, for example, the payer will be unsuccessful in offering premium that is not tied accurately to loss probabilities and proper safeguards against IBNR exposure.

The payer having inaccurate operational and forecasting data negatively impacts both providers and practitioners who are contractually bound for the risk associated with a population that has not been accurately measured. Providers are particularly susceptible due to the high prices per case that occur in institutional settings; forecasts that are too low, for example, mean that the provider is at risk for an understated population (who, perhaps, may also be associated with greater consumption of inpatient and emergency services relative to a normal distribution) while receiving less capitation than is due.

The next two chapters cover topics that are rarely included in books about managed care. Chapter 4, "Managed Care Accreditation," provides an appropriate setting to include the application of payer and payer/provider operations within the guidelines set by various accrediting agencies. Chapter 5, "Managing the Managed Care Enrollee," is particularly unique, as member compliance and health adaptation are the key to any successful plan, yet enrollees are traditionally viewed as cattle, requiring a gatekeeper to push them into the appropriate pens before they consume the wrong resources. By contrast, futurists had been predicting since the mid-1990s that members will participate in their healthiness in unprecedented ways. While history has shown that people need to take more responsibility for their own health status, the actual transformation of public and private policies under managed care thus far in the 21st century has not entirely lived up to this ideal.

# 4 Managed Care Organization Quality Benchmarking

## INTRODUCTION

In Chapter 1, we considered the quandary in defining the nature of quality in health care organizations. In the public sector, we recognized that measuring satisfaction, documentation of care required versus provided, and reviews of medical necessity could be implemented when one defined quality based on the health status of populations in need of care based on a public health standard. At the same time, such measures were poorly understood in the private sector, for which quality remained elusive and commensurate with a definition that was poorly conceived all along. The managed care implications of these discussions focused on care provided (or not, in fact, provided) at the levels of providers and practitioners of managed care and the third-party organizations contracted with them to implement managed care objectives. Examples of such organizations were discussed in Chapters 2 and 3, particularly related to third-party administrators (TPAs), management service organizations (MSOs), case managers, utilization managers, and even hybrid organizations (such as administrative service organizations or ASOs), which are carved out from public-sector managed care organizations (MCOs) to handle authorizations, utilization management (UM), and meeting of administrative benchmarks (such as reduction of incurred but not reported [IBNR] exposure in reporting encounters on a timely basis).

What has not yet been discussed is how "quality" is defined and measured among health plans, integrated networks, ACOs, and among larger independent practice association [IPAs] seeking to differentiate themselves on the basis of managed care quality. Historically, such MCOs have sought to define and benchmark the quality of their plans through accreditation. Unlike hospitals seeking accreditation through organizations like the Joint Commission—which typically accredits hospitals based on operational parameters and with an increased emphasis on allowable tolerance for certain clinical errors as a result of both random and representative chart reviews—MCOs have relied on their accrediting organizations in response to concerns of regulators, purchasers, and the general public about the effect of managed care on the quality of health care. There is a variety of accrediting organizations for a variety of managed care-related operations. (Federal qualification of health maintenance organizations was discussed in Chapter 3 for example.)

The original purpose of accrediting organizations was to respond to the demands of HMO customers for accountability and, increasingly, measurable quality. Initial objectives, especially in accrediting MCOs, centered on administrative processes such as streamlining, rationalizing, or attempting to forestall regulation, reducing risk and liability for purchasers, and strengthening the quality process itself within the MCO. Unlike with the Joint Commission, entire datasets of encounters, and both quality and operational benchmarks attained within them, were always part of accreditation procedures of the National Committee for Quality Assurance (NCQA) and later the Utilization Review Accreditation Commission (URAC), now known simply as URAC, which has become the dominant accrediting organization for health care organizations in all aspects of managed care today. The dataset used for NCQA, known as the Healthcare Effectiveness Data and Information Set (or HEDIS), also evolved, particularly since 1995 when it started to zero in on quality of health adaptations, especially key aspects of certain chronic diseases that were responsible for significant excess hospitalizations when the disease was poorly managed.

As mentioned, the Joint Commission, originally just for hospitals, has begun to accredit some group and staff model HMOs as well as PSOs. While the Joint Commission still accredits these types of MCOs, key MCO clients (such as governmental and private-sector purchasers of care, state health exchanges, ACOs developed by health plans and hospitals, as well as underwriters in general) typically put far more credence in URAC or NCQA accreditation, rather than on Joint Commission accreditation for overlapping MCO entities.

The federal government has also gotten into the accreditation business, initially with the quality improvement standards for managed care (originally known as QISMC) of the U.S. Department of Health and Human Services (DHHS), on which the Health Care Financing Administration (HCFA) (and later, the Centers for Medicare and Medicaid Services, CMS) began to rely in the participation of MCOs in federal programs such as Tricare, managed Medicare (particularly Part C), as well as managed Medicaid plans. These standards have been adapted for health care practitioners and their related organizations (such as IPAs, integrated and specialty care networks, and medical groups) under the Physician Quality Reporting Initiative (PQRI), which represents a "safe harbor" in awarding performance bonuses for participants who exceed applicable benchmark standards, particularly for their respective specialization.

## ACCREDITATION OF HMOS UNDER NCQA

HMOs and POS plans were originally accredited by NCQA. To be eligible, the MCO must meet the following criteria:

- It must provide comprehensive health care benefits to enrolled members, through a defined benefit package, in both inpatient and ambulatory settings.

- It must have been operational and actively providing health care services for at least 18 months.
- It must have access to clinical information about enrollees.
- It must have an active quality management system.

Established in 1979 by the Group Health Association of America (GHAA) and the American Association of Foundations of Medical Care, the NCQA became an independent entity in 1990. Its original purpose included bringing some consistency to the tangle of regulatory and consumer requirements for HMOs as well as ensuring quality of care and service.

## NCQA Accreditation Process

The HMO accreditation process begins with a preliminary information form, which includes descriptions of the delivery system of the plan, including quality assurance, UM, and credentialing. NCQA uses this form to schedule an on-site review, including the size and members of the review team and the estimated time the review will take. Both factors determine the price of the review. The review team normally consists of an administrative reviewer, who is a nonphysician clinician or quality assurance expert, and two or more physician reviewers, who are MCO medical directors or quality management directors.

Before the review team arrives, the MCO provides more detail on the compliance of the plan within each review area. The on-site review will generally last 3 days. The review team confirms compliance with each of the NCQA standards and will normally sample, test, and/or review all of the following:

- Quality assurance studies, reports, and case files
- Member satisfaction and disenrollment surveys
- UM review criteria, reports, and files
- Policies and procedures relating to quality
- Physician credentialing files
- Complaint and grievance files
- Provider contracts
- Minutes of quality assurance and board meetings
- Interviews will be conducted with some or all of the following:
- Chief executive officer (CEO)
- A member of the board of directors
- Medical director(s)/chief medical officer (CMO)
- Selected network physicians
- Director of quality assurance
- Members of the quality assurance committee
- Director of UM
- Director of provider relations
- Director of member services

At the end of the on-site review, the team delivers a summary of its findings and submits a report to the NCQA. The report is reviewed by staff and by the review oversight committee, which judges compliance on each standard and makes an overall accreditation decision.

Plans that meet the standards are accredited for up to 3 years. If the plan has deficiencies that can be remedied in 90 days, it may be given accreditation with recommendations. Once the deficiencies have been addressed, which may require another site visit, the plan is accredited. Plans that have more serious compliance problems may be granted provisional accreditation for 15 months. After 12 months, the plan is reviewed again. If the problems have been corrected, the plan is accredited for 21 months. If not, accreditation lapses.

## AREAS OF NCQA REVIEW

An NCQA review covers six areas, all of which must be comprehensive and well organized as well as meet the highest clinical and administrative standards:

- Quality assurance
- Utilization management
- Credentialing
- Preventive and adaptive health services
- Medical records
- Member rights and responsibilities

The first priority of NCQA in reviews is the internal quality assurance program of the MCO. The quality assurance program must be well organized and comprehensive and report to the highest administrative levels in the organization to meet NCQA standards. Review criteria for the quality assurance program include the following:

- It must cover the full range of services delivered.
- It must include all providers who either agree to cooperate with the quality program of the MCO or allow the MCO to monitor its own.
- It must focus on clinical issues that have a major impact on enrollees' health.
- It must demonstrate effectiveness in improving service and care.

As mentioned, the review team evaluates all relevant quality documentation (from procedures to meeting minutes), interviews staff members, and tracks specific issues through the system to check for resolution and documented improvement, at the reviewers' discretion.

The review of UM will include documentation review and interviews looking for the following characteristics of the UM function:

- An organized system for UM
- Written UM protocols based on medical evidence

- Monitoring for underutilization as well as overutilization
- Review decisions made by qualified medical professionals
- Adequate appeals process for patients and physicians
- Timely decisions and communications

The credentialing review will include reviews of selected provider files and tracking of specific issues through the complaint system as well as reviews of policies and procedures and interviews with staff. NCQA requires the credentialing process of an MCO to include two or three of the following:

- The MCO must verify such information as licensing, malpractice history, hospital privileges, DEA (Drug Enforcement Administration) certification, and other basic physician credentials.
- If the physician entity of the MCO is an IPA, the MCO must conduct a review of physician offices before credentialing physicians within the IPA.
- The MCO must conduct periodic physician performance appraisals, including the areas of quality assurance, risk and UM, member satisfaction, and member complaints.

Because the focus of an MCO should be on preventing health problems, the NCQA standards require that the MCO adopt clinical policies, practice guidelines, quality benchmarking, or balanced scorecards focusing on preventive health care and proactive management of chronic diseases. These guidelines must be communicated to providers and patients. In addition, the delivery of two preventive services (chosen from an NCQA list) must be measured yearly, and the reported results audited by the NCQA. Several defined measurement systems have been enacted, more recently centered on accountable care (the late 2010 ACO standards of the NCQA) and patient-centered medical homes (PCMH; 2011 NCQA PCMH standards).

A sample of medical records is reviewed by the NCQA physician reviewers for quality of documentation and quality of care. Reviewers use a detailed review form to assess the preventive services, diagnoses, and appropriateness and continuity of care provided to patients; outcomes reported; accountability of primary care or overall health status; or balanced scorecard benchmarks reportedly attained.

The NCQA reviews the interactions of the MCO with its members as they relate to member rights and responsibilities. The standards for accreditation include the following:

- A system for resolving complaints and grievances and a system for using complaint data to improve quality;
- Written policies that recognize member rights, such as the right to receive information about the organization and its providers and services and the right to make complaints; and member responsibilities, such as the responsibility to provide needed information and the responsibility to follow physicians' instructions;

- Communications of the MCO to members covering the benefits and charges, procedures for notifying members about changes in benefits or services, referral procedures, emergency and after-hours procedures, disenrollment procedures, and procedures for appealing decisions or lodging complaints;
- Policies and mechanisms for ensuring the confidentiality of medical records; and
- A system of measuring and improving member satisfaction, including satisfaction surveys and disenrollment surveys, and a system for using these data to improve quality.

## CLINICAL INDICATORS MEASURED THROUGH MCO ACCREDITATION

Examples of clinical indicators for MCO accreditation include Joint Commission quality indicators and HEDIS.

### Joint Commission Quality Indicators

Most provider-based MCOs comply with accreditation standards of the Joint Commission (formerly known as the Joint Commission. Starting in the early 1990s, the Joint Commission initially implemented disease staging—a nomenclature that means stratifying patient discharges by the severity of a condition within each single DRG (diagnosis-related group)—as a condition of accreditation and implemented on a staggered basis.

In mid-February 2000, the Joint Commission announced more specific quality-of-care measurements that went far beyond the HEDIS Version 3.0 standards as applicable to provider-based MCOs. These quality-of-care measurements were, at the time, specific to five areas of provider practice (Table 4.1).

### Health-Plan Employer Data and Information Set

The HEDIS dataset of the NCQA represents a set of benchmarks to evaluate the value health care payers provide to their customers. Annual updates to the HEDIS dataset represent the current set of benchmarks against which health plans are measured, which now include conformance to performance indicators that increasingly make HMOs accountable for the health adaptations of certain members with chronic diseases, which is particularly seen in the more recent ACO standards. In general, HEDIS comprises a set of over 60 measures that are used to evaluate, compare, and track performance of health plans, plus examine financial stability, clinical performance (quality of care), access to care, member satisfaction, and preventive care. These data, as well as HEDIS MCO report cards, are compiled and published by NCQA and are available via their Web site or by published reports.

Compared to the previous quality-of-care indicators of the Joint Commission referenced previously, the first set of disease adaptation indicators given by NCQA under HEDIS 3.0 were much less intrusive in payer operations. Previous versions of HEDIS focused on administrative concerns, such as answering calls in a timely

## TABLE 4.1
## First Five Joint Commission Focus Areas of Provider Performance (ca. 2000)

1.  **Acute Myocardial Infarction (AMI)**
    - **Smoking Cessation Advice/Counseling**—AMI patients with a history of smoking who are given smoking cessation advice or counseling during hospitalization.
    - **Aspirin at Arrival**—AMI patients who are given aspirin within 24 hours of arrival or within 24 hours prior to arrival at the hospital.
    - **Reperfusion Therapy: Time from Arrival to Initiation**—Timely reperfusion (opening blocked arteries) of eligible AMI patients; time from arrival to initiation of thrombolysis medication administration or primary percutaneous transluminal coronary angioplasty procedure (PTCA).
    - **Aspirin at Discharge**—AMI patients who are prescribed aspirin at discharge from the hospital.
    - **Beta-Blocker at Arrival**—AMI patients who receive beta-blocker medication within the first 24 hours of arrival at the hospital.
    - **LVEF (Left Ventricular Ejection Fraction) < 40% Prescribed Angiotensin-Converting Enzyme Inhibitor (ACEI) at Discharge**—AMI patients with low LVEF (index of how well the heart functions) who are prescribed an ACEI medication at discharge from the hospital.
    - **Beta-Blocker at Discharge**—AMI patients who are ideal candidates for beta-blocker medication who are given a prescription for a beta-blocker at discharge.
    - **Intrahospital Mortality**—Patients with a primary diagnosis of AMI who expire during hospitalization.

2.  **Congestive Heart Failure**
    - **Patients with Atrial Fibrillation Prescribed Warfarin at Discharge**—Patients with heart failure with atrial fibrillation (irregular heartbeat) who are given a prescription for oral anticoagulation therapy (warfarin) at discharge from the hospital.
    - **Diet/Weight/Medication Management Instructions at Discharge**—Patients with heart failure who receive patient education (as documented on their written discharge instructions) regarding all of the following: all discharge medications, weight monitoring, diet, activity level, follow-up appointment, what to do if symptoms worsen.
    - **Assessment of Left Ventricular Function**—Patients with heart failure not admitted on ACEIs or angiotensin receptor-blocking (ARB) agent medications who have LVEF evaluated before or during admission.
    - **LVEF < 40% Prescribed ACEI at Discharge**—Patients with low LVEF who are prescribed an ACEI medication at discharge.
    - **Smoking Cessation Advice/Counseling**—Patients with heart failure with a history of smoking who are given smoking cessation advice or counseling during hospitalization.

3.  **Community-Acquired Pneumonia**
    - **Pneumonia Screen or Pneumococcal Vaccination**—Patients age 65 or older who are screened for or given pneumococcal vaccination during hospitalization.
    - **Smoking Cessation Advice/Counseling**—Pneumonia patients with a history of smoking who are given smoking cessation advice or counseling during hospitalization or advice or counseling is given to pediatric caregiver about effects of secondhand smoke.

(continued)

**TABLE 4.1 (continued)**

**First Five Joint Commission Focus Areas of Provider Performance (ca. 2000)**

- **Oxygenation Assessment**—Patients who receive oxygenation assessment (determination of amount of oxygen in blood) within 24 hours of hospital arrival.
- **Blood Cultures**—Patients who have blood cultures collected, had them drawn prior to first dose of antibiotic administration in the hospital.
- **Antibiotic Timing**—Time in hours from initial presentation at hospital to first dose of antibiotics.
- **Empiric Antibiotic Regimen, Non-Intensive Care Unit (ICU)**—For patients with pneumonia *not admitted* to an ICU, the antibiotic given is consistent with current consensus guidelines (e.g., of the American Thoracic Society, Infectious Disease Society of America, and the Centers for Disease Control and Prevention).
- **Empiric Antibiotic Regimen, ICU**—For patients with pneumonia admitted to an ICU, the antibiotic given is consistent with current consensus guidelines (e.g., of the American Thoracic Society, Infectious Disease Society of America, and the Centers for Disease Control and Prevention).

4.    **Surgical Procedures and Complications**
- **Surgical Site Infection within 30 days (for Selected Surgical Procedures)**—Patients undergoing selected surgical procedures who develop a surgical site infection (SSI) within 30 days of the procedure.
- **Timing of Prophylactic Administration of Antibiotic**—Timing of when patients were given prophylactic (preventive) intravenous antibiotic administration for selected surgical procedures.

5.    **Pregnancy and Related Conditions**
- **VBAC (Vaginal Birth after Cesarean) Rate**—Patients who have had a cesarean delivery who have a vaginal delivery.
- **Third- or Fourth-Degree Laceration**—Patients who have vaginal deliveries with third- or fourth-degree laceration (tear).
- **Neonatal Mortality**—Infants who expire within 28 days of birth.

manner, having an appropriate percentage of practitioners who were board certified, as well as standard "report cards" that allowed for cross-MCO comparisons by employers choosing MCOs for their benefit plans as well as guidance for medical directors of quality assurance within MCOs themselves. These report cards represented a pioneering effort in the development of hospital and even physician report cards that are popular today, particularly used by health plans to create value equations of their provider network stratified on both quality and price. In fact, the state of Oregon was among the first in the nation to utilize such MCO report cards with full transparency to purchasers of care (such as employers) and to the self-employed shopping for individual plans to offer or join.

The 10 more in-depth disease indicators included in the contemporaneous HEDIS standards (relative to Joint Commission indicators) focus on key areas whose omissions are likely indicative of poor network management and poor member health status. While these indicators become more specific each year,

NCQA has been steadily adding disease states and specifications since HEDIS Version 2.0. The intent of NCQA in updating these HEDIS disease management and wellness indicators remains to put MCOs increasingly accountable to member health status adaptation of chronic diseases and key lifestyle strategies for improved wellness and disease prevention. Examples of HEDIS 2000 indicators—contemporaneous to Joint Commission indicators shown in Table 4.1—are presented in Table 4.2.

It should be noted that staying abreast of NCQA accreditation standards is particularly important. New NCQA standards are announced in July, and new HEDIS standards are announced toward the beginning of each calendar year. Because of the timing involved, some aspect of MCO accreditation will likely change about every 6 months.

## URAC ACCREDITATION PROCEDURES

Utilization management firms or non-HMO MCOs were originally accredited by URAC with the purpose of bringing some uniformity into the UM process. URAC was established in 1990 based on an initiative led by the American Managed Care and Review Association. Its original purpose was to head off legislation fueled by provider frustration with UM diversity by championing standards and consistency in UM. URAC accreditation was designed to simplify life for the provider, not to evaluate the effectiveness of any UM process.

Since its original creation, URAC has evolved just as substantially as NCQA. The two organizations overlap in nearly all aspects of health plan benchmarking, with the possible exception of ACO standards (as of this date of publication). That said, both URAC and NCQA accredit patient-centered medical homes and even maintain accreditation standards for credentialing providers.

### URAC Accreditation Process

Accreditation begins with a detailed application from the UM organization. Once received by URAC, the application is reviewed over the telephone with the applicant. The applicant is given 90 days to supply missing data or clarify unclear data based on the telephone review.

If the application passes the telephonic review, it goes on to the accreditation committee. Identifying information is removed from the application for review by the committee, so the organization is reviewed anonymously. If this review is passed, the application proceeds to the executive committee of the URAC board of directors for final approval. Accreditation is granted for 2 years.

### Areas of URAC Review

URAC standards apply to prospective and concurrent UM for inpatient admissions to hospitals and other facilities and to outpatient admissions to surgical facilities and

## TABLE 4.2
## Sample HEDIS 2000 Disease Indicators

| HEDIS 2000 Indicator | Applicability | Criteria |
|---|---|---|
| 1 Immunizations | Children and teens | Specific combinations of immunizations/ vaccinations (while a common medical criterion, compliance with tetanus boosters every 10 years among adults has not yet become part of HEDIS but is widely expected to become an indicator over the next few years). |
| 2 Mammography | Women ages 52–69 who have been continuously enrolled for 2 years | Mammogram every 2 years; a 52-year-old woman should have had a test over last 2 years; women at significant risk for breast cancer < 52 are not yet included in this indicator or tested more often. |
| 3 Pap (Papanicolaou) smear | Women ages 21–64 | Pap every 3 years; a 21-year-old woman should have had a test when she was over 18; women at significant risk for uterine cancer are not yet tested more often under HEDIS. |
| 4 Comprehensive management of type II (age-onset) diabetes | Adults ages 18–75 with type II diabetes mellitus | (a) HgA1C test done with value < 9.5 (higher clinical standard is < 7.5); (b) lipid profile done with low-density lipids (LDLs) <130; (c) diabetic retinopathy ophthalmological screening once every 3 years; (d) evidence of screening for nephropathy (leads to renal complications, including end-stage renal disease [ESRD]). |
| 5 Beta-blockers | Patients with previous acute myocardial infarction (ami) | Beta-blockers started within 7 days of hospital discharge. |
| 6 ACE inhibitors | Patients with congestive heart failure (chf) | Compliance with medication regimen. |
| 7 Atrial fibrillation | Patients with atrial fibrillation (chf /or coronary artery disease [cad] comorbidity) | (a) Compliance with anticoagulation therapy (e.g., warfarin); (b) evidence of prothrombin time (PT) lab test using International Normalization Ratio (INR) standard. |
| 8 Asthma | Patients with asthma | Evidence of compliance with asthma medication regimen. |

(continued)

**TABLE 4.2 (continued)**
**Sample HEDIS 2000 Disease Indicators**

| HEDIS 2000 Indicator | Applicability | Criteria |
|---|---|---|
| 9  Psychiatric (major depression) | Patients prescribed antidepressants or hospitalized | Follow-up psychiatric management after hospitalization and ensuring that antidepressants (e.g., Prozac) are properly prescribed and medically managed. |
| 10  Chlamydia | At-risk women | Evidence of chlamydia screening for at-risk women. |

*Source:*   National Committee for Quality Assurance. *HEDIS 2000 List of Measures*, May 2000.

include the following: responsibility, information, procedures, appeals of denied authorizations, confidentiality, staff and program requirements, and accessibility.

## Responsibility

A UM firm or department must allow any licensed hospital, physician, or patient representative to assist in the responsibility for obtaining certification/authorization.

## Information

The organization may collect only the information necessary to certify admission, length of stay, and treatment/procedure and may not routinely request medical records on all patients reviewed. When medical records are needed, only the pertinent sections are to be requested. Copies of medical records may be requested for retrospective review of services, quality, and coverage. Data elements that can be required are limited to those considered necessary for UM review.

## Procedures

Reviews must be prompt. Certification/authorization determinations should be made within two working days of receiving the relevant information. UM organizations may or may not conduct daily review of ongoing inpatient stays. The organization must have specific procedures for providing notification of decisions and for addressing the failure of the responsible person to provide information for review.

## Appeals of Denied Authorizations

Patients/enrollees and practitioners have the right to appeal denied authorizations, and the UM organization must have provisions for these appeals. The standards define the specific elements that must be included.

## Confidentiality

The UM organization must have written procedures for confidentiality of patient information. Patients' personal health information must be certified to be compliant with the Health Insurance Portability and Accountability Act (HIPAA). Any subcontractors or third-party benchmarking measurement firms must have signed business associate agreements that are compliant with both HIPAA and the Health Information Technology for Economic and Clinical Health (HITECH) Act of 2009 (the latter enacted as part of the American Recovery and Reinvestment Act of 2009). Such business associates agreements are executed on behalf of the MCO or its UM organization. Summary information is not considered confidential if the patient cannot be identified from it.

### Staff and Program Requirements

Staff must be properly trained and supported by written clinical criteria and review processes created with the participation of physicians. While nurses or case managers may recommend that prescribed treatments do not meet UM standards for medical necessity or that care does not meet established clinical care guidelines (such as Milliman Guidelines), only a physician can deny authorizations and only on an independent review of prior decisions or adverse treatment recommendations made by nonphysicians.

### Accessibility

The standards generally require a toll-free telephone line to be available during regular business hours in the local time zone with written procedures for handling after-hours calls. Nearly all firms maintain secure online servers for processing such requests via the Internet. Other URAC standards cover on-site review.

## ACCREDITATION OF PREFERRED PROVIDER ORGANIZATIONS

Preferred provider organizations (PPOs) are accredited by the American Accreditation Program Incorporated (AAPI), which was jointly founded in 1989 by the AAPI and MedStrategies Incorporated, a consulting firm. The original purpose of the AAPI accreditation process included forestalling further regulation as well as ensuring quality. It emphasized reducing risk and liability for purchasers as well as assessing the value of a PPO. The accreditation process has been administered by MedStrategies. It should be noted that, more recently, PPOs have increasingly sought URAC accreditation to improve its differentiation among purchasers of care and employers, rather than simply relying on AAPI accreditation alone.

### AAPI REVIEW PROCESS

The AAPI accreditation process starts with the PPO submitting a 100-page questionnaire, which is then reviewed by the primary accreditation team, consisting of a physician, a lawyer, and a PPO administrator. If this step is passed, the next is a 2-day site visit. The on-site review team consists of PPO professionals with experience and expertise in finance, UM, information systems, medicine, administration, and law. The team verifies questionnaire answers, reviews records, and interviews staff.

In each review area, the PPO is given a numeric grade, based on a 100-point scale, indicating degree of compliance, plus a level rating of I to III indicating the complexity of the system. The final accreditation decision is made by the on-site team.

PPOs that meet standards in all eight areas are accredited for 2 years. If a PPO meets standards in five of the eight areas, it may be granted provisional accreditation and 6 months to correct deficiencies. At the end of 6 months, the PPO is either granted full accreditation or denied accreditation, depending on whether the deficiencies have been corrected.

### AREAS OF AAPI REVIEW

The AAPI reviews PPOs for compliance in eight areas but does not publish its standards for compliance. The areas of review are as follows:

**Managed care network**, including its scope, stability, nonnetwork referral capabilities, and patient access

**Financial stability**, including the budgeting process, controls, adequacy of reserves, insurance coverage, and a review of the financial statements

**Provider selection**, including selection criteria and their application, verification of provider data, and credentialing procedures

**Utilization management**, including its standards, scope, effectiveness, the experience and training of staff, and the integration of UM with management information systems (MIS)

**Payment methods and levels**, including the responsiveness of the PPO to purchasers, the competitiveness and incentives of the compensation system, whether incentives reward cost-effective behavior, and how fee increases are handled

**Quality assessment**, including the scope and effectiveness of the program, experience and training of staff, quality of the data, and use of the data in provider credentialing

**Management capabilities**, including the structure, information systems, marketing, member relations program, provider relations program, and the training and experience of staff of the PPO

**Legal structure**, including provider and purchaser contracts, litigation history, antitrust provisions, and provisions for due process

## INTRODUCTION TO SIX SIGMA QUALITY BENCHMARKING METHODOLOGY

Six Sigma was first developed by Motorola in the early 1980s to respond to the challenge of management to achieve 10-fold improvement in product reliability over a 5-year period. To achieve this goal, Motorola was forced to identify root causes of product failures and to correct them quicker than their previous performance. It was not until a decade later, after winning the Malcolm Baldrige National Quality Award, that Motorola removed the proprietary nature of Six Sigma by sharing its details with the business world, at which time other large manufacturers, such as General Electric (and its CEO Jack Welch, one of the first to dub Six Sigma as the "Holy Grail" of industry), quickly adopted it as a quality improvement framework.

The goal of the Six Sigma methodology is to reduce the number of defects a process generates to the point at which it would cost more, in the long run, to correct the defects themselves than to prevent the defects in the first place. A particular Six Sigma strategy in Japan called *Poka Yoke* (or "error proofing") demonstrates this goal by developing key performance standards that actually serve to prevent such defects from occurring. Defects, per Six Sigma standards, are not just possible errors that may occur; rather, they are factors that directly affect customers' requirements to the point that the customers might refuse to pay or to return an item purchased. Defects meeting this standard of customer dissatisfaction are thus known as "critical to quality" or simply CTQ.

Health care processes, particularly in the managed care industry, have a variety of customers, both internal and external, whose satisfaction is critical to the generation of cash; such factors that directly affect these customers' satisfaction are by definition considered CTQ. For example, the claims management function of an MCO is a customer of its member services department; mistakes made in validating a member's subscribed managed care plan generate CTQ errors when receiving authorizations and attempting to process claims payments at an anticipated pricing standard. Other examples can be found in Table 4.3.

Six Sigma is concerned only with such defects, which by definition are process defects that are CTQ. Focusing on CTQ factors is key to many industrial quality improvement endeavors, such as the International Organization for Standardization ISO 9000 standards family, and amply reveals that increased defects result in increasing losses of customers as well as reduced profitability and cash flow.

There are three key metrics used in Six Sigma, all of which are interrelated; knowing one means that the other two can be determined. They are simply

---

**TABLE 4.3**

**Examples of CTQ Defects for Health Care Finance Under Six Sigma**

- Incorrect mailing address for fiscal intermediary
- Receiving ancillary charges too late to be timely billed
- Misidentifying capitated patients as fee for service in admitting
- Materials management overpayments

alternative ways of measuring the effectiveness of a given process. These three are the following:

- **Defects per million opportunities (DPMO)**: DPMOs are the number of CTQ factors that are defective for every 1 million opportunities for such defects to occur. The level of performance that the Six Sigma methodology hopes to achieve is 3.4 defects per DPMO. Of course, a process does not need to generate 1 million observations, or 1 million observations do not need to be reviewed, to calculate its DPMO. That is why sampling is such an important tool for every aspect of Six Sigma, especially in calculating DPMOs. Indeed, the lower the DPMO of a process is—from 1 million all the way down to 3.4—the better the process is performing. A process that generates 100,000 DPMO is less effective than a process that produces 10,000 DPMO.
- **Error-free yield (EFY)**: EFY is the percentage of a process that is free of defects. The reciprocal of an EFY $(1 - EFY)$ represents the percentage of defect, or "defect rate," observed (e.g., 80% EFY = 20% defect rate).
- **Sigma level**: Sigma is the Greek symbol—$\Sigma$ for uppercase and $\sigma$ (the more common use) for lowercase—for the statistical concept of a standard deviation. A standard deviation is the square root of the average squared differences between a set of data points and its common average (or "mean"). It is less important to understand the mechanics of the calculation as it is to understand what it means for a process to be operating at a certain sigma level. For example, what does it mean for an operation that produces widgets to run at a sigma level of 3.0? What it means is that over 93 of every 100 widgets are defect free. Conversely, it means that almost 7 of every 100 widgets produced is flawed in some way that is critical to quality. Thus, the higher the sigma level at which a process is operating (or simply, its "process sigmas"), the higher the chances that the process will produce nondefective output.

At Motorola, its sigma level went from $4.2\sigma$ in 1986 (99.65% EFY corresponding to 3,467 DPMO) to $5.6\sigma$ by 1996 (99.9979% EFY corresponding to 21 DPMO). During this 10-year period, a 33% increase in process sigmas corresponded to a 99.4% drop in measured defects. In comparing its experience, Motorola determined that

- The average industry runs at $4\sigma$, corresponding to a DPMO of 6,210, meaning that some industries run both above and below this quality benchmark; a four-sigma level suggests that a defect rate of 6 of every 1,000 widgets is tolerated, thereby being a benchmark for appropriate procedural performance;
- An example of a lower-than-$4\sigma$ operation would be the phone-in tax advice service of the Internal Revenue Service (IRS), running at roughly

$2\sigma$ (DPMO = 308,537), meaning that appropriate service is defined by the IRS as providing erroneous tax advice for 30 of every 100 calls; and

• An example of a higher-than-$4\sigma$ industrial measurement would be domestic airline flight fatalities, running at better than $6\sigma$, meaning a DPMO of less than 3.4 deaths for every million passengers (thank goodness).

Not all processes can achieve Six Sigma performance in a cost-effective manner. For example, hospitals and MCOs, whose processes require a large quantity of human intervention, as well as the intervention of contracted professionals such organizations cannot directly control, should not expect to ever achieve a Sigma Level of 6. But, it is far from the truth to construe that Six Sigma cannot be successfully used for health care. With the goal of eliminating process defects, Six Sigma can be used to improve any process, up until the inherent limitations of the process.

## QUALITY IMPROVEMENT AND BENCHMARKING APPROACH FOR SIX SIGMA

Like all process improvement methodologies, Six Sigma has a unique project approach. In Six Sigma, this quality improvement approach has the acronym DMAIC. The various aspects of DMAIC are as follows:

• *D*efine the purpose and scope of a project, especially the CTQ factors of the output;
• *M*easure by creating a performance baseline against which data evidencing errors can be compared, both leading to a more precise refining of the problem statement;
• *A*nalyze root causes that are quantified by actual data;
• *I*mprove performance by implementing procedures that get at root causes of errors; and then
• *C*ontrol the process through evaluating performance both before and after improvements were attempted, initiating a monitoring system to reduce future errors, and documenting results as well as both recommendations and lessons learned. DMAIC is also cyclical, in that controlling leads to more precise defining, measuring, and so on.

Approximately 48 quantitative tools are utilized as part of the DMAIC framework, many of which are used for multiple stages. Some of these tools go back to the days of Walther Shewhart in the 1920s. Indeed, many of the so-called total quality management (TQM) initiatives that invaded the health care industry in the late 1980s used some of these tools. But, this is the closest that DMAIC comes to most all of the TQM programs. The various TQM programs are tied to fixing health care enterprise *problems* on a periodic, phased basis. DMAIC, by contrast, is tied to fixing *critical processes*—which are tied to CTQ factors—on an ongoing, perpetual basis. The Poka Yoke tool mentioned is an example of the "I" (or improvement) aspect of the DMAIC framework.

## UTILIZING SIX SIGMA BENCHMARKING IN MCO OPERATIONS

Six Sigma is neither the fabled "black box" nor the "silver bullet." Real and lasting solutions are never that easy. Rather, Six Sigma is concerned with CTQ defects, not just any measurable error that can be discerned in a given process. Furthermore, by forcing managers to deal with CTQ defects, this technique removes the excuse of plausible deniability, a common excuse for managers who are "too busy fighting fires," handling critical line management situations, and claiming to be less concerned with less-urgent procedural errors. But, if procedural errors are defined as CTQ—and directly related to customer requirements—Six Sigma cannot be brushed off as simply too "touchy-feely," as many of the former quality improvement initiatives for health care have been perceived (such as "quality circles" and "centers of excellence").

Let us look at the admitting department of the total process of a hospital as an example of what Six Sigma could mean for a hospital-based MCO. (One reason for choosing this perspective is that one of the "customers" of the admitting department is all nursing and ancillary departments dependent on accurate information gathered at admission; thus, any errors that later prevent clean claims submission are truly CTQ.) Let us make the following assumptions:

- Of all the data entered by admitting personnel for each inpatient admission, only 10 data fields are critical to getting paid (which is an extremely low assumption);
- The hospital processes 10,000 admissions/registrations per month;
- Each month, 50 admissions are audited for accuracy; and
- In any single audited sample, 50 CTQ errors are detected (whether as low as 1 error per admit or as high as 10 errors in each of five admits observed).

Now, let us "count the beans." Each sampling has 500 potential defects, of which 50 CTQ errors are observed, equating to both a 10% error rate and a 90% error-free yield; this EFY corresponds to 2.8 process sigmas. Should a Sigma level of 2.8 be considered tolerable to most MCO managers? If you have no opinion, consider that a 10% defect rate per 10,000 monthly admissions means that the personnel of the MCO must correct 1,000 CTQ errors each and every month to get paid correctly.

Still not convinced? Well, if each such error required 10 minutes to correct, corrections require 10,000 minutes per month and therefore 120,000 minutes per year. Incidentally, 120,000 minutes per year corresponds to 2,000 hours per year, which approximately equates to one paid FTE (full-time equivalent employee)—or what is paid to keep the equivalent of one employee working *entirely* on correcting critical errors in the admitting department. Is that less tolerable enough not to be satisfied with 2.8 process sigmas?

Also, consider the irony of the admitting department having to run one FTE short simply to correct the errors generated by the other staff in the admitting department. The result of this error-correction strategy is inevitably cyclical: With the full complement of admitting staff generating a 10% defect rate (which necessitated the corrective action described), and without attacking the root causes of this defect rate, the error rate the following month will necessarily be higher, necessitating a greater complement of FTEs to correct them for the following month. The month after that, the admitting department will have even fewer staff available to comply with an increasing work load (even assuming that the overall volume of admissions remains stable).

Since nursing and ancillary departments are customers of the admitting department of this MCO, what cascade effect might occur as the error rate attributable to the admitting department escalates as a greater complement of staff are assigned to correct CTQ errors? Remember that just the process of correcting CTQ errors in the admitting department is also subject to another defect rate. As more staff are allocated to fix the first level of errors, and as there is less time available to validate that the errors corrected were successful in correcting the errors, the admitting department will experience a new defect rate of errored admissions identified that were either overlooked or insufficiently corrected. Further, the secondary defect rate will be higher than the primary one because each such secondary error will be spread over a smaller amount of claims as in the primary defect rate.

This cyclical nature of correcting process errors without correcting their root causes cannot be dismissed by throwing FTEs at a problem that has never been corrected. So, let us go back to the original question: Is this level of rework tolerable for a process running at 2.8σ? Obviously not. An error rate such that 1 of every 10 accounts is wrong is intolerable for almost every proprietary enterprise using Six Sigma in the larger marketplace (which excludes the IRS, for example).

Besides the cyclical nature of assigning one FTE to address each encountered problem, rather than preventing it (Poka Yoke, for example) or fixing its root causes, consider other impacts of our assumptions:

What if a number of errors require substantially more than 10 minutes to correct? For every average 10 minutes more, that is another FTE wasted.

What about the hidden costs? Examples of hidden costs relative to admitting errors are increased days, small balances that are written off that will never be collected, collection fees charged by early out agencies, and perhaps the largest source of hidden costs, opportunity costs: With follow-up staff correcting admitting errors, they are not achieving their own collection quotas, or they need to incur overtime to do so.

What about the impact on customers themselves? As uncorrected admitting errors start occurring, or as inappropriately corrected ones are not caught by those assigned to fix the original mistakes, at what defect rate will physicians stop referring patients to the MCO? At what defect rate will health plans continue referring their members to that hospital, especially if the CTQ errors result in health plans underaccruing authorizations and IBNR exposure? It does not take too many of that type of errors for health plans to stop contracting with the MCO on all products that pass through either inpatient or outpatient registration areas of the admitting department (which is just about everything).

It is important to recognize an important caveat about using Six Sigma as a benchmarking initiative. That is, that certain levels of error are tolerated at all. In past dealings with colleagues in both MCO and health care practitioner settings, and consistent with the training of physicians in general, no error is too small. Physicians covered under malpractice policies consider even the slightest error in judgment or clinical practice to be completely intolerable. This attitude represents a cascade effect on most practitioner organizations, even when they are running well below a sigma level of 2.8. This same attitude would consider an operation running at $6\sigma$ to have 3.4 errors per million opportunities too many to be tolerable. The same attitude would persist in an organization implementing the procedures promulgated by the ISO (or, for example, ISO 9000), with quality measured as part of a learning organization committed to improve its performance, not the absence of any errors—CTQ or otherwise.

## LEARNING FROM CLINICIANS: HEALTH CARE FINANCE'S BEST RESPONSE TO SIX SIGMA

The seeds of Six Sigma came to the health care industry in the early 1990s but could have arrived even faster. When the Joint Commission changed its accreditation standards in the late 1980s to require disease staging, evidence of customer satisfaction scoring, and documentation of outcomes, it was clear that the clinical side of health care needed to ramp up quickly to set up processes and document results by 1993, the first year that accreditation inspections would be held to this higher standard. Instead, the consulting industry chose to focus on hospitals adopting a quality-focused culture and philosophy, training educators in teaching others to perform general quality process appraisals and measurements (e.g., Pareto charting and Ishikawa ["fishbone"] diagramming), as well as creating corporate slogans that attest to a general quality focus (such as various acronyms for the word TEAM, like "*Together Everyone Achieves More*" or "There's no 'I' in TEAM"). This fetish for quality-promoting slogans seems no different from the slogans and taglines adopted by private-sector health plans during the same period, rather than focusing on documenting or benchmarking the quality they perceived themselves as possessing.

Moreover, an actual cottage industry was also created of educators offering nothing more than basic training about the different methodologies for documenting quality improvement and for training in-hospital trainers and educators to become familiar with the need for quality improvement, as part of new employee orientation, and to assist others in the data management functions. The same can be said about early Six Sigma initiatives for corporations focusing on training trainers, rather than working to change attitudes, particularly in health care. In short, this approach to quality improvement made millions in engagement fees for

**TABLE 4.4**

**The Four Keys to Success Under Six Sigma**

1. Commitment from senior management to improve processes to increase performance

2. Advanced knowledge of $6\sigma$ techniques

3. Ability to utilize all available hospital data, not just data needed to work accounts receivable

4. Expert, applied knowledge of health care finance and operations areas, especially revenue cycle, materials management, central supply/ancillaries, and nursing

the consultants but completely side-tracked the original focus of hospital MCOs: to achieve Joint Commission accreditation quickly. It was not until the last 9–12 months prior to the initial change in focus of the Joint Commission in 1993 that much of the consulting industry changed gears, forcing clinicians to work feverishly, at the last minute, to provide the benchmarks and statistical measurements that the Joint Commission required all along.

Health care finance has much to learn from their clinician counterparts, who have nearly a 20-year head start in data-driven approaches. Training in-hospital educators and trainers in using every DMAIC tool so that they can attain so-called green belts and black belts in the field of Six Sigma is as much an appropriate solution today as it was two decades ago. Rather, Table 4.4 summarizes the four keys to success under Six Sigma.

The unavailability of any of these key success factors will hobble a Six Sigma installation from the outset and doom it to repeat the failures of the past. Six Sigma will absolutely work in all areas of the practitioner and hospital-based MCO as long as every one of these key success factors is available and operational.

Six Sigma is not voodoo. To the contrary, it depends on a constant stream of data, data analyses, and objective points of view. Politics, favoritism, sacred cows, and all other subjective criteria for decision making play absolutely no part in moving toward a Six Sigma paradigm. For hospitals, MCOs and health care enterprises unafraid to make decisions based on data, Six Sigma should not be feared but embraced and incorporated into the efforts of every hospital to reduce process errors, achieve better customer satisfaction, as well as improve cash collection and retention.

## CONCLUSION

As MCOs continue to compete for market share, accreditation becomes an ever-greater differentiation tool. Medicare is increasingly requiring contracted MCOs to obtain and retain accreditation, as are most all state regulatory agencies and a growing number of state health care exchanges. The participation of every ACO practitioner in PQRI, and the attainment of defined benchmarks to affect their respective incentive compensation, is commensurate with an accreditation standard for ACOs also. In the most mature markets, employers and benefit trusts look to accreditation as an indicator of quality, even though previous accreditation standards have done little to measure quality accurately and appropriately. Even the "granddaddy" of accreditors, the Joint Commission, has measured quality in terms of acuity adjustments and maintaining efforts to improve quality within the entire enterprise.

Only within the last decade has the Joint Commission required its accredited providers to measure quality indicators in certain diseases. Concomitant to Joint Commission's efforts, NCQA had again "upped the ante" with HEDIS 2000 for MCOs to assume greater responsibility in the health status adaptation of selected disease states for which member mismanagement creates avoidable high-cost claims. Expect to see even greater adaptation standards for even more disease states under HEDIS in the years to come, in addition to greater adoption of classical quality benchmarking tools, like Six Sigma and ISO 9000, as health care organizations are actually continuing to transform into "learning organizations." It is also hoped that the unrealistic practitioner standard of a "zero tolerance" for administrative errors is bifurcated from the clinical milieu of the operating room in which such an attitude is more welcome.

# 5 Managing the Managed Care Enrollee

## INTRODUCTION

The content of this chapter is noticeably absent from many managed care books, particularly those focused on operational and financial perspectives to "win" at managed care and capitation; moreover, the topic is included here to offer an opportunity to reorient managed care delivery to encompass all *four* sides: payer, practitioner, provider, *and enrollee.*

The reorientation has to start from the moment employees are solicited to join a managed care organization (MCO). The concept of the wellness model, as described in Chapter 1, must enter any discussion of participation. Potential members must understand that the wellness model is vital, and that managed care cannot work without it. The practitioner is no longer the fount of all knowledge, considering that computer software and Internet resources often far exceed the knowledge of any single practitioner, particularly among those members or their children afflicted with an incurable chronic disease.

The entire schema by which practitioners/providers dispense health services as well as *both* the optimal payer relationships *and* the preferred method of how enrollees are taught to consume or not consume services has to be part of the same equation. Under capitation, for example, payers assume a provider liaison role different from when they acted as providers themselves. All of these changes are not openly discussed in most managed care educational resources. As a result, the content of this chapter is blazing a new trail in payer and provider relationships with their end-line customers.

At the same time, consumerism is starting to enter the payer's point of concern, primarily due to relaxing of state and ERISA (Employee Retirement Income Security Act of 1974) protections that health maintenance organizations (HMOs) have had from member lawsuits arising from denied or unapproved services based primarily on cost and secondarily on the risk of resulting comorbidities. The consumerism, however, is currently serving to attack the managed care industry unfairly and not to reorient everyone concerned to how managed care is supposed to work. The necessary dialogue between MCOs and their enrollees sometimes first occurs when there is dissatisfaction with practitioners/providers or specific care consumed.

The lack of such dialogue is not meant to disparage practitioners and providers in dealing with enrollees—quite the contrary. Practitioners tend to be caught up in the minutiae of their contractual obligations, all the while presuming that they need no direction in caring for enrollees. The basic problem, as stated so well in Chapter 2, is that managed care contracts reflect the exact opposite of traditional practitioner operations because the contracts are in line with the insurance industry and not with the health care delivery industry. Too often, the fantastic potential of enrollees managing their own health is often overlooked in favor of insurance industry perspectives, such as stringent authorization, financial disincentives, and high stop-losses.

Here is the basic managed care equation: If practitioners lose money for every incident of care consumption, then change the consumption behavior instead of relying on gatekeeping and case management to ensure that providers and practitioners lose less money. An even more basic equation is this one: Providers and practitioners make more money when enrollees demand less inappropriate care. *The issue is not how much money or monetary resources providers and practitioners spend, but how much less inappropriate demand enrollees require.*

So, just exactly how should practitioners change enrollee demand and influence reduced inappropriate consumption behavior? The question itself is an indictment of much of American managed care and the dominant public reaction to the HMO industry: The question asked simply recognizes that behavior plays even any role at all. And, it is more than a psychological equation because somewhere along the line the managed care enrollee needs to self-monitor whether any such demand for care is appropriate.

As any psychologist would readily espouse, behavior is changed through positive incentives, rather than harsh disincentives and treating enrollees like 2-year-olds. The fact that psychology plays any part in changing both demand and consumptive behaviors is itself a revelation. Moreover, if the insurance industry model of disincentives, gatekeeping, authorization and preauthorization, second opinions, lost bonuses tied to enrollee noncompliance, and stringent case management protocols really worked in the health care service industry, then health plans would have had no incentive to outsource this business (via capitation) in the first place. Changing demand behavior is the linchpin, not how and where care is consumed.

Recognizing that incentives hold more promise than disincentives in changing demand behavior should also be a revelation for practitioners. Take smoking, for example, as an obvious example of the disintegration of enrollee health status. How do practitioners typically manage nicotine addiction? Is it by stating authoritatively, "You should be ashamed of yourself, smoking in the house with small children around! What could you possibly be thinking?" or "If you don't quit soon, you're facing congestive heart failure, lung cancer, or emphysema, if you're not already dead anyway!" Scaring or shaming can be successful for some enrollees, especially those under the age of 3, but is more likely to be interpreted negatively by most members. In fact, it is also possible that the scolding they receive from physicians, however well intentioned, may constitute negative reinforcement that unconsciously causes them to demand even more nicotine.

Continuing with the smoking example, how many practitioners would take the opposite approach of inquiring of the enrollee-patient? For instance, they might say: "What benefit does smoking provide you?" or "Is it possible for you to obtain this benefit without spending all that wasted money on cigarettes?" or "What incentive can you provide yourself to quit smoking? How can I help you do that?" or "How many days has it been since you last smoked a cigarette. ... Congratulations, that's a fabulous achievement! You're doing great and I'm proud of you!"

Yes, it is certainly possible that most enrollees are not used to compliments from their practitioners, but isn't bringing out the good things in people much more effective at influencing their behavior than magnifying the times they mess up? Whose ego really has to be massaged in practitioner-enrollee relations?

It is often said that, in changing behavior, one should use honey instead of vinegar. Taking this adage to the field of managed care, all that payers and practitioners have largely tried are "vinegar" interventions to change behavior. What happened to incentives for enrollees while incentive pools were being created for practitioners and providers by the payers? Dangling drops of honey in front of the noses of practitioners will do nothing to change the appropriateness of services that enrollees demand, and ignores that more appropriate demands (and less-inappropriate ones) influence practitioner behavior. This strategy is failing miserably in mature managed care markets. What happened to real incentives that have never been tried?

Might enrollees be more interested in health status improvement if their practitioner offered a rebate of a premium payment for a month if all family members attained their annual objectives of their respective lifestyle improvement contracts (LICs; see discussion in this chapter)? Think about the economics: A $400 rebate could be offered for a family of four in return for 12 months of no admissions and minimal demand in the office (except to check that objectives were obtained twice per year, given that experience rating formulas from Chapter 2 assume 3.5 office visits PMPY [per member per year]). Let us say the practitioner is paid $20 per member, per month (PMPM). For 1 year, the practitioner receives $960 of capitation, before any incentives the practitioner might earn based on the healthiness or disease adaptation of enrollees.

## MANAGED CARE EXPECTATIONS OF ENROLLEES

Enrollees have specific expectations, and MCOs must be accountable to achieving their reasonable ones. At the same time, enrollees need to take responsibility as adults, not children. Practitioners and providers bear the risk of members who persist in behaving unhealthily; to place the entire onus on the practitioner is naïve. For example, a smoker who is informed about the risks of smoking and the harms of secondhand smoke to other family members, who is encouraged to quit smoking and who is provided education and guidance to quit, that enrollee bears at least a shred of responsibility if the risk occurs, such as lung cancer.

This is an inherent limitation in the Affordable Care Act passed in 2010. While much of the public outcry has been focused on the requirement that people be covered by some form of health insurance, all that policy does is indemnify someone else (specifically the strained public health systems at the state and federal levels) from the responsibility of paying for medical losses. It does nothing to ensure that healthier lifestyles are adopted to cost everyone less money and to improve the healthier adaptation should a chronic disease occur. Even so, the personal accountability of covered members is completely absent: The smoker who never quits—but dutifully pays his insurance premiums each month—will still create an enormous drain on some insurer when he develops congestive heart failure (CHF), chronic obstructive pulmonary disease (COPD), and lung cancer in his mid-40s. Is the financial responsibility of paying his insurance premiums an absolution for his unhealthy and expensively inappropriate lifestyle choices? And, since the Affordable Care Act provided no additional funding for actual care, how would this example substantively change the public health equation of the public sector having ultimately to pay for providing expensive care that could have been avoided, or at least severely mitigated (on the basis of comorbidity risks) with more personal responsibility for changing lifestyles, diet, medication compliance, exercise, sleep patterns, or better stress management?

The problem with blaming the primary care physician (PCP) for poor lifestyle and compliance choices of managed care enrollees is basic. After all, surgeons are indemnified if they obtain informed consent prior to a surgery in which a previously stated complication indeed occurs; why should PCPs be held to a higher standard than say, neurosurgeons? Second, only health insurance—so far, at least—bases premiums on community ratings and, to some extent, on the overall claims experience of employer customers (see Chapter 2), rather than the individual lifestyle choices and mistakes of individual enrollees. Consider the parallel to automotive insurance, which in most states is based on some type of experience rating. Bad automobile drivers pay more for auto insurance than drivers with clean driving records. It is the same thing with the life insurance industry: Healthy policyholders pay less for life insurance than obese diabetic smokers with cancer and high cholesterol. Ditto for professional liability insurance: Physicians with a large number of guilty negligence lawsuits pay more malpractice insurance than better physicians pay.

There is no consequence to enrollees, yet, in any aspect of health insurance for those who have lousy health and no desire at all to improve it. However, it is the capitated practitioner who bears all of this liability for poor health status. Furthermore, most all of these practitioners do not recognize that the underlying behavior that creates demand is the issue, and not the fact that the enrollee eats unhealthily, smokes, is sedentary, or is overdue for a physical exam.

It is also reasonable to believe that enrollees are not given the opportunity of self-determination in improving the health status of both themselves and their family, as well as maintaining good health. Like most every other American, enrollees are tempted every day to practice bad health: to eat fast food (with ever-increasing fat content) instead of healthier home cooking, to allow their children to crave sugar-laden snacks and excess carbohydrates instead of more sensible eating habits, as well as to spend more time in sedentary activities like video gaming and television watching instead of exercising. Adults are reinforced to substitute caffeine for sleep, to eat poorly balanced breakfasts (if any breakfast is eaten at all), and to consume alcohol and over-the-counter medicines rather than dealing with the root causes of their behavior.

Consequently, practitioners (especially capitated ones) are mistaken to believe that enrollees are substantively different people than the rest of America, yet that enrollees have an ever-expanding array of resources to help them manage their own health if truly given the opportunity to do so. In fact, a foundation of capitation-based health plans is for otherwise-healthy enrollees to, in fact, be kept healthy and subsequently reduce their inappropriate demand for acute care services.

The expectation of enrollees of MCOs is a blank slate, a tabula rasa. The family chose a MCO product for a reason. The reason differs by individual and may include cost, protection beyond simple "major medical" coverage, the opportunity to participate in becoming healthier, or even a brand identity with the thousands of HMO advertisements that help form consumer decision-making habits. Yet, at no time does a practitioner typically ask an enrollee why the enrollee checked the MCO box on their health benefit election form.

This initial period is especially critical for capitated practitioners in shaping enrollee expectations. For whatever reasons they chose the MCO product, enrollees' expectations typically first arise in waiting for the practitioner to make the first move in effecting wellness management. Most practitioners do not realize that the "ball" has been dropped between the time the enrollee becomes a member (of a defined population of covered lives) and the first contact with the PCP. Since the PCP typically has no outreach to enrollees, the gatekeeper is dependent on member decision making in accessing the practitioner; as a result, the gatekeeper will see the enrollee only as a patient, when the patient is sick.

This crucial first contact, where the enrollee has no contact from the PCP other than receipt of a membership card, continues to be based on the "illness model" (see Chapter 1). The illness model is perpetuated only as a "default," simply because the MCO and PCP have missed the golden opportunity to define enrollee access under the wellness model (also per Chapter 1). If, on the other hand, the PCP takes a small amount of initiative to introduce new enrollee expectations under the wellness model, true profitability under capitation and from managed care operations is entirely possible.

If practitioners truly demonstrated that they cared about the individuals they are entrusted to keep healthy, practitioners might have the slightest chance of changing members' behavior in their consumption of money-losing resources, especially in inappropriate circumstances (like seeking primary care at a trauma center—the most expensive emergency room [ER] available). Such caring can be as simple as trying to reestablish a doctor-patient relationship under managed care.

A capitated practitioner who believes that managed care medicine is all about being more productive in shorter blocks of time, while triple booking all appointments, is missing the point. One important point is that encouraging members to manage their own health status is the end product of a trusting and supportive relationship between enrollee and practitioner. Yet, given the opportunity to repair the damage of improperly executed managed care during the last two decades, many practitioners intentionally or inadvertently repeat past mistakes, as depicted in Table 5.1.

So, what can be done to improve enrollee expectations in ways that benefit practitioners under the wellness model other than perpetuating the money-losing, unmanaged default approach as the illness model? The simple increase in initiative is tied to enrollee access.

## MANAGED CARE ENROLLEE ACCESS AND ACCESSIBILITY MODELING

From the moment an employer, employee, beneficiary, or even a general consumer evaluates an MCO product to include the independent practice associations (IPAs) or independent medical groups (IMGs) associated with each health plan, potential customers and members must be told that they will need to access health and medical care in different ways, such as seeing a practitioner when they are not sick. Assuming HITECH compliance by practitioners' information technologies over secure Internet servers, there are ample opportunities to make "wellness-based" physician access more convenient to managed care enrollees. With poor economic conditions in general, especially with overall desires to minimize time off from work to seek health care, being able to e-mail health status updates or to accept cell phone videos from enrollees curious about a rash (which may be something serious, but not a condition most enrollees would think important enough to take a sick day to have evaluated) would help facilitate with wellness model practitioner initiatives. This can even be extended to brief (no more than 5-minute) exchanges over Skype, at a time mutually convenient for both practitioners and enrollees.

To allow purchasers to believe that managed care is just about economies of scale and cost efficiencies does a great disservice to this vital field. Just as payers, practitioners, and providers must change their operations under managed care, so must enrollees change their consumption patterns and expectations of access.

The most important difference in access is that members must be accountable for their own health status, and the role of their practitioners and providers is to help them to return or achieve a mutually agreed-on healthy state. At the same time, these goals have to be achievable in a health enhancement approach that does not require practitioners to lose money through unnecessary office visits.

The accessibility to health enhancement is, by its very nature, different from simply consuming care directed toward treating episodes of illness or minimizing costs associated with entire care continuums.

In fact, providers and practitioners are increasingly aware of adverse selection, whereby a given enrollment is less healthy than expected. The adverse selection could be due to a payer pooling less-healthy enrollees at the point of sale (a version of a once-common insurance practice called "redlining") or due to a larger proportion (relative to average selection measurements) of less-healthy enrollees selecting a given provider or practitioner organization. Because of redlining, this

## TABLE 5.1
## Examples of How Cost Decisions Have an Impact on Enrollee Managed Care

| Practitioner Decision | MCO Reaction (Positive/Negative) | Effect on Enrollees (Positive/Negative) | Ramifications (Positive/Negative) |
|---|---|---|---|
| Reduce days and hours of operation | Reduces opportunities for losses to occur; reduces need for higher staffing; reduces productive labor expenses; reduces some fixed costs (e.g., janitors); reduces some premium costs (shift differentials/overtime) | Increased waits for appointments, possibly violates NCQA standards; less time spent per patient; less time spent with each patient | FFS patients will seek care elsewhere; practice will become dominated by MCO and Medicaid clientele; reputation can be hurt as quality harder to achieve/maintain if time too limited |
| Take McDonald's® approach to medical care: reduce all costs and charges, and improve staff productivity; initiate phone-based care and/or management; implement social networking | Improves primary care efficiencies; reduces need for additional PCPs; improves logistics for lower PMPMs | Reduces enrollees to cattle; less personal interaction hurts Medicare enrollees harder than commercial risk members | Increases member dissatisfaction in era of increased HMO litigation; initiating social media and phone-based care for all enrollees needlessly increases some members' morbidity and mortality risks |
| Change job descriptions where possible to substitute extenders for physicians and lower-level clinicians for LVNs/RNs; improve inpatient care efficiencies by hiring hospitalists | Derives more FTEs for less labor expense; improves accountability at each job description: RNs manage care, not bedpans; hospitalist use may equate to reduced inpatient stays | Depersonalizes care (each member must remember 3–5 names, not 1 or 2); miscommunication increases (caregiver requests made by patients might have to be assigned to other caregiver) | Upgrades professionalism of most FTEs; destroys doctor-patient and nurse-patient relationships; use of hospitalists might violate federal law (see Chapter 8) |

Boldface = Positive Ramifications
Roman = Negative Ramifications

reality should not be unexpected under capitation, especially in least-mature managed care markets, where high-cost or high-risk populations are capitated before less-consumptive ones are.

## ACCESSIBILITY TO APPROPRIATE SPECIALTY CARE

As an adjunct to risk stratification techniques mentioned, the timely referral to specialists is enhanced and is made more appropriately. For example, specialists are suggested by the PCPs, typically as part of disease management approaches (see next paragraph), rather than demanded inappropriately by enrollees, putting the practitioner in the position of approving access to effect higher enrollee satisfaction. Instead of practitioners *allowing* themselves to be put into this no-win situation, more appropriate access to specialty care can be directed by the PCP, who is the one who is supposed to direct patients to specialists.

In addition, the creation of innovative disease management approaches for chronically ill enrollees recognizes that primary care gatekeeping is an inappropriate managed care approach for members with specific disease states. However, it is an appropriate managed care approach for otherwise-healthy individuals if such members can be segmented from all covered lives and managed by PCPs, instead of specialists and without the need for expensive in-office history and physicals (H&Ps).

The adoption of this approach also serves to create new types of practitioners: ones who humanize enrollees and guide them in managing themselves rather than the typical figureheads, who believe that they are the founts of all health care knowledge. Adopting this low-tech risk-stratification approach cuts inappropriate specialist referrals, improves the public relations of the PCP practice with its enrollees, and even cross sells participating hospitals (which provides an opportunity for full, or even partial, subsidies associated with community health education activities of many providers).

The enrollee directly benefits when such risk stratification allows for more informed care management. Mismanaged care, on the other hand, requires enrollees to be "bounced around" between specialists, labs, and clinic settings, with the enrollee paying a minimum $10 to $20 copay to each such practitioner. To the enrollee, the notion of being seen by specialists—for whatever reason—could be misperceived as an opportunity for the health plan or MSO to "nickel and dime" the patient with an endless series of copays (for little perceived benefit) and requiring excessive missed time from work. In the end, much of the mismanagement could have been prevented had the PCP "handed off" the patient to the appropriate specialist who is given the authority to diagnose, not just to perform a single, specialized task set by the gatekeeper.

A perfect example of this phenomenon is seen with specialty referrals to optometrists (see Chapter 1 and Chapter 9). Without the recognition that optometrists are trained as PCPs with specialized knowledge of the eyes or that many systemic medical conditions could be more appropriately diagnosed at less cost during primary medical eye examinations (not simply subcapitated vision testing), a tremendous opportunity for optometrists to act as unique primary care extenders at lower cost is wasted.

A hospital becoming involved in wellness activities, as a team partner of the PCP, has collateral provider benefits beyond mere marketing. For one important reason, the hospital will see reduced MCO-specific ER visits due to lack of proper PCP access in time of urgent need. The urgency of the needs can be reduced if the enrollee and the PCP have an initial understanding, the value of which is enjoyed by providers due to low reimbursement by MCOs for emergency care as well as the marked potential for retroactive denials by health plans.

## Provider/Practitioner Autonomy

Many practitioners resent the fact that their actions in many managed care situations are questioned by nonproviders, many of whom are not physicians. At the same time, providers who have relatively more expensive charges (e.g., emergency physicians, hospitals, ambulatory surgery centers, and surgeons) face more retrospective denials regardless of the appropriateness for which the care was consumed. To be sure, retrospective denials represent "hindsight" management, which is especially important for emergency department providers: Regardless of how care was managed *at the time it was incurred* (e.g., charges for services consumed for a patient who presents in the emergency department unconscious who later turns out just to have fainted), charges for care consumed could be denied based on an outcome that might not have been positive had care been withheld.

Finally, restrictive access to specialists via stringent gatekeeping is a methodology of the insurance industry, not the health care industry. After all, insurers live and die by the medical loss ratio (MLR), and specialists are notorious for running up excessive costs. What insurers do not understand, however, is that specialists "run up" these charges because they have no access to meaningful, disease-oriented capitation and are selected by PCPs for very specific activities, and "running up" charges is their only means of being paid.

From a health care perspective, however, specialists are masters of selected disease states, and generalists (e.g., PCPs) are not. Therefore, compensation should be set on the basis of the appropriate level of expertise, where such practitioners are incentivized for doing their job well rather than compensated for the job regardless of the patient's outcome or disease adaptation. These specifications of diagnosis or treatment protocols include both clinical pathways and clinical practice parameters.

Much of what passes for subcapitation in mature markets like Southern California is not tied to any actuarial basis, but rather to the lowest price that a market will bear. For example, in 1993 the state of California published an all-inclusive price, per AIDS patient (not PMPM), of $1,883 per identified patient per month; at the same time, commercial risk-participating immunologists were being paid 8¢ PMPM—that is, per unidentified member per month. At this PMPM (which continues today in Southern California, by golly), an immunologist bearing the AIDS risk of 100,000 covered lives would get $8,000 each month. A single admission for any one of 0.1 million enrollees would bankrupt each such physician. There has to be a better way to increase access to measurable, quality care.

## ACCESS TO NON-ALLOPATHS AND ALLIED HEALTH PROFESSIONALS

Allopathic practitioners (e.g., MDs, podiatrists, optometrists, etc.) represent the vast majority of American physicians. Because of the competition of nonallopaths (such as osteopaths, chiropractors, acupuncturists, herbalists, etc.), a war has existed for decades among allopaths, osteopaths, homeopaths, and other nonallopaths to disparage the competition and hold onto market share. This revolt continues in markets dominated by fee for service, based on the premise that patient needs can be satisfied in a variety of locations, and that high billings equate to high net revenues. This equation is commonplace between chiropractors, for example, and typifies conflicts with competing practitioners, such as orthopedists, neurologists, and osteopaths.

Under capitation, however, these historic battlegrounds can very well become moot. It makes no sense, for example, for a capitated orthopedist to squabble over one member for a single incident of care with a chiropractor, who has no access to capitated business at all. Chiropractors claim that orthopedists charge more for every unit of service, and orthopedists claim that chiropractors consume higher volumes of service that are higher cost relative to the per case fees for which orthopedists generally bill.

If, however, the chiropractor is given access to managed health care by virtue of a subcapitated contract tying both PPPM (per patient, per month) and comorbidity prevention/management for specific disease states, the battleground is obviated. After all, why should a subcapitated practitioner care what the degree on the office wall is? If each such professional receives a single subcapitation based solely on the basis of successful management—and they will lose their contracts equally if they do not perform up to contracted standards—everyone's interests are safeguarded. More important, enrollees have increased access to any provider/practitioner with enough confidence in their product or service to fulfill their contractual obligations.

This concept is vital to understanding the future of enrollee access to nonallopaths, including allied health practitioners (AHPs). The health care industry has succumbed to these petty turf squabbles because practitioners' livelihoods have been tied to receiving provider and independent medical group/IPA franchises. These squabbles exist solely because of fee-for-service billing. They also exist in high-penetration managed care markets because nonallopaths and AHPs have no access to managed care populations *except* by promoting their services using market segmentation strategies to convince enrollees to go out of their plan or network to access care touted as "higher quality." Without the market ban, the benefits of specific promotion by a desirable market segment are eliminated. Furthermore, practitioners given the opportunity to benefit from successful services can receive incentives, rather than simply overcharging or stealing business from internal and external competitors.

This strategy of incentivizing based on performance is the same concept as employee stock option purchases, performance bonuses, and promotions in the general business community. These strategies exist because they work. It is indeed tragic that the health care industry has, to this day, largely ignored one of the cornerstones of traditional business and labor management for providers and practitioners assigned through managed care to populations of enrollees.

## MANAGED CARE CHOICE

Freedom of choice has been known for years to be a strong indicator of how employees and their dependents choose from among multiple MCO plans available to large employers. MCOs entering markets with low managed care penetration attempt to get as many local physicians as possible contracted, typically through contracting entire medical groups or forming (or contracting) IPAs with all such practitioners. The purpose of this plan design is to promote to prospective enrollees that they can have a choice of provider and practitioners, many of whom they may already be seeing.

Unfortunately, there is a catch. While it may appear that the enrollee has a choice of practitioners, for example, what might not be divulged is the existence of subcapitation arrangements with other practitioners, often ones they *did not* choose. To make the legal exposure of these relationships even riskier, enrollees might not be informed that the responsibility for all or part of their care has been resold to practitioners they did not choose. If matters are still not risky enough for the reader, consider that most commercial risk plans offer no self-referral option for the enrollee. And, what if the enrollee's choice of PCP is also resold to other practitioners for a gatekeeping subcapitation? Oddly, and amazingly, the "other shoe has yet to drop" on highly subcapitated markets, such as in Southern California.

The big risk to the managed care industry is that the public and the media do not know that this "subculture" exists in the health care industry. This area is likely one that cannot be blamed on MCOs because undisclosed, subcapitated arrangements are completely without the knowledge of the payer based on its good faith efforts. Two exceptions are that (a) the actuarial and underwriting processes are based on fee-for-service costs that may no longer reflect a mature capitation market; and (b) capitation contracts do not specifically prohibit reselling risk to reinsurers, providers (e.g., tertiary capitation; see Chapter 2), or other licensed practitioners. In addition, subcapitated arrangements, and their impact on enrollee referrals of loss-generating resources, are rarely—if ever—factored into both the actuarial and underwriting processes, thereby allowing these relationships to be based simply on whatever the market will bear.

Managed care specialists need to be especially careful of maintaining the balance between the choices enrollees think they are making and the realities of subcapitation contracts that may exist. Enrollees do not even know the word *capitation*—and may even believe it to be a French form of capital punishment—let alone the accepted convention of *subcapitation*. They are honestly shocked to learn what these terms mean and are even more aghast at the consequences of their choices given the fact that subcapitation exists.

## MANAGED CARE QUALITY AT THE ENROLLEE LEVEL

A new approach to capitation that measures service excellence, as a substitute to practitioners running scared solely because of a volume-based price that they poorly understand, is the key determinant of new contracts. Service excellence, and the quality management that goes with it, will have the effect of reducing inappropriate utilization by enrollees anyway and without the hand-wringing over practice expenses and poorly understood price controls.

To affect improved managed care quality, appropriate specialists need to be identified to utilize their expertise in managing specific populations of patients. For example, pulmonologists manage patients with COPD, cardiologists manage patients with CHF, and endocrinologists or certain vetted internists manage diabetics. Such specialists can be given access to capitated pricing that is specifically tied to disease-specific costs of care, instead of a PMPM set for generally healthy enrollees (which is an undifferentiated population for whom specialty care is impossible), with the end result promising to measurably improve health adaptation quality.

What are the steps in such a management approach to PMPM contracting? The basic managerial steps for disease state populations are described in Table 5.2.

The establishment of LICs see separate section in this chapter) can constitute a measurable basis for practitioners receiving incentive compensation for work done well, thus moving the health care industry back to a service basis and away from an unfortunate rationing basis, in managed care.

A strategy to remove inherent risk from homogeneously sold populations so that proper gatekeeping can occur is outlined as follows: Here is a possible solution for practitioners. Instead of the MCO mailing the membership card and registration materials to new enrollees, the payer can *easily* include a customized introductory letter about the PCP practice that the MCO could include in this mailing. If the MCO has too much trouble accomplishing this simple change, it can also easily send the computer-generated mailing labels and inserts directly to the practitioner; the practitioner then mails each of the new packets to his or her new enrollees using the logo of the practice and establishing an identity beyond that achievable by the MCO directly.

So, what is this introductory letter? A sample one is shown in Table 5.3. This sample should no doubt shock many readers. Raffles, tours, gifts, and refreshments—what kind of medical practice is this? The answer is that for minor cash outlays (envelopes, postage, use of word-processing software, about an hour of administrative time each month, and either one or two 45-minute Welcome Wagon meetings each week—with even less cost if these letters are mail merged and transmitted electronically, albeit less personably), huge rewards are possible. In short, the wellness model will be presented, and members will receive vital information about properly accessing providers and practitioners, in addition to accessing services during the least-busy times, thus evening out call volumes. Smoothing call volumes increases staff productivity, reduces stress, enables staff to be less harried and friendlier in scheduling welcome wagon appointments and

## TABLE 5.2
## Five Strategies to Improve Subcapitated Specialty Care Quality

1. Identify a disease state (e.g., HIV+/AIDS, congestive heart failure, etc.) or a specific service line of business (e.g., neonatal intensive care) that is better served by specialists than generalists under capitation.

2. For disease states, map out all of the currently known comorbidities of the disease and determine specific outcomes that can prevent the comorbidity entirely or lessen its severity (e.g., optometrists preventing and comanaging diabetic retinopathy [with retinology-specialized ophthalmologists contracted for treating it surgically], neurologists preventing and managing diabetic neuropathy, nephrologists preventing and managing diabetic nephropathy, cardiologists preventing and managing hypertension comorbidities of diabetes, etc.). For service lines, map out clinical practice parameters (using either published approaches or original research) and determine optimal performance objectives (e.g., specific "superstat" lab tests that require a result within 5 minutes for specific ER enrollee presentations).

3. Determine the responsibilities of each such practitioner or provider to document to ascertain contract compliance and engage an actuary's services to determine risk exposure and minimum acceptable capitated price. Also determine the role of an administrative body (e.g., MSO, third-party administrator [TPA], or administrative service organization [ASO]) to measure and manage contract compliance as equitably as possible.

4. Develop subcapitation contracts tying together per patient, per month (PPPM) prices with specific comorbidities to manage, with incentive provisions that reward highly aggressive management, successful enrollee health adaptation, or measurable prevention of specific comorbidities among at-risk family members of the patient-enrollee.

5. For nondisease individuals, for whom gatekeeping is more likely appropriate than inappropriate, PCPs need to be incentivized for enrollees who adopt healthier lifestyles that can reduce new incidence of preventable disease states. This is especially the case for so-called prediabetics or those who are not yet diagnosed with diabetes but do meet criteria for metabolic syndrome. While some incentives exist for PCPs in mature managed care markets, they are obtainable through reducing overall care consumption (which, in this decade, may prove to be a violation of legal duty and possibly an illegal health care practice). In addition, PCPs have no current access to be incentivized for doing good work, only in receiving disincentives for performing bad or expensive work, regardless of outcomes.

general office visits, and improves the public's perception of the professionalism that the practice exudes to new patients. This is, incidentally, a model that has been poorly adapted even by "concierge care" internist practices in recent years. If I know my readers, they are probably asking aloud, "What's the cost savings for new members to receive several incentives to come to a physician's office when they are not sick and to give the practitioner even the *opportunity* to improve health status separate from treating an illness?"

In short, the cost savings are tremendous. First, and most important, this program is vital in creating basic management data of each and every covered life. Data, you must ask—which data? (The letter says that no medical information will be asked.) The answer is simple: Another expense the PCP bears is to hire a triage

## TABLE 5.3

## A Sample PCP Introduction Letter (Underlined Fields Customizable)

Dear _____ [or use phrase *New Enrollee* instead of customizing this letter]:

I and my staff at XYZ Medical Group are very happy that you chose us to be your primary care physician of the health plan you previously chose. We'd like to become your partner in achieving good health and keeping you free from diseases and conditions that could adversely affect the quality of your and your family's life.

Our approach in helping you stay well is unique. First, my staff and I want the opportunity to give you a proper welcome to our group: to meet me, to meet my staff and colleagues, to tour our offices, to receive vital information about access to our health care services, and to receive our special welcome gift (one to each family in attendance).

Don't be concerned about coming in to see us because WE WILL ASK YOU NO MEDICAL QUESTIONS. Yes, that's right … no needles, no prostate exams, and no embarrassing questions. This is not the point of us meeting; we sincerely want to meet you and your family beyond just names and identification numbers on some computer report.

Your health depends on us working together. Enclosed is an RSVP to join us for one of our "Welcome Wagon" evenings, every Tuesday or Thursday evening at 6:30 p.m. (these evenings never run longer than an hour and are early enough for your children to come along); refreshments will be served, and every complete family in attendance will receive our special gift. Plus, it will give you an opportunity to meet some of your neighbors in a relaxed, stress-free environment. Can we count on you to take advantage of this unique opportunity? Please give us a call at (555) 555-5555. Thank you, and welcome again!

Very Truly Yours,

Manfred Manfreddy, MD

Enclosures: Membership packet, XYZ Medical Group "Quick Facts," family raffle ticket (raffle tickets require validation in our office), and Health Status Information Questionnaire (if you won't be able to accept our invitation)

---

nurse from his or her provider hospital to moonlight by attending each Welcome Wagon meeting and to be introduced as a member of his or her wellness team.

Why a triage nurse? A triage nurse is experienced at making basic medical judgments appropriate to severity of condition, but typically based on sight and speech alone. Lab tests, histories, and physicals, in this context, serve only to validate a fairly expert opinion that is rarely wrong.

Take shaking an enrollee's hand, for example. The physical proximity of the triage nurse to the enrollee can detect the smell of tobacco, the breath of an alcoholic, and the pupil dilation consistent with a substance abuser. A clammy hand can signal medical conditions as well, as could a refusal to shake hands (the proverbial "fist bump" instead), indicating someone who is currently contagious (or just a germophobe). This type of information is very basic, but it lends itself to risk-based medical decision making, which is a welcome substitute for widespread rationing and withholding care based solely on

## TABLE 5.4
## Reengineering Capitated Primary Care by Risk Stratification

A reengineered approach to practitioner decision making can encompass the following risk strata:

- Which enrollees are the "ticking time bombs" (e.g., substance abusers, smokers, morbidly obese, asthmatics, morbidly uncontrolled diabetics, or any other screening observations that the PCP wants the triage nurse to unobtrusively assess) who need to be seen immediately and possibly transitioned into disease management programs?

- Which enrollees are at risk of being abused, based solely on observation and listening to vocal cues, which may indicate an immediate risk to life or limb or likelihood of mental illness?

- Which enrollees cannot be entirely ruled out as having a likely health risk, again based on observation alone, and whose health status can definitely benefit from an in-office H&P examination?

- Which enrollees can be ruled out and judged, based on visual and auditory observations (including touch), to "pass" this low-tech "screening exam" and not require an in-office examination?

its expense. Examples of this reengineering approach using triage nurses are shown in Table 5.4.

These four simple questions in Table 5.4 can be answered by quality triage nurses based solely on "gut instinct," without any reliance on an H&Ps. This approach to population management reengineers it by creating the following three risk stratifications:

1. The high-risk people (e.g., the ticking time bombs), such as smokers who need to be seen in the office immediately;
2. The low-risk people who can be monitored every 6 months by phone or by Internet (and not involve low-value in-office expenses), and
3. The enrollees who fall out of the stratification equation, thus creating a need for less-urgent H&Ps.

Providers and practitioners need to manage the populations for whom they are capitated, and there are many sophisticated population-based risk stratification tools available today to make that job easier, provided that the capitated provider knows that it is their duty to address. Payers sell these populations in good faith, and many providers/practitioners misrepresent to MCOs their true skill sets and population-based management capabilities. Because capitated populations are sold as a homogeneous group (with PMPM closer to an appropriate per member cost), the capitated practitioner—if possible, with the assistance of the capitated provider—needs to dichotomize this grouping into "specifically unhealthy" and "otherwise healthy" subpopulations, a process that could be called *heterogenizing*. Four of the advantages of such a low-cost, high-value interaction with new enrollees, which heterogenizes a population sold as homogeneous, can be seen in Table 5.5.

**TABLE 5.5**

**Four Advantages of "Heterogenizing" Covered Lives**

1. Office productivity can be enhanced by scheduling new patients on certain days or at certain times, managing certain risk factor enrollees on certain days (which increases the opportunity to hire locum tenentes to perform certain screenings), and keeping control of member demands better because the PCP took the first step to manage enrollees' needs;

2. Practitioners can spend more time with high-risk enrollees during relatively slow periods of the workday, such as late afternoon or during the traditional lunch hour;

3. Managing a risk-stratified population appropriately is what managed care was supposed to have as its goal, not the stringent gatekeeping and cattle herding that typify most practitioners' organizations; and

4. Enrollees can be guided in taking responsibility for their own health status and that of their family with a minimum of distractions.

The statistical approach suggested in Table 5.4, and with advantages detailed in Table 5.5, represents added bonuses to both the PCP and the MCO. For example,

- The PCP learns information about the Welcome Wagon attendees without providing medical care;
- The PCP can identify first-degree, at-risk relatives of ticking time bomb enrollees, even if they were not present at the Welcome Wagon event;
- The enrollee has a tacit incentive to attend the Welcome Wagon events and provide basic screening observations in the PCP's office: They have to fill out a health status questionnaire (e.g., SF-36 or some ominous-looking, lengthy questionnaire that requires far more than 5 minutes to complete), which yields even more critical data, if they do not attend Welcome Wagons (and staff should regularly "hound" these enrollees to get their instrument filled out and sent back or to schedule a more convenient Welcome Wagon evening); and
- The PCP can control variable practice expenses by controlling who are to be called for appointments (entirely outbound, per the wellness model, instead of partly inbound, as is prevalent in the illness model) and who do not require appointments for effect health maintenance.

What about all of the costs of the Welcome Wagons? These costs are thankfully minimal because the premium gift can be nothing more than a first aid kit (with the practitioner's name, as well as both provider's name and its ER phone number on the exterior of the kit, at a one-time cost of under $25, which can also be a marketing aid) per family and provider promotional materials (e.g., personalized pens, refrigerator magnets, etc.) that can serve as the individual giveaway items. Refreshments can be fresh fruit, ice water, and vegetable crudités, for example, or other food that reinforces the healthiness paradigm.

At the end of the Welcome Wagon presentation, enrollees can be invited to find out their health status by completing an SF-36 or the proprietary "health track" instrument by signing their names on a clipboard that is passed around (peer pressure may convince a percentage of enrollees to provide this increased level of information—and risk stratification that results from it—by indicating their basic interest). The PCP staff can also pass around a second clipboard to find enrollees interested in providing health adaptation mentoring for certain diseases (preferably those included in disease management approaches), joining an online discussion board with other patients (after waivers of disclosure of personal health information pursuant to both HIPAA and HITECH are signed), or even of general health. Again, some peer pressure may convince some enrollees to participate, especially if the most fit enrollees volunteer to mentor others.

Even if the Welcome Wagon evening produces no "takers" for health status measurement and for mentoring others, the invitation can remain open, and names can be added in subsequent months of the same capitation term. By the practitioner simply asking for their help, the dynamics of enrollee access to health care services and enrollee-enrollee cooperation in improving health status could measurably improve. Similarly, a physician working with an agency that supplies promotoras can also yield collateral lifestyle improvements, especially among Latino members, at least initially, and again at minimal cost relative to immediate benefits. And, the human incentives for enrollees to be treated as competent and contributing members of a population under managed care can increase their satisfaction, a quality measure for which such practitioners typically receive bonuses, and can influence them to reduce inappropriate utilization without the need for a PCP to "play the bad guy" and impose stringent authorization and gatekeeping for every enrollee. The result of this approach is to risk stratify using a methodology that minimizes disincentives and squarely puts the onus back on the enrollee to improve his or her own health status rather than keep him or her dependent on the PCP.

## MANAGED CARE ENROLLEE IMPACTS ON PROVIDER/PRACTITIONER COSTS

The management of enrollees in the PCP's office is alone considered by many in the field to be a false sense of success. This place of access is considered as more cost effective than seeking inappropriate care in a hospital. It is not unusual in Stage 4 (approximately 75%) managed care penetration markets, for example, for patients to self-diagnose conditions that previously would have resulted in their running to the nearest ER. In such markets, the standard $50 ER copay, particularly for Medicare beneficiaries, is deterring enrollees from accessing emergency care unnecessarily.

There is a discontinuity of logic at play in such markets. Why do MCOs believe in imposing high copays, especially given that higher copays are inversely proportional to costs; namely, higher copays, which are better tolerated in mature markets, are correlated with less health care consumption. In the insurance industry, in which MLR is king, this inverse relationship incentivizes benefit plan designs with high copayments.

In the health care industry, however, reducing access to everyone is the same strategy that awarded numerous multimillion-dollar judgments against the MCOs. Why is this strategy considered desirable by the capitated providers and practitioners of today? Moreover, if reducing access to everyone *itself* is the management strategy, what cost effectiveness has occurred? In reality, the financial management strategy is to improve cost efficiency through improved health care financial management, not cost effectiveness alone.

Through capitation, managed care providers and practitioners are obligated to make sense of enrollee consumption and provide basic health care management to large blocks of covered lives. Reducing utilization for those needing care, in a new era in which provider/practitioner lawsuits are now possible for financially tainted clinical decision making, is a mistake for the health care industry. Statistically speaking, saying "no" to everybody, all the while running the risk of "false negatives" (e.g., practitioners saying "no" when they should have said "yes") are still errors of commission. Encounter data or claims submitted with *ICD-9 (International Classification of Diseases, Ninth Revision)* and *CPT (Current Procedural Terminology)* codes are "smoking guns" that are discoverable in litigation to document provider and practitioner rationing based on financial influences. (Other implications for compliance, illegal managed care practices, and relevant federal sentencing guidelines are described in considerable detail in Chapter 8.)

But, who is really benefiting from stringent gatekeeping, reducing all practitioner costs (without selectivity regarding performing even basic health care financial management, such as weighing costs and benefits in decision making), cutting off ER access, pushing more provider business down to the practitioner level, and pushing more specialty practitioner care down to the primary care level?

- **Capitated practitioners do not benefit by restricting enrollee access.** The practitioners are hardly benefiting by getting a $15 copay to provide services that have just a fixed cost above the copay, let alone any variable costs consumed (e.g., consumables and lab tests).
- **Capitated providers typically do not understand how enrollee access affects them.** Providers with capitation business lose money on every patient presentation, whether treated in the emergency department, in ambulatory care settings (such as diagnostic radiology), or as inpatients. Relying on case management and utilization management (including preadmission visits) as the answer merely minimizes these losses; it does not change the fact that the provider loses lots of money every time an enrollee accesses a care location and does nothing to change the behaviors that drive such inappropriate access patterns.

- The lack of understanding of the effect of enrollee access on provider operations is demonstrated every time a manager (within a provider organization with capitation business) measures success simply by the census of a day. Hospitals, for example, still have in their mission statements the provision of care, and census serves to validate how much care is being provided. Every bed filled by a capitated patient is a financial drain; why should that census day be viewed as a financial success? The only way to answer that question is to acknowledge a lack of understanding about the effect of enrollee access on optimal provider operations under capitation.
- **The capitating payer has nothing to gain by restricting or allowing member access.** The capitating payer, whether an ACO (accountable care organization), an MCO, an IPA, just an independent medical group offering subcapitation to other practitioners, has already been indemnified through monthly capitation payments. The actuarial assumptions and rating methodologies were created for the benefit of determining a capitation premium price, which has already been offered to, and accepted by, one or more customers. Thereafter, any aftermarket fluctuation in capitation price is due either to changes in member volumes (which affect the total capitation received, not the PMPM specifically), to changes in product line profit margin expectations, or to changed elasticity of market prices.

Any specification by the capitating entity regarding the place of enrollee treatment or the name of a practitioner rendering care to enrollees—except for a catastrophic condition that is *known* to have an impact on a reinsurance policy, and then *only* when such policy is held in the name of the payer—is simple micromanagement. A payer that micromanages its customers (practitioners/providers) by interposing itself in the way managed care is practiced is committing *slow suicide* by

- alienating practitioners/providers;
- setting itself up as a scapegoat to its membership, "med-mal" (medical malpractice) attorneys, and politicians; and
- destroying marketing objectives of each product line.

The only logical explanation for a capitating payer to micromanage is its own unwillingness to accept the distribution role that it now plays in the marketplace.

- **Enrollees are harmed by inappropriate restrictions to access.** Restricting enrollee access sends a contrary message that undermines the "doctor-patient" relationship. Enrollees are told that they are incompetent to make their own access decisions, and that they must play "Mother may I?" with their PCP any time they wish to self-refer. Enrollees are taught to be dependent on a PCP rather than independent health adherents.

# HEALTH GUIDANCE SERVICES FOR MANAGED CARE ENROLLEES

The goal of proper health care management of enrollees is tied to improvement of health status and, if appropriate, to disease adaptation. This new goal also transforms the role of providers and practitioners. Since they lose money for every incident of office- or clinic-based medical management, their new role is to provide proper guidance so that enrollees can self-manage with appropriate guidance.

Numerous opportunities for improved health guidance by enrollees exist in 21st-century America, some of which are available for free: community-based health information, payer- or MCO-provided consumer education, and enrollee health guidance Internet sites.

## COMMUNITY-BASED HEALTH INFORMATION

Many provider organizations have health information services, such as TeleCare, Ask-a-Nurse, or even prerecorded CDs/DVDs, many of which are provided by the National Institutes of Health (NIH) and other national public health organizations. Hundreds of free health information Web sites are available on the Internet, including sites that have online physicians available to provide health management information. The trick to health information is not in obtaining it, but in improving its use by enrollees.

## PAYER- OR MCO-PROVIDED CONSUMER EDUCATION

An unexplored option to improve enrollee health guidance is for capitated practitioners to recognize that they have a conflict of interest in balancing provider desires for admissions with their desires to keep their capitated enrollees out of provider settings.

Two strategies for providing consumer education to enrollees exist:

1. Involve the provider in accessing provider health information resources (see previous discussion) that have already reconciled the balance between health information and resulting admissions; or
2. Recognize that the practitioner cannot provide effective consumer education cost effectively, which can be managed by creating a health information carve-out that can be sold to a proprietary health guidance service (such as Ask-a-Nurse) or even to resell this responsibility back to payers (and subsequently create this practitioner responsibility as a contractual carve-out).

## ENROLLEE HEALTH GUIDANCE INTERNET SITES

Hundreds of health guidance resources certainly exist on the Internet. A plethora of health management sites (both public sector and private-brand labeled) exist to ensure quality health care information and encourage users to share their personal information to allow a health care professional to provide health guidance on a customized basis.

A new Internet approach to health guidance is in granting access to intranets with appropriate firewalls and encryption schemes to protect consumer privacy and that guarantee that the names of registered participants will not be sold to others, such as list management companies.

Another Internet approach, rarely used yet, uses member-specific content for demand management, such as harnessing proprietary "push" technology (same concept as vendors sending e-mails or text messages based on Internet cookies and browsing experiences) to customize health guidance for online enrollees (who can be traced using their e-mail address provided at the time of the Welcome Wagon meetings or at initial patient registration in the practitioner's office). Some health plans themselves are harnessing this technology, such as Aetna, which specifically shares each member's personalized health record (complete with every prescription, lab test, practitioner seen [and all dates of service, for example, in each practice location]), all of which is maintained and updated on Aetna's secure server and can be downloaded to a "thumb drive" or USB device on one's key chain, so that up-to-date medical histories are available when presenting to an ER or to a new physician's office. This same push technology can scour the Internet each day to create customized e-mail of disease-specific news stories, lifestyle improvement techniques, and local fitness-oriented programs available within or near the enrollee's zip code. In short, much of what practitioners consider to constitute health guidance can be accomplished automatically and for free. There may even come a day when large IPAs and IMGs create their own, HIPAA-compliant intranets that provide these types of services for subscribed users, which it is hoped will include their capitated enrollees.

Another approach bridges consumer-based needs for managing health with MCO needs for ensuring that consumers take more responsibility for guided, self-management. One approach taken is by Blue Shield of California, which established its mylifepath.com Internet site as a combination of consumer-based self-care with a regional discount program negotiated for consumers in such areas as vitamins, therapeutic massage to reduce stress and improve circulation, acupuncture services for pain management, and initiation discounts to join certain health clubs.

## ENROLLEE RESPONSIBILITY TO COMPLY WITH STRATEGIES FOR TREATMENT, DISEASE ADAPTATION, HEALTH STATUS IMPROVEMENT, AND HEALTHINESS MANAGEMENT

One of the most critical elements of enrollee managed care involves the enrollee's participation in improving health status and disease adaptation. Resources to assist the member exist in community-based and provider settings, as well as thousands of Web pages every day, some of which are even moderated by trained health care professionals. But, the responsibility to ensure compliance has rarely been transferred from practitioner to enrollee.

This transfer of responsibility itself is critical to the success of enrollee management under managed care. A practitioner who transfers the responsibility is transformed to an advocate or coach of wellness from the "know-it-all" who dispenses easy-to-digest snippets of information based on specific questions asked. Many periodicals, for example, feature stories that emphasize improved communication with their practitioners. Some practitioners can become great communicators, although filtering of some information based on a specific enrollee's capacity needs to occur, which confounds people intent on improving communication skills. Still others are poor communicators and know they are.

Transferring the onus of care management back to the enrollee creates something else: It restores the doctor-patient relationship that was last seen in the 1970s, well before the managed care era that now exists. This relationship can flourish based on alternative technologies that now exist to provide lifestyle improvement and disease adaptation. For example, a practitioner who establishes Skype connections or conducts virtual doctor-patient conferences using video-enabled cell phones can infuse new interest in disease-specific, parenting and wellness-oriented support groups. Even using such cameras to have visual conversations with loved ones living far away is important for reducing stress and improving family support, especially during times of illness or infirmity.

## APPROPRIATENESS OF PROVIDER RESOURCE UTILIZATION OF ENROLLEES

Enrollee utilization of provider and practitioner resources must be recognized as relative to, rather than a static component of, stringent authorization and gatekeeping. *Gatekeeping works only for otherwise-healthy individuals.* Gatekeeping for enrollees who indeed require practitioner intervention is the source of many lawsuits that cost payers millions of dollars in damages. Rather than imposing gatekeeping universally, capitated practitioners must identify the populations who need to see practitioners immediately and identify the remaining subset for whom gatekeeping should continue to be utilized without problem.

This basic strategy is critical to any form of management in a business, even more so for managed care. Think about how care can be managed if the populations defy traditional medical management. If all a practitioner knows of the covered population is "name," "address," "Social Security number," and "date of birth," how can informed management occur? The simple answer is that informed management has *no chance* of occurring. In the absence of such basic management data, many providers and practitioners have chosen to manage populations based on price alone.

But, what is management by price? It was suggested in Chapter 3—and is discussed in detail in Chapter 6—that most provider organizations perform little cost accounting other than simple ratios of Medicare costs to charges; practitioner organizations have even less wherewithal to perform detailed cost accounting. Therefore, if little cost accounting occurs among providers and practitioner organizations, how can capitated price management occur at all? Obviously, this question is rhetorical. Management simply does not occur. Worse, the rationing of care for all enrollees is what passes for informed management of covered lives. And, rationing care for enrollees reduces their accessibility to health care services, some of which are necessary to protect life and limb. Why would any practitioner knowingly restrict a diabetic's access to glucose-monitoring supplies, insulin, glucagon for severe hypoglycemic events; to access to a registered dietician to learn how to eat properly; and even to specific guidance to know when to dial 911 in cases of extreme hyper- or hypoglycemia?

## METHODS OF TRANSFORMING BEHAVIOR OF CAPITATED ENROLLEES

With disease management populations for whom providers and practitioners are capitated, much of their remaining lives involve one or more specific disease progressions. The long-term costs involved in managing disease-state populations are much more significant management challenges than cross-sectional approaches aimed at managing individual incidents of consumption. For these populations, more significant financial returns are realized by how successfully enrollees, on an individualized basis, adapt to their chronic conditions, improve their health, and reduce their need to consume expensive health care commodities more often. This management shifts the responsibility of transforming behavior from the practitioner to the individual enrollee.

For this population, the overall strategy involves spending some money on the front end to reduce more expensive outlays on the back end. For example, consumptive services spent on people with type 2 diabetes, such as visits with a dietician, private health club memberships (which are subsidized only to the extent that the individual uses the benefit at least three times each week) with counseling by a trainer, and regular periodic blood work can have benefits far in excess of consumption spent by the capitated provider. In this example, the members of this disease management population can be taught

- How to reduce fat and increase fiber in their diet to effect healthy weight loss that can be sustained and, at the same time, eliminate the need for insulin and, perhaps, oral hypoglycemic medications;
- How to engage in appropriate exercise on a regular basis that sustains aerobic activity at a level that represents 85% of their target pulse rate, all aimed at aiding in healthy weight loss and in replacing fat tissue with muscle tissue, which will reduce the tendency to return to obesity; and
- How to make adjustments in their lifestyle and eating habits to compensate for blood sugar fluctuations and maybe, just maybe, "cure" themselves of this disease, as there is medical documentation that complete changes of lifestyle can bring about "remission" of type 2 mellitus diabetes.

Variations of this strategy can also be applied to patients with other chronic, as well as catastrophic, diseases. The items that need to be documented in the example of type 2 diabetes mellitus involve more than the visits the patient has and the consumption on the part of the provider for which he or she may not be immediately reimbursed. ***The missing element is the enrollee's behavior.***

It also needs to be said that diabetes can also be put in remission as a result of certain types of gastric bypass surgeries. While this may be true, neither the Affordable Care Act nor almost any public- or private-sector health plan willingly covers these costs, or even is receptive to the very discussion. Assuming the enrollee remains compliant with aftercare instructions following gastric bypass surgery, at what price for such a surgery are the benefits and reduced comorbid expenditures not cost effective? The willingness of some payers to cover laparoscopic bands or duodenal sleeves—instead of the more expensive gastric bypass surgery—speaks to a softening of gastric surgery policy exclusions and expensive medical riders in recognition of the obvious benefits to enrollees' health status, quality of life, productivity, and functional adaptation (especially in the earliest stages of such diseases).

## LIFESTYLE IMPROVEMENT CONTRACTS

Increasingly, provider and practitioner observations of enrollee's behavior need to be documented and tracked within electronic health records. Equally important, the inherent behaviors of individual enrollees, at the time they are initially screened (whether in a physician's office or at a Welcome Wagon presentation as described in this chapter), must also be incorporated into an LIC.

An LIC is similar to a capitation contract executed between a payer and a provider or practitioner; it specifically documents what the agreed-on duties are, what the rewards are for success, and what the consequences are for failure. Enrollees must be treated as partners in managing care if managed care is intended to be successful.

An LIC must be part of the enrollee's clinical record because it is behavior that is the longitudinal measurement to determine if individuals are taking responsibility for their own health status. In this case, the data that are most important for documentation are not the weight measurements, the interpretations of the radiologist in reading a smoker's chest X-ray, or the lab results of a toxicology screen. No, the more important data in this case are not for what you can bill but for what influences future consumptive activity:

- What is the patient's observed reaction to good news?
- Is he or she happy at the achievement or more concerned that the results were not good enough?
- Does the patient smile when the data indicate a less-than-optimal or even poor result?
- Does the patient seem depressed and beaten, or does he or she pledge to do better?

- More important to others who may be reviewing this scenario years later, how does the practitioner respond to a poorly motivated enrollee?
- Does the practitioner try to get the patient to recognize the bigger picture: that lasting, overall improvement in health status takes time, in that one cannot often turn around the progression of an entire life over the course of a few months?
- Does the practitioner demonstrate to the patient that all efforts in the right direction are meritorious, in and of themselves, and not just the biggest or most drastic incidents of improvement?
- Is the practitioner solicitous or genuine in his or her respect for the enrollee's efforts toward lifestyle improvement?
- What behaviors are occurring from both sides? All behaviors, positive and negative, should be observed. Videotaping behaviors could be advantageous, if the patient consents, in documentation, especially if the digitized videos could be included within any electronic health records (EHRs).

The demonstrated behavior to change is the catalyst that can lead to lasting effects on the overall progression of the disease state; the lifestyle change and the greater health status responsibility are the "commodity" that generates the payback for the practitioner and payer. For such practitioners, lifestyle improvement and documented behavior in assuming health status responsibility represents his or her return on investment (ROI).

## Incentivizing Enrollee Compliance

The onus for moving to that ROI behavior must be on the part of the capitated enrollee, not the practitioner. Hence, the first step is letting the enrollee know that his or her own behavior is important to the patient-practitioner relationship.

A strategy for enticing patients to consent to such a contract could involve incentives for meeting lifestyle improvement objectives or measurable progress toward meeting each objective. As suggested, examples of such incentives could be monetary (e.g., $20 per pound of weight lost, $5 per pound of lost weight that is not regained after 3 years); motivational (magazine subscriptions to a self-help publication, membership dues in a support organization, sponsorship in a walkathon, a charitable contribution to a medical research foundation, etc.); or personal (a smile, a kind word, or a demonstration of admiration or respect). People are best motivated if their actions please others, and doubly so if, in the process, they are pleasing themselves.

The cost of incentivizing others to achieve milestones in their personal lives is negligible compared to the "rewards" of a healthier lifestyle and a new outlook on "beating" their disease or minimizing the effects of the disease on leading a useful, productive life. Good health and healthy lifestyles should be associated with pleasure; this association is part of the behavior modification approach to wellness. To become part of this end result is also why many practitioners chose their respective professions.

## ESTABLISHING ENROLLEE "FEEDBACK LOOPS"

A principle of continuous quality improvement, especially when it entails introducing a change, involves collecting and managing feedback. The process by which evaluative information is collected, and the results of all such collections shared with the respondents themselves, is what is known as a *feedback loop*. In capitation management, the feedback loop defines and refines the relationship between the practitioner and the disease management enrollee, especially in measuring individuals' demonstrative progress in improving their lifestyle and in taking responsibility for their own health status.

As discussed, a practitioner's positive feedback for a job well done, evidenced both tangibly (with a cash or in-kind incentive) and intangibly (with words, gestures, and other nonverbal feedback), is a powerful motivator for change. In conjunction with both documentation and the referenced behavior modification, modeling approaches need to be taken under capitation management to assess whether incentives provided are translated into demonstrable improvements in behavior related to lifestyle improvements and self-management of health status. This modeling approach and the data generated (both documented "gut feelings" and actual test and observational results) represent the level of feedback that the provider should be generating for him- or herself for each capitated enrollee, especially so under a disease management approach.

The level of sustained and measurable positive feedback practitioners provide to their enrollees constitutes their feedback. The observable and documented reaction by the enrollee to the positive feedback generated by the practitioner is also the basis of the practitioner's feedback from the enrollee.

## TYPICAL MEMBER RIGHTS AND RESPONSIBILITIES

For many years, ERISA, has allowed MCOs a measure of protection from medical malpractice of member care, even though ERISA was enacted to preempt state laws about employee benefits, but not of insurance plans. While this apparent contradiction is still being worked out in the courts, state legislation passed in late 1999 allows aggrieved members to sue their HMO for the negligence or wrongdoings of its contracted or employed practitioners as well as its contracted providers.

Generally, patient issues fall into the general categories of responsibility for negligence and contractual responsibilities.

### MCO RESPONSIBILITIES FOR IMPROPER CARE

MCOs may be held responsible for adverse outcomes in several ways:

• Administration of medical management programs

- Credentialing of network providers
- Actions of employees and contracting physicians

A managed care plan may be liable if a defect in the design of its medical management program contributes to a reasonably foreseeable injury to an enrollee, even if the determination to deny a service is not challenged by the attending physician. The MCO must usually demonstrate that the decision was made in accord with documented internal procedures and generally accepted medical management practices, and that the MCO exercised reasonable care when making the determination. The result is that the utilization management programs of most MCOs are similar to establish an accepted and appropriate standard of care.

The MCO must exercise reasonable care in recruiting and supervising physicians. A Missouri court found that an HMO that did not verify credentials for specialists it was recruiting had created a foreseeable risk of harm for members.

The MCO, like all organizations, is responsible for the actions of its employees—the legal concept of *respondeat superior.* Staff model HMOs are thus liable for the actions of their employed physicians/staff, but the liabilities of HMOs with other models are not yet so clear. Despite the independent contractor language in a typical contract, an MCO may be held liable for a contracted physician. For example, Kaiser Foundation Health Plan (KFHP; a health plan generally with a network of exclusive practitioners) was held liable for the malpractice of a network cardiologist because, the court held, KFHP restricted members to a limited number of physicians, paid those physicians to perform services that the HMO was obligated to provide, and had some control over the physician's behavior—attributes more of an employer-employee than independent contractor relationship.

In a 1969 case (*Pogue v. Hospital Authority of DeKalb County* [Georgia]), however, a court held that since an HMO cannot practice medicine and cannot control practitioner behavior and judgment, it thus cannot be held liable for medical negligence. Two other cases showed that an MCO may create the impression through its marketing materials that a physician is acting as an agent of the MCO and therefore may be liable for the physician's negligence. As stated, court decisions are increasingly holding MCOs liable for practitioner negligence, and certain states are giving members the right to sue their HMO, without protection from the ERISA statute.

## MCO Contractual Responsibilities to Enrollees

Employers are increasingly searching for ways to avoid liability for the medical management decisions of contracting MCOs. Some groups require the MCO to indemnify or hold the group harmless against any medical management liabilities and include this provision in the contract. The MCO is then liable for expenses and damages from any lawsuits.

Most medical management problems have dealt with denial of authorization or benefits that the enrollee believed should have been covered. The case generally hinges on whether the denial was reasonable, based on the terms of the agreement or, in other words, whether the MCO breached its implied duty of good faith and fair dealing when it denied authorization or benefits. Examples of behavior confirming bad faith include failing to contact the enrollee's physician before denial, failing to obtain or review the appropriate sections of medical records, and failing to inform the enrollee of his or her right to appeal a denial. Bad faith judgments can include compensatory and punitive damages, which have been awarded in the millions of dollars.

If a plan is determined to be governed by ERISA, participants or beneficiaries can initiate civil actions to recover benefits due under the terms of the plan, to enforce rights under the terms of the plan, or clarify rights to future benefits under the plan. The court may award reasonable attorney fees and costs but not compensatory or punitive damages.

The administrator of the managed care plan is required to act as a fiduciary when making benefits determinations. This duty prohibits arbitrary and capricious behavior when making determinations, such as using undisclosed medical criteria that are more restrictive than those of other policies. Again, the courts look for reasonable behavior. Currently, legal fees and costs may be recovered by the member in these cases, but the scope of damages may be enlarged in future cases.

## CONCLUSION

Much of this chapter described a level of effort that still does not exist. The crucial role of understanding enrollee requirements and helping them to manage themselves represents the entire goal of managed care. If enrollees voluntarily reduce their patterns of inappropriate demand, why would gatekeeping and stringent preauthorization be required at all? The answer should now be obvious. The health care industry can radically redefine itself under managed care by paying more attention and guidance to their defined population of enrollees, each and every one of them.

# 6 Enrollee-Based Financial and Mathematical Prediction Models

## INTRODUCTION

Through the timely and accurate recording and reporting of revenues and expenses, the managed care organization (MCO) monitors its progress toward financial goals and in predicting operational consumption. To these ends, this chapter introduces the basics of managing, reporting, and auditing enrollees' clinical services and some simple mathematical modeling to improve predicting clinical loss ratios and operational requirements to maintain profitability. These services are at the heart of MCO operations because of their impact on the medical loss ratio (MLR) and MCO budgeting and capitalization requirements.

## OVERVIEW OF CASE MANAGEMENT/ UTILIZATION MANAGEMENT

All MCOs use utilization management (UM) to control the costs of health care. UM techniques include a wide range of procedures enabling the MCO to review treatment before, during, and after it takes place. UM may be provided by a UM department internal to the MCO or by a contracted UM firm.

UM plays an important role in the managed care industry. First, it is generally the first and always the most important tactic employed by any organization to begin to manage care. Second, UM produces a "sentinel" effect on physicians, whose practice patterns change when they know they will be reviewed. Last, UM that takes place before services are rendered is becoming more important, enabling costs to be controlled through planning rather than through retrospective reviews when it is too late. In addition, UM techniques are being developed for specialized services, such as mental health care.

UM procedures are based on standards and norms of appropriate medical practice. They are developed from regional medical practice standards and adjusted for individual circumstances.

Case management (CM) shares a linkage with UM, even though both disciplines are somewhat different. Their common bond is that they help a provider, management service organization (MSO), accountable care organization (ACO), or physician-hospital organization (PHO) "to lose less money." Even though both operate in real time—unlike their predecessors, quality assurance (QA) and

**TABLE 6.1**

**Case Management Standards**

| | |
|---|---|
| 1 | Coordination of treatment |
| 2 | Delivery of patient services |
| 3 | Physical and behavioral factors of injury or illness |
| 4 | Cost benefit of treatment |
| 5 | Cost effectiveness of care with best possible outcomes |
| 6 | Community resources to facilitate discharge |
| 7 | Consideration of accreditation and regulatory compliance |

utilization review (UR)—they are not oriented to improve revenue or to equalize value derived from cost consumed (which itself could become an outcome). They are designed merely to reduce clinical expenses or to have an impact on the potentiality for accountable care (and the potential for financial incentives).

The CM position is primarily a liaison between the provider and the practitioner as they interrelate with the patient member. CM positions are typically held by registered nurses or certified nurse practitioners (CNPs). A summary of CM standards is shown in Table 6.1. The goal of CM is to ensure that facility objectives are being met by facility practitioners. Examples of such objectives might include adherence to medical staff bylaws, care compliance (including Milliman clinical care guidelines and/or adoption of "best practices" as they might be established for certain clinical parameters), as well as conformance to facility-established clinical pathways or product line standards.

CM strictly speaking falls into the category of concurrent review, but it is really a process of its own. The concept of CM (or large CM or catastrophic CM) is that cases with the potential for incurring extremely high costs can be identified early and managed to control the services provided and their related costs. This type of CM is called *precertification*. Cases requiring precertification might include AIDS cases, high-risk pregnancies, spinal cord injuries, and transplants.

CM usually involves one UM nurse (the case manager) who manages the case from beginning to end. A case may be identified when it arrives at the emergency room of a hospital (the spinal cord injury) or by the primary care physician (the high-risk pregnancy). Especially in pregnancies, CM staff can work closely with patients to coordinate care early and control costs. CM can go beyond normal UM in coordinating care for patients from hospital to rehabilitation to home care.

Utilization Management is primarily concerned with the conformance of care received relative to accreditation requirements—such as Joint Commission or NCQA or URAC—as well as meeting objective UM criteria, such as those established by Milliman USA®. In the case of the latter, its Milliman Care Guidelines represent a combination of proprietary administrative and clinical guidelines that govern utilization management, and are the basis for certain accreditation criteria.

In facility practice, the UM position is primarily an in-house liaison that manages the patient member's consumption of institutional services. While the practitioner demand for such services is a CM responsibility, the UM nurse coordinates with the admitting physician and any referred practitioners rendering care to ensure primarily that patients are discharged as quickly and expeditiously as possible—in concert with both the provider liaison of the MCO as well as the discharge planner of the facility—and within clinical standards for doing so. Expediting discharge also requires that treatments ordered are promptly received, that managed Medicare (HMO or PSO) admissions meet federal compliance and "medical necessity" regulations, that required documentation and procedures are followed by the facility (e.g., for managed Medicaid and managed workers' compensation patients), and that transcribed reports and medical record cover pages are signed prior to discharge.

## USE OF FINANCIAL DATA DERIVED FROM CM/UM

The financial statements of an MCO may be reported in conformity with generally accepted accounting principles (GAAPs) or statutory reporting requirements, which vary by state. These monthly financial statements of operation should optimally reflect income on both a total and per member, per month (PMPM) basis. MCOs operated by state and local governments are subject to statements and interpretations of the Governmental Accounting Standards Board (GASB), American Institute of Certified Public Accountants (AICPA), and Financial Accounting Standards Board (FASB) statements made applicable by the GASB. Moreover, the so-called "Orange Book" of standard reporting forms for state regulatory agency reports developed by the National Association of Insurance Commissioners (NAIC) may be helpful to comply with state-specific requirements. The chapter describes the financial accounting and reporting of revenues, medical benefits and administrative expenses, plus guidance on recognizing loss contingencies under short-term contracts for an MCO.

Specific data elements captured from the CM/UM departments are shown in Chapter 7. However, four factors most influence MCO costs derived from UM:

1. Inpatient hospital use rates,
2. Hospital contracted payments,
3. Practitioner payments and ordering/referral patterns, and
4. Frequency of office visits.

## INCURRED-BUT-NOT-REPORTED CASE MANAGEMENT DATA

The expenses of an HMO fall into two categories: medical benefits expenses (Table 6.2) and administrative expenses (Table 6.3). The larger category is medical benefits, the cost of providing health care services to enrollees. The identification, correct categorization, and accurate prediction of these costs in financial accounting

### TABLE 6.2
### Typical Medical Benefits Expenses

- Inpatient services
- Outpatient services
- Practitioner services
  - Primary care
  - Specialty care
- Other medical services
- Ancillary services
- Prescription drugs
- Reinsurance premiums
- Other costs

### TABLE 6.3
### Typical Administrative Expenses

- Administration
- Sales and marketing
- Medical management
- Occupancy
- Other expenses

and reporting are vital for a successful MCO. Reports of these expenses, in addition to revenue and membership data, are normally provided monthly.

### INDICATORS OF INAPPROPRIATE IBNR LEVELS

There are various methods used to estimate IBNR (see IBNR definition and modeling in Chapter 2). Typically, the methodology is developed and periodically reviewed by an actuary either employed or contracted by the HMO.

HMOs generally account for medical benefits in the categories of inpatient services, outpatient services, physician services, other medical services, ancillary services, prescription drugs, reinsurance premiums, and other medical costs. The following sections consider each such IBNR methodology.

### Inpatient Services

The largest segment of HMO health care costs is inpatient services, the cost of provided services in an inpatient facility, generally a hospital, including facility charges—operating room, radiology, laboratory, pharmacy—and other charges connected with the admission and treatment of the patient.

The UM department of an HMO is responsible for capturing actual admissions and length-of-stay data, and by using authorization information, is able to compile regular reports on total admissions and days incurred. These reports should provide the finance department with such information as number of admissions by type (surgical, maternity, etc.), total days incurred, and the facility where they were incurred. The data on these reports may be used in the IBNR estimate for reported services as well as an identification of high-cost cases (catastrophic cases or shock claims), which may be used to set up additional reserves and share with the CM department of the HMO.

The UM reports are typically used in combination with "lag reports" of claims paid statistics. Lag reports are so called because they summarize claims paid by the month of service and the month of payment, and there is a lag, or time elapsed, between the date of service and the day the HMO is billed for and pays for the service. Lag reports can be based on

- Date of service versus date of receipt of bill
- Date of service versus date of payment of bill
- Date of receipt of bill versus date of payment of bill

The lag report is laid out so that months of service are along one axis and months of payment on the other. Lag reports are updated monthly to include all claims paid during the current month, by month of service. The result is a "lag triangle," the basis for calculating "completion factors" for each month of service based on historical patterns. Estimates of the total incurred claims liability for a given month may be calculated by applying the completion factors to the total claims for that month. Table 6.4 presents an example of a lag triangle.

Estimates of inpatient expense for a given month may be based on the UM inpatient reports and the lag reports. Two specific methodologies are specific inventory and completion factor.

**TABLE 6.4**

**A Lag Triangle**

| | | Date Claim Incurred | | | | | |
|---|---|---|---|---|---|---|---|
| | | **Dec 199X** | **Nov 199X** | **Oct 199X** | **Sep 199X** | **Aug 199X** | **Jul 199X** |
| | Dec 199X | $100 | $195 | $200 | $175 | $150 | $90 |
| **Date** | Nov 199X | XXXX | $110 | $190 | $210 | $180 | $150 |
| **Claim** | Oct 199X | XXXX | XXXX | $100 | $210 | $220 | $180 |
| **Paid** | Sep 199X | XXXX | XXXX | XXXX | $130 | $200 | $240 |
| | Aug 199X | XXXX | XXXX | XXXX | XXXX | $120 | $210 |
| | Jul 199X | XXXX | XXXX | XXXX | XXXX | XXXX | $135 |

*Estimating Inpatient IBNR: Specific Inventory Method*

From the UM report, historical cost per day data for each type of service and each facility may be used to calculate the current liability. This inpatient estimation methodology is also known as the *specific inventory method*. This method involves inputting the number of days incurred for the current month, sorted by type of service and facility used, into a worksheet with the historical costs. These historical costs per day for each type of service and facility are calculated by dividing the total amount paid by the total number of days paid.

For example, if current paid claims information shows that a total of $160,000 for 200 surgical days was paid to Community Memorial Hospital, its cost per day is $800 for surgical admissions. (Note: When coordination of benefits [COB] results in another carrier paying some portion of a claim, the cost per day should be adjusted to reflect the liability amount to the facility. Otherwise, subtracting the other carrier's payment from the net claims paid amount will result in understating the average cost per day.)

The days incurred for the month are multiplied by the appropriate cost per day for the inpatient liability for each facility. The total of these is the overall inpatient liability. The next step is applying estimated IBNR claims. IBNR claims are for activities that have occurred but have not been identified by the UM department. There are many reasons for IBNR claims: out-of-town emergencies, incorrect procedures such as lack of precertification, provider not billing in a timely fashion, and so on.

The IBNR factor is again calculated using historical data: paid admissions versus admissions reported by UM. The IBNR reserve plus the estimated liability for the month is the total estimated liability. This total appears on the income statement as inpatient expense and on the balance sheet as a liability for inpatient claims.

*Estimating Inpatient IBNR: Completion Factor Method*

Another method of estimating inpatient liability is by using historical completion factors derived from lag reports. The completion factor is applied to the inpatient claims paid for the dates of service for the current month to arrive at the liability for the current month. Lag reports and completion factors should be updated frequently to avoid under- or overestimating liabilities.

The completion factor method may be the best option if the HMO is not able to track and report admissions and days incurred data prospectively. However, there are several disadvantages to this method. First, inpatient utilization, usually expressed as days per thousand members covered per year, can vary tremendously from month to month. Recent changes in inpatient expense reimbursement methods or unexpected backlogs in the claims-processing department can cause the completion factor system to be inaccurate. Also, if membership in the HMO is increasing rapidly, historical admission trends may prove ineffective at estimating admissions and inpatient costs.

## Outpatient Services

Outpatient services are typically provided by ambulatory surgery centers or hospitals. In financial reports, the outpatient services category may include emergency room charges and ambulance transportation charges as well as services provided by the outpatient department or ambulatory surgery center of a hospital.

The outpatient services part of the medical expense budget of an MCO has grown rapidly in recent years as outpatient care is increasingly seen as a cost-effective alternative to inpatient services. Hospitals are major factors in outpatient medical expenses. To replace revenues lost through declining occupancy (caused primarily by efforts of MCOs to reduce inpatient admissions and reduce lengths of stay), hospitals have developed the technology and facilities for outpatient procedures. As inpatient revenues decline, outpatient charges rise.

Hospitals have typically been reimbursed for outpatient services based on discounts from allowable charges. Rising charges have caused HMOs to explore alternative contracting mechanisms. Newer reimbursement methods include case rates, global rates, and discounts with maximum reimbursement limits. These and other contracting methodologies are covered in Chapter 1.

As with inpatient expenses, outpatient liabilities depend heavily on trends in service costs and utilization. Reports on the number, type, and facility used for ambulatory surgery based on precertification information are generally produced by the UM department in the same way that inpatient reports are produced. Lag reports for outpatient services may also be produced in the same format as lag reports for inpatient services.

The specific inventory and completion factor methods can also be used to estimate IBNR for accrued outpatient services. The disadvantage of the specific inventory methodology is that radiology, laboratory, and emergency room services are rarely captured as part of specific inventory provided on an outpatient basis. As a result, most MCOs use the total of the completion factor method in combination with the specific inventory method.

Here, the completion factor method calculates the estimate for the current month using a historical PMPM claims expense. (Note: UM efforts to control costs can be quite successful, so historical cost factors must be kept up to date.)

## Practitioner Services

Capitation is the simplest payment method from the finance point of view. It is usually automated. Liabilities for total primary care provider (PCP) capitation, incentive withholds, referral and hospital pool allocations, and stop-loss protection are estimated monthly by the automated system. PCP capitation is recorded as an expense when it is paid, while allocations to the referral pool and hospital pool are recorded as specialty care expenses and hospital expenses, respectively, when funded. Accruals to the withhold, referral, and hospital pools are recorded as liabilities. As claims are paid, the liability balances are reduced, and except for amounts needed for IBNR, pool balances are cleared at year-end settlement. Retroactive adjustments in membership per PCP must be accounted for in accordance with restrictions set forth in the HMO contracts with PCPs and the employer group. Tight reconciliation and balancing controls between the capitation system and the enrollment system are crucial.

IBNR for primary care physicians reimbursed under some form of fee for service is estimated using the completion factor method. Expenses are projected on a PMPM basis using PCP expense lag analysis and historical trends. Again, any changes in the procedures of the HMO—fee schedules, primary care physicians billing for additional services—need to be included in the analysis of current and historical trends and reflected in the IBNR estimate. Once the PCP expense liability is calculated, it appears on the income statement and as a liability on the balance sheet. The net amount of claims paid is charged against the liability account.

Specialists are generally reimbursed on a fee-for-service basis; however, specialist capitation—either as contact capitation or subcapitation (see Chapter 2)—is a growing trend. If PCPs are also reimbursed by fee for service, the same fee schedule, containing *Current Procedural Terminology* (*CPT*) codes and fee maximums, can be used for specialists. While the services of specialists are generally more expensive than those of PCPs, the volume is typically controlled by the PCP through the referral and authorization system. IBNR estimation for specialist under fee for service is often the same as for PCPs under fee for service.

## Other Medical Services

Other medical expenses can be defined as those outside the gatekeeper control of the PCP, such as vasectomies, maternity care, chemotherapy, and so on. They may also include potentially catastrophic cases managed directly by the HMO. The volume of these cases is generally low, except for maternity care, so they do not pose a significant financial risk.

Generally, other medical services are reimbursed on a discounted fee-for-service basis. Unlike with specialists, churning and upcoding are generally not issues, although unbundling can be. This is because authorizations are usually more specific or limiting. The IBNR estimate is typically calculated in the same way that the liability for specialty care is.

## Ancillary Services

Ancillary services, a very small part of medical expenses, include allergy, mental health, laboratory, radiology, and substance abuse services, often subcontracted to specialized providers. Subcontracting can be done by plans, medical groups, and most MCOs. Because the services are so specialized, the HMO will often be able to capitate them in return for exclusivity for the provider. The provider is willing to accept capitation and its attendant risk sharing in exchange for being the sole provider of the service for the enrollees of the HMO.

Laboratory services are one example of where this system works well. The HMO cannot control the frequency of laboratory referrals, so must find a way to control overall cost instead. Capitation provides one way to do this and provides other benefits as well, such as avoiding self-referral problems with physicians holding financial interests in laboratories. (The Healthcare Financing Administration [HCFA] prohibits referrals of this nature.) Laboratories can offer competitive rates and leverage the additional volume to reduce their costs internally. The HMO gains cost control; the laboratory gains market share.

Some HMOs may reimburse providers of ancillary services on a discounted fee-for-service basis. The IBNR estimate typically follows the methods established for capitated and fee-for-service medical expenses.

### Prescription Drugs

The percentage of medical benefits expense represented by prescription drugs for an HMO is rising faster than any other major component of medical expense, even though each individual expense is relatively small and not relied on in rating methodologies (the industry standard is to assume prescription drugs as comprising only 10% of experience-based rating methodologies). Pharmacies are generally reimbursed at a discount from the average wholesale price, plus a dispensing fee per prescription filled. Reimbursement may also be controlled by use of maximum allowable charge pricing.

IBNR estimates for prescription drug benefits are typically calculated using lag reports. Lag reports for pharmacy claims differ from those for medical services in that pharmacy billings are usually processed more quickly than physician billings due to the rapid turnover of medications. Processing claims is also quicker since referrals are not involved. The time of year and epidemics (colds, flu) will cause variations in prescription drug use. Also, enrollees approaching the end of their HMO coverage will often take advantage of their HMO benefits and refill prescriptions, an effect sometimes called the "end-of-year run on the bank." These variations will need to be taken into consideration when the estimate is prepared.

### Reinsurance Premiums

For IBNR purposes, reinsurance premiums are considered benefits expenses because recoveries are considered an offset to medical benefits expenses. Premiums are usually paid monthly based on enrollment and are recorded as expenses when paid.

### Administrative Expenses

For an HMO, administrative expenses cover all of the expenses incurred in administering enrollees' medical benefits, from salaries to supplies. Accounting and reporting for these expenses follow GAAPs. Please note that the Affordable Care Act restricted all health plans to 15% of an HMO's total expenses or to 20% of every premium dollar. HMOs exceeding administrative expense thresholds in 2011 were required to start rebating excess expenses to customers starting on January 1, 2012.

Administrative expenses will be classified differently depending on whether the HMO uses the staff model, paying salaries to physicians and owning facilities, or uses one of the other models and contracts with physicians and their facilities. They are generally categorized as administrative, sales and marketing, medical management, occupancy, and other expenses. It should be noted that few purely staff-model HMO still exist in the new millennium.

### Administration

Administration expenses include the salaries, benefits, and expenses of departments that provide nonmedical member services, such as customer and member service, claims processing, finance, underwriting, management information systems (MIS), human resources, and executive staff.

### Sales and Marketing

For IBNR estimation purposes, sales and marketing expense includes the salaries, benefits, and expenses of the marketing staff plus the costs of their activities, including broker and agent commissions as well as such marketing communications expenses as advertising and printing.

### Medical Management

Medical management includes the salaries, expenses, and benefits of the medical director, UM, provider relations, physician advisors, and QA.

### Occupancy

For IBNR estimation purposes, occupancy expenses include space and equipment. In an HMO based on a nonstaff model, this includes utilities, rent, maintenance, and depreciation for furniture, fixtures, and office equipment. In a staff model HMO, the equipment depreciated will include medical equipment.

### Other Expenses

State and federal regulatory reporting requirements, as well as some contracts, will affect accounting and reporting of administrative expenses. For example, a Federal Employee Health Benefits Program (FEHBP) contract requires detailed accounting for the cost of administering the benefits of the group and does not allow the allocation of certain administrative expenses (advertising, interest) to the contract for an experience-rated plan.

## MANAGED CARE-SPECIFIC FINANCIAL INDICATORS

Besides the basic financial indicators used in health service organizations, a few indicators are specific to MCOs. The first indicator, the MLR, has been discussed in detail in Chapter 1, particularly Figure 1.2 and Figure 1.3. Other managed care ratios can be generally categorized as utilization measurements or cost measurements. Utilization measurements are usually expressed in terms of utilization per thousand members per year, although sometimes utilization per member per year (PMPY) is used.

## PAYER INDICATORS

As described in Chapter 1, one financial ratio peculiar to the MCO is the MLR. In the insurance industry, however, loss ratios that benchmark claims paid against premium revenue received are not at all peculiar; in fact, loss ratios are a necessary part of the actuarial and underwriting processes, particularly for experience ratings, on which the entire insurance industry depends.

Besides its use as an insurance industry barometer of acceptable risk per premium dollar, the ratio can also be used as an indicator of the percentage of premium revenue available to cover medical expenses. The remaining percentage (one minus the MLR) indicates what portion of premium revenue remains after payment of medical expenses to cover administrative expenses and profit. The benchmark for national MLR is usually between 70% and 80%. Regional characteristics will cause this ratio to vary. Some regions are associated with lower expenses (e.g., Mississippi) while others with higher expenses (e.g., Hawaii).

## PRACTITIONER INDICATORS

### Average Visits PMPY

One common indicator of practitioner productivity is measured in terms of PCP office visits. As discussed in Chapter 2, costs associated with office visits represent 40% of an adjusted community rating and are critical for capitated PCP budgeting and projection of fixed practice expenses. The average visits per member per year (average visits PMPY) are graphically depicted as Table 6.5. This indicator is primarily measured for primary care physicians or practitioners but is also suitable for specialty IPAs. The total number of member visits per year is divided by the total number of members. This ratio is usually calculated in total and on an individual practitioner basis.

The benchmark for this ratio is between 1.5 and 5.0 PCP visits. A ratio of less than 1.5 office visits PMPY might indicate denied or restrictive access, while a ratio of greater than 5.0 might indicate poor CM or churning attempts of IPA members relative to contact capitation.

### Referrals PMPY

An alternative member access indicator, and one that helps zero in on IBNR risk, is to measure the number of practitioner referrals PMPY. This ratio, depicted in

---

**TABLE 6.5**

**Number of PCP Visits PMPY Benchmark**

$$\frac{\text{Total Number of Annual PCP Visits by Members}}{\text{Sum of Actual Monthly Members}}$$

PCP BENCHMARK = 1.5 to 5.0 PCP Visits PMPY

## TABLE 6.6
## Number of PMPY Referrals Benchmark

Total Number of Annual Member Referrals

Sum of Actual Monthly Members

BENCHMARK = 0.5 to 3.0 Referrals PMPY

Table 6.6, is calculated by dividing the total number of referrals for the year by the number of plan members. The referrals PMPY indicator is usually calculated both in total and on an individual practitioner basis. The benchmark for this indicator is 0.5 to 3.0 referrals per member year. Less than 0.5 referrals indicate denied or restrictive access, while more than 3.0 might primarily indicate poor referral control.

### Authorization Compliance

Compliance with authorization requirements may be measured to evaluate the practitioner's participation in the network. It is calculated as a percentage of cases, for example, total precertified admissions divided by total hospital admissions. Most plans have a target of 100% compliance, with tiered disincentives for noncompliance.

## MCO INTERNAL CONTROL

The bottom line for gatekeeper models (not loosely managed preferred provider organizations [PPOs]) is that claims for anything but primary care services should not be paid without an authorization unless such services are specifically excluded by policy. Two areas are required to ensure proper internal controls: linking authorizations to claims (and thus reducing IBNR) and ensuring the cooperation of the PCP.

### CONTROLLING CLAIMS BY LINKING TO AUTHORIZATIONS

The first required area is accomplished by assigning a unique authorization number to each authorization issued. That number must then accompany any and all claims related to that authorization. In a paper-based system, in which the primary care physician fills out an authorization form (which may double as a referral or admission form), the MCO assigns the number when the authorization is received. In a telephone-based system, in which the primary care physician calls the MCO, the authorization is issued essentially as an authorization number, which is immediately entered into the computer system and available for claims processing. Online or electronic systems, undoubtedly the wave of the future, turn the number assignment and information entry into one process, with the information ready and waiting when the claim is processed.

## PCP Cooperation in Enhancing Controls

Lack of cooperation from the primary care physician is a stickier problem, best dealt with through education and incentives. However, if an authorization for a service is missing, the MCO has a limited number of options. Most dramatically, the MCO can refuse to pay the claim or refuse to include services consumed as part of a capitation contract (making the provider/practitioner liable for the full costs of care). Since most contracts with providers forbid balance billing, and a violation of the False Claims Act may result in doing so, the provider will not be paid the balance. This option, however, punishes someone other than the uncooperative primary care physician. Another (rather frequently used) option is to create authorizations retrospectively, as mentioned, calling them prospective or concurrent depending on the claims processor's belief about the primary care physician's original intent. These retrospective authorizations should be tracked for administrative follow-up with problem physicians.

Problems of simple confusion and error can be at least partially avoided by considering the possible complications with authorization in advance and determining the best ways to deal with them. This is particularly vital in the case of point of service (POS) plans (for which self-referral is often permitted), in which some services are expected to be provided out of the network—the possible complications are endless. Most MCOs have an authorization system coordinator who acts essentially as an internal auditor of the authorization system. It is his or her responsibility to track the system on an ongoing basis, find and fix problem areas, and recommend changes and improvements to the system.

## CONCLUSION

Sound financial management of MCOs requires taking the enrollee perspective in driving health care consumption and the demands to do so. This effect on demands is the impetus for all of the areas covered in this chapter. Unless enrollees are guided to change their behaviors and adopt the wellness model, strategies such as CM and UM will forever be "band-aid" approaches and will fail in improving practitioner consumption. Even more telling is the fact that IBNR will likely increase if practitioners perceive that MCOs are out of touch with the needs and demands of their enrollees.

# 7 Management of Managed Care Information for Modeling Purposes

## INTRODUCTION

In the health care industry, unlike the insurance industry, providers and practitioners are constantly challenged to obtain meaningful market intelligence and operations indicators to manage resources efficiently and effectively. This challenge is not specific to health care financial managers, but extends to all aspects of health care operations. The problem in the health care industry is not that providers/practitioners have no data, but rather that they have no easily digestible information on which to base management and clinical decisions. Hence, the challenge to provider- and practitioner-based managed care organizations (MCOs) is to harness the right data to yield the right information. What typically happens, however, is that some of the right data are not recognized as such. What is even worse, is that much of the data, including some of the "good" data, are discarded as meaningless.

Take, for example, the problem about lack of outcomes data to create clinical practice parameters and optimal clinical treatment strategies. Provider enterprises process hundreds of medical records each month in order to generate UBs for inpatient care and practitioner enterprises process hundreds more to send out CMS-1500 claim forms for outpatient and ambulatory care. What happens to those medical record fields that were not essential to the processes of preparing and mailing a single claim form or encounter report? What happens to clinical information, such as in a standard dictated discharge report, about the nature of the patient's symptoms relative to the discharge diagnosis and the aftercare treatment prescribed? Such fields are not required to submit a claim for payment or an encounter to close an authorization. Yet, looking at these two additional fields would yield significant outcomes data. If the same inquiry were practiced and stratified by physician and by diagnosis code or stratified-severity adjustment within diagnosis-related groups (DRGs; as practiced by providers to comply with Joint Commission on Accreditation of Healthcare Organizations quality-of-care guidelines first implemented in the early 1990s), approximately 1 week's worth of work would yield very significant intelligence for a single month: How many Medicare patients of the same diagnosis and the same physician were readmitted within 72 hours for the same condition (especially since this is now considered a "never event" for which most payers no longer reimburse providers)? How many within 1 week? Even within 1 week for readmission, it should be clearer which treatments might work better than others might and which practitioners have better outcomes than others do. This single inquiry is a start.

Instead of properly analyzing their own data, providers and practitioners generally create scapegoats, wringing their hands that they have no "executive information" in real time. Few hospitals nationwide have true cost accounting systems; they rely instead on the ratio of reported Medicare costs (in total) to reported Medicare charges (in total) as a "reasonable" substitute for cost accounting. (There should be an exclamation mark after the previous sentence, but most every financial manager knows how true that statement is.) What do providers actually know about their operating costs to be able to complete a simple per diem or discounted fee-for-service (DFFS) managed care contract, let alone complex all-inclusive case prices and PMPM (per member, per month) costs?

Against this dubious backdrop is the information technology industry, and its recognition that information systems are not achieving what managers and contracting staff feel they need to have. As a result, practitioners and providers—not MCO provider liaisons, as widely believed—are the ones accepting "what the market will bear" in lieu of careful costing and strategizing based on appropriate executive information of fixed and variable costs by relevant department. The belief is that health maintenance organizations (HMOs) have destroyed managed care markets by offering below-market PMPMs. The more likely reality is that practitioners and providers asked the MCOs for opening bids rather than the other way around. The likely culprit for managed care contracting staff's blindness about their costs, and what the lowest price points are, is their information systems.

In addition, management staff may be unaware of how files are actually created in the computer software, such that the managed care information desired is reliably collected. And, to keep training costs down, management staff rarely participate in user training at the time of installation; they must then rely on subordinates to create reports that meet their needs. This type of rationale is crazy: Managers have a level of understanding about the data and objectives required that subordinates generally do not possess. Even if this "upside-down" bureaucratic approach works, there is still an untenable belief that the information systems cannot be trusted and need to be made more "user friendly"; in other words, no matter how user friendly the information system, the perception remains that it will never be user friendly enough. This is another reason why the information technology industry will always have customers for their products.

## DATA ELEMENTS AND SOURCES

The scenario given is not to suggest that the information technology industry has been designing and selling inferior products and inadequate software. True, there are some bad systems in the industry. Also true is that the vast majority of information technology products sold in the health care industry are excellent. At the same time, the "Tower of Babel" phenomenon (see section on integration of managed care databases) has an influence in which specifications are requested, which features and integration software are specifically installed, and which standard reports are created to give management staff the "information" that they desired in the first place. There is a huge difference between the standard reports of a company and a custom report that *"could* be created" to capture managed care-related data promised to management.

The source of market and operating intelligence is information, and the source of that information is data. Obtaining accurate and adequate data at enrollment is critical. Those data are used to bill groups (mostly via age/sex tiers) as well as build the member database that uses everything from designing disease management programs to distributing member identification cards.

Reports on the cost and use of health care are meaningless without information about the group using the services. The sex mix, age mix, and size of the group described by cost and frequency reports provide the context in which the reports may be meaningful. Is $300,000 in prescription drug costs high or low? If 40% of your total expenditures are on maternity costs, is that good or bad? Are medical costs of $2,500 per enrollee high, low, or average? Without knowing the size of the group, the percentage of women in the group, and the age mix of the group, these questions cannot be answered as absolutes.

The following data were captured from the claims-processing (per Chapter 2) and both the case management and utilization management activities in Chapter 6.

## DATA CAPTURED FROM CLAIMS PROCESSING

- Patient or enrollee ID
- Social Security number
- Patient age and sex
- Provider ID (and referring provider ID if appropriate)
- Date of service
- Type of service
- Type of diagnosis/major diagnostic category
- Procedure code
- Primary, secondary, and other diagnosis codes as necessary
- DRG classification
- Episode-of-care identifier
- Cost center (UB-04 or later UB revision than 2004) code for hospitalization
- COB information
- Detailed inpatient pay classifications (medical/surgical, intensive care unit [ICU], etc.)

## DATA CAPTURED FROM CASE AND UTILIZATION MANAGEMENT

- Admission date
- Diagnosis

- Type of service (surgery, maternity)
- Type and timing of procedures planned
- Admitting physician
- Consultants
- Anticipated discharge date
- Discharge planning necessary

The information gathered from these two MCO functions is combined then "sliced and diced" in numerous ways. Provider profiling and financial reporting are two vital analyses derived from costing data.

## ENROLLMENT DATA SOURCES

Each enrollee's name, address, employer/division/location, salary, length of employment, employer standard industrial classification (SIC) code, plan design deductible and copayments, and other coverage if any must be recorded. In addition, the employee's (and covered dependent's) age, sex, family status, primary care physician, dates of coverage, type of coverage, and history of past coverage (if available) should be recorded (see Table 7.1).

---

### TABLE 7.1
### Enrollment Data per Member

- Name
- Address
- Social Security number
- Date of birth
- Employer (including department or division location)
- Salary (if part of benefit design)
- Length of employment
- Employer standard industry classification (SIC code)
- Deductible
- Copayment
- Other insurance coverage, if any, for coordination of benefits (COB)
- Ages of covered dependents
- Sex
- Family status
- Primary care physician
- Dates of coverage
- Type of coverage or insurance product name
- History of past coverage (if available)

---

Enrollees must be required to complete enrollment applications, and the enrollment information must be entered into the computer of the MCO as soon as possible for use in authorizations, claims processing, or capitation payments. Enrollment applications may also include the necessary consent for the MCO to have access to enrollees' medical records as necessary. Restricted access and medical information confidentiality are important risks to consider in respect to any enrollee database.

The enrollee database can also produce information of use to the management of the MCO. These reports may be high-level profiles of enrollee behavior and illness patterns, or they may be straightforward reports of health care service patterns based on demographics: age, sex, industry classification, and so on. Reports like these can be compared to industry norms and standards, with some caution. Parameters of the industry norms may not be comparable to your population or market.

As the managed care industry continues to shift from focus on the employer group to retail marketing (focus on enrollee), high-quality data and flexibility of enrollee databases will remain important.

## Provider/Practitioner Data Sources

Practitioners and providers are a key part of the information flow concerning enrollees: They *need* information from the MCO to serve members, and they *provide* information about patients and their own activities that is vital to the operations of the MCO.

The most important element of the provider information flow is simple: using the same identifier or ID number for all services provided by a specific provider. Using tax identification numbers often will not work since providers may have several of them. The MCO itself will need to develop its own system of assigning provider IDs and insist that providers use it. The ability to study patterns of care by provider is of immense benefit to the profitable management of the MCO and the delivery of high-quality care to members.

Thus, providers will also need to be "enrolled." Health plans follow a credentialing process that enables the plan to ensure that only qualified providers constitute the network accessed by members. Both the National Committee for Quality Assurance (NCQA) and URAC (formerly Utilization Review Accreditation Commission) look for a rigid and thorough credentialing program in reviewing health plans. The name, address, locations, types of institution/specialties, and contractual relationships with the MCO will need to be recorded along with a great deal of other background details; the required data for medical practitioners are shown in Table 7.2, for nonphysician practitioners in Table 7.3, and for providers are shown in Table 7.4.

## Authorization Data Sources

One of the major areas in which provider information and enrollee information are used together is authorization. HMOs and EPOs/PSOs generally require

### TABLE 7.2
### Application Data per Medical Practitioner

- Board certification
- Group and site affiliations
- Tax ID number
- UPIN (universal provider identification number)
- Social Security number (SSN)

### TABLE 7.3
### Application Data per Nonphysician Practitioner

- Name
- Tax identification number/Social Security number
- Billing address
- Office location(s)
- Type of service (e.g., chiropractic, acupuncture) contracted
- Contractual relationship with the managed care organization

### TABLE 7.4
### Application Data per Institutional Provider

- Name
- Employer identification number (state and federal)
- Billing address
- Secondary care institution, primary care facility/clinic, satellite, or owned retail pharmacy or home health/hospice locations
- Type of institution and in-house specialties
- Tertiary care facilities and any tertiary capitation purchased
- MCO contractual relationship, especially all-inclusive case rates that bundle hospital and hospital-based practitioner services
- For hospital-billed physician practices:
  - Board certification
  - Group and site affiliations
- Hospital-owned specialty care centers (e.g., hemodialysis, radiation therapy, chemotherapy, level 2 and 3 cardiac rehab)
- All other contractual relationships with the managed care organization

---

**TABLE 7.5**

**Data Captured from Authorization Services**

- Authorization identification number
- Name of referring provider
- Provider referred to
- Date of authorization
- Patient name, age, and sex
- Diagnosis
- Range of dates for services authorized
- Type and quantity (number of days/services) authorized
- Specific procedures and aftercare management authorized
- Amount paid for service
- Quantity of service actually used

---

authorization for specialty services, as do accountable care organizations (ACOs). PPOs may require authorizations for inpatient and some outpatient services. Authorization is covered in detail in Chapter 2. The requirements for prior authorization are steadily loosening as members with the muscle of state legislation are seeking more direct access to specialists (e.g., many states now mandate that women have direct access to obstetricians/gynecologists [OB/GYNs], rather than relying on family practitioners who possess many overlapping skills on a less-surgical level).

Authorization of services is one of the major ways in which the enrollee database will be used. The database will enable the MCO to verify that the patient is eligible for the service and provide any benefits information that may be relevant to the situation (lower coinsurance, for example). A well-designed enrollee database will also be able to check the appropriateness of the treatment to the demographics and diagnosis of the patient (a hysterectomy for a man?), indicate whether the treatment requires a second opinion, list the reimbursement amount, and identify the data needed to determine medical necessity and perform financial modeling. It can also provide the names and locations of preferred providers for a procedure. The specific data captured from authorization services are listed in Table 7.5.

## DEFINITION OF DATABASE AND CLAIMS PAYMENT INFORMATION FLOWS

An accurate and all-encompassing database is critical for MCOs. Accurate identification of members and their patterns of consumption of managed care resources are vital data for projecting resource consumption, maintaining budgeted per product medical loss ratios (MLRs), as well as providing accurate experience-based ratings for underwriters (such as the adjusted community rating methodology in Chapter 2).

## BASIC MCO DATABASE INFORMATION FOR AUTHORIZATIONS

Prior authorization enables the MCO to gather information in advance and identify potential problems. One of these is potentially catastrophic cases, which, if identified early, can be taken under case management. Usually a function of the utilization review department, case management seeks to improve the continuity and quality of care as well as control costs in these situations. It involves such activities as special agreements with and referrals to tertiary care facilities, specialists, home health care, and durable medical equipment (DME) providers. Early identification of these higher-cost cases can serve as an aid in setting claim reserves. (More on incurred but not reported [IBNR] is in Chapter 6.) Prior authorization also helps track these high-cost cases.

Prior authorization also provides a means of studying referral patterns, such as inappropriate referral relationships and physicians who under- or overrefer. Prior authorization records initial diagnoses at the beginning of the case. Combined, these records make it possible to profile providers for appropriate diagnoses and, by comparing the outcomes of similar diagnoses, create quality profiles of providers.

To manage the authorization process, the database of the MCO will need the following: an authorization identification number; the names of the referring provider and the provider referred to; the date of the referral; patient name, age, and sex; diagnosis; the range of dates for services authorized; the type and quantity (number of days/services) authorized; and the specific procedure authorized. After the authorized service has been provided, the amount paid for service and quantity of service actually used should be added to the database (see Table 7.5). As mentioned, the database provides information to the provider during the authorization process as well: verification that the patient is eligible for the service, relevant benefits information, such as copayments, deductibles, and noncovered services.

## CONCURRENT REVIEW INFORMATION FLOWS

Another area in which provider and enrollee data intersect for management purposes is concurrent review. Concurrent review is an assessment of care that determines medical necessity or appropriateness of services as they are being rendered. Changes in diagnosis can be tracked as well as clinical data, including

- The frequency of complicating infections in a particular hospital;
- Extended fevers that may have been controlled inadequately;
- Sequences and combinations of procedures; and
- The final/discharge diagnosis as compared to initial/intake diagnosis, indicating both diagnostic accuracy and possible complications.

The types of clinical data can be studied to produce provider effectiveness profiles, another management tool for the MCO.

## EPISODES-OF-CARE INFORMATION FLOWS

The information generated by the authorization process plus the information tracked by concurrent review can be used by a utilization review clinician to link various incidents and treatments into one illness or "episode of care." This enables the information in the database of the MCO to be linked as well. Identifying episodes of care can allow additional appropriate treatments and levels of treatment to be determined and recommended.

Using episodes of care in combination with data on a provider's billed charges can allow the MCO to profile a given provider's effectiveness in treating certain conditions and help determine whether the provider may be overtreating or undertreating enrollees. In addition, when an episode of care has been identified, further services can be reviewed for appropriateness or compared to such norms as those reported by PAS (see Chapter 3) for lengths of hospital stays.

To reach its goals of containing costs and ensuring quality of care, an MCO absolutely must continue to monitor its provider network. Collecting and processing information from patients and providers, as we described, is vital.

## DISTINCTION BETWEEN LOGICAL AND PHYSICAL UNITS OF MANAGED CARE DATA

The way in which data are kept on storage devices and accessed is called its *physical design*. The way the data are viewed by different applications and individual users is called its *logical design*. One logical record can extend across multiple physical records, such as depicted in Figure 7.1. That is, what a user in claims processing sees as one logical record may include data from the enrollee records and from utilization management processes. Conversely, one physical record may contain parts of more than one logical record. For example, a logical record of an enrollee's name and address and a logical record of an enrollee's age and sex both come from the physical enrollee record.

In a database system, data are analyzed logically according to their relationship to other data, then designed physically for the most efficient processing or accessing. Users can access a logical view of data without any regard for its physical storage at any specific physical location. Information obtained from the

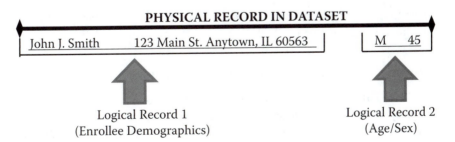

**PHYSICAL RECORD IN DATASET**

| John J. Smith | 123 Main St. Anytown, IL 60563 | | M | 45 |

Logical Record 1
(Enrollee Demographics)

Logical Record 2
(Age/Sex)

**FIGURE 7.1** Logical and Physical Records.

Internet is a perfect example of viewing graphics and music as part of a logical design, such as HTML (hypertext markup language) or JAVA, even though pieces of data, from which an HTML screen page may derive, can be physically located anywhere in the world (and perhaps even in outer space), all in a manner that is completely hidden from end users who access that logical screen page.

## DATA AND SYSTEM SECURITY ISSUES FOR MCOS

MCO authorization services represent an internal control issue that works much like a purchase requisition. The segregation of responsibility rule in internal control says that the ability to issue a purchase order should not be given to the same person who issues checks. By analogy, the information system should not allow personnel in the claims area to add, change, or delete authorization records.

The maintenance of provider records similarly should be handled outside the claims department. Record creation must follow carefully defined procedures to ensure that only genuine practitioners and real facilities, with valid tax ID numbers, are added to the system. Changes in name, address, or tax ID should always be provided in writing, never over the telephone. To avoid duplicate records, full names (or if space limits, standard abbreviations) should always be used. For example, if the name of Community Memorial Hospital is entered Community Meml Hosp, searching for records for Community Memorial Hospital using its full name will sometimes turn up a blank (unless the system has a browse look-up function). The puzzled searcher may then create a new record—and eventually, confusion.

Confidentiality is another data access issue and, with medical records, a particularly sensitive one. Access to these data must be severely limited to only those who are authorized and genuinely need it. Certain types of records, such as mental health claims, may be restricted to only a few individuals. (A more thorough discussion of legal requirements in the electronic transmission of member medical and encounter records is found in Chapter 8.)

## DIFFERENCES AMONG MANAGED CARE REPORTS

Several types of routine reports are used by most MCOs. The characteristics of these reports are presented as Table 7.6.

### STATISTICAL INDICATORS OBTAINABLE FROM STANDARD MCO REPORTS

Routine reports of an MCO will usually focus on costs and utilization. For example, hospital utilization management data entered daily by the utilization nurse can be summarized on a monthly basis in a report that might include the following: planwide statistics, service-specific statistics, provider-specific statistics, and other MCO statistics.

**TABLE 7.6**
**Standard Report Characteristics**

| Report Type | Data Presented | Report Advantages | Report Disadvantages |
|---|---|---|---|
| 1  Plan average | Average performance for entire plan that ties closely to financial performance of plan | Consistent cross-plan comparisons; often required by regulations | Inconsistent in identifying causes of performance problems |
| 2  Independent practice association (IPA)/ health center/ regional center | Provides managers data for their scope of supervision | Imperative for management | Does not explain causes of problems |
| 3  Individual practitioner | Provides PCP/ network practitioner profiling data | Basis for cross comparisons of practitioner patterns of practice, referrals authorized, and IBNR | Does not explain causes of variances (such as vacations and new data entry staff) |
| 4  Service/vendor | Provides profiling data for non-PCPs and nonpractitioners | Useful for utilization management and contract negotiation | Does not explain causes of variance (e.g., supply chain) |
| 5  Employer group | Tracks utilization attributed to employer customers | Identifies problems with experience ratings and community-rated groups | Does not explain variances (e.g., layoffs affect MLR) |

## Planwide Statistics
- Inpatient days and admissions per 1,000 members
- Average member inpatient length of stay
- Average per diem expenses per member length of inpatient stay
- Average total cost per member admission (case)

## Service-Specific (e.g., Psychiatric, Surgical, Obstetric) Statistics
- Service-specific admissions and inpatient days per 1,000 members
- Average member inpatient length of stay by service (useful for intrahospital transfers, such as to telemetry from coronary care unit or to medical/surgical services from intensive care unit)
- Average per diem expenses per member length of inpatient stay by service
- Average total cost per member admission (including intrahospital transfer, e.g., to obstetrics from the emergency department)

## Provider-Specific Statistics

- Admission and inpatient day use rates (statistic per 1,000 members) among all network facilities
- Average member inpatient length of stay by service (useful for comparing member length-of-stay data to approximate outcomes data, for example)
- Average per diem expenses per member length of inpatient stay by facility (useful for contract renegotiation, especially for members with similar acuity)
- Average total cost per member admission by facility (critical as one component of evaluating value derived from inclusion of a particular facility in a network)

## Other MCO Statistics

- Summary of retrospective and pended authorizations
- Number and percentage of authorizations denied
- Summary of in-network versus nonnetwork services
- Primary care encounter rates: Rates of primary care provider (PCP) encounters include visits per member per year, percentage of new patients/visits, and revisit intervals.
- Referral utilization rates: Referral rate per 1,000 members per year; cost per referral by primary care practitioner, by specialty care practitioner, and by plan or plan product; average referral cost per member per year; average referrals per primary care practitioner or by specialty care practitioner; and comparison of initial referrals to total referrals.
- Prescription statistics: Prescriptions per member per year, average number and average wholesale cost of prescriptions per PCP and per specialist; and comparisons of percentage of brand-name versus generic prescriptions as well as percentage of prescriptions ordered versus those filled.
- Ancillary statistics: Clinical, reference, and pathology lab CAP units and cost per member case; radiology RVUs (relative value units) and cost per member case; ambulatory surgery minutes and cost per member case; and so on.

These reports and derived statistical indicators are utilized primarily for the managers, underwriters, and individuals preparing HEDIS (Healthcare Effectiveness Data and Information Set) reports for an MCO. A powerful use of these indicators is to share them with providers and practitioners because they are likely to change their consumption habits. The positive change in consumption simply by recognizing that a problem exists is well documented in social science and total quality management (TQM) research. And of course, as contracts are negotiated and renegotiated, hard data are a necessary and powerful bargaining tool, especially considering the dearth of providers that practice department-specific cost accounting.

**TABLE 7.7**

**The "Tower of Babel" Effect: Different Perspectives on Authorization**

| | Managed Care Organization | Provider/Practitioner |
|---|---|---|
| DATUM: Date/time of PCP authorization for emergency care | Critical datum for managing loss attributable to a PCP and if in or out of network | Critical "hoop to jump through" to get emergency room care paid |
| Information yielded from date/time of PCP authorization for emergency care | Critical information about the extent of PCP IBNR and how delinquent unreported, incurred care may be, down to the minute | Complete headache: If authorization obtained *before* lifesaving emergency care rendered, the datum may be discoverable as "evidence" that the emergency room violated federal Emergency Medical Treatment and Active Labor Act (EMTALA) statute, which could jeopardize the Medicare certification of entire hospital |

# INTEGRATION OF MANAGED CARE DATABASES

The MCO, like all organizations, is a system. The related elements (departments of employees) are working together toward a common goal (the success of the organization). When the MCO is thought of as a system, it becomes possible to study it as such and, more to the point, study the information flow through the system.

Each department is also a system. The method that an individual system uses to collect data, process them, and distribute the resulting information is its information system. An information system receives data as input, processes them using a computer or a person's intelligence, and produces information. Employees provide feedback within the system of the organization. Finance needs information from utilization management (internal feedback), and utilization management needs information from hospitals (external feedback).

There are two complicating factors to this noble desire to have information technologies deliver the executive information needed to manage MCO business. The first complication is the modern equivalent of the "Tower of Babel," in which information technology employees speak a language different from operations and financial management staff and different from the language spoken by most clinicians. Everyone at the practitioner, provider, and payer enterprise levels has a unique language that is poorly spoken within enterprises, or even single departments, that are supposed to be integrated and sharing common data. A single factoid or datum has different informational meanings depending on the enterprise or the individual department. This Tower of Babel is one of the basic problems of managed care, as seen in Table 7.7.

The second complication is that reports that integrate managed care data from different departments or even entities are no longer sufficient as information, at least not since the personal computer started appearing on most managers' desktops in the mid-1990s. In fact, spreadsheets and integrated database access now govern many management decisions concerning contracts and MCO covered lives. Managers need the freedom to shape the data into information that meets their personal needs, specific and flexible enough to handle any given situation; they should no longer rely on subordinates to know how to generate reports of the data interrelationships that they need to know. This level of freedom with confidential data is more than most information systems managers would prefer to allow, and with the best of reasons. Hardcopy reports were staples in the 1970s but have a much lower value in the 21st century. If executives need to spend precious time to rekey summarized data just so they can perform simple "what if?" scenarios for a pressing management or contractual problem, whose benefit does this attitude serve, and whose interest is being protected?

## ELECTRONIC CONNECTIVITY OF MANAGED CARE INFORMATION

The future of management information systems specific to MCOs and operations will necessarily require electronic connectivity. As the move to electronic connectivity began when the Medicare program, as payers, imposed cash flow delays for organizations *not* submitting claims electronically, vital managed care information is increasingly available online. Such critical operations as monthly eligibility lists, electronic claims submission, electronic claims error checking, as well as electronic funds transfer in lieu of check receipt have been available since the mid-1990s. Providers and practitioners prefer this electronic connectivity because of time savings, reduced days in accounts receivable, and less propensity for errors and delay.

A classic example of the need for connectivity is in authorization. Authorization can be a win-win opportunity for both the MCO and providers/practitioners. Referring to Table 7.7, the problem facing the MCO is that data so critical to claims prediction are prone to noncompliance by providers/practitioners because of the operational headache of obtaining authorization (busy telephones, busy fax machines, and the need to allocate scarce and overworked full-time employees for obtaining authorizations). Using a computer that accesses the Internet via thousands of portals and allowing for hundreds of users to access a single database could eliminate the majority of noncompliance causes by providers/practitioners while improving MCO compliance.

## CONCLUSION

The world of information systems has gone through a complete metamorphosis in the managed care industry in just 5–10 years. As the need for better and quicker information to manage this industry has improved tremendously, MCOs and providers/practitioners have found that their operations have changed just as tremendously. It was not that long ago that MCO eligibility lists were printed on green-bar computer paper, at great cost to the payer industry, and eligibility checking was a painstaking problem. Not only was the process of eligibility checking a problem, but also the fact that it was so labor intensive resulted in significant provider/practitioner noncompliance from two perspectives.

The first case of noncompliance occurs when eligibility lists are not checked if "members" present an MCO identification card. There were some good reasons for this noncompliance. For example, because some lists were voluminous and the MCOs sought to reduce mailing costs by using lower-priority mailing classes, lists were sometimes unavailable at the beginning of the month. In addition, there were "catch-up" periods between the time new married names started appearing on the listings.

In response to not checking authorizations, many MCOs had exactly the worst-possible reaction: They penalized the provider/practitioner by reducing capitation payments when care was provided to nonmembers, notwithstanding the fact that many cards lacked a logo or special colored ink and that most cards listed no expiration dates. The MCOs sought to keep their administrative costs as low as possible and passed the resulting headache on to providers/practitioners. The result was a provider/practitioner rebellion.

This rebellion, whereby authorizations are obtained but encounter data or claims are not reported, has done far worse damage to payer-provider/practitioner relations than the retroactive denials that started this vicious cycle. Because of the dire IBNR implications, payers had to spend far more money on making eligibility lists electronic, creating firewalls and intranets to accept electronic authorizations, and instituting 24- to 48-hour grace periods in obtaining authorizations. They have probably spent far more money in improving their management information systems than if they had made it easier for providers to obtain authorizations with easily recognizable cards, making their cards fraud resistant, and helping them comply rather than slapping them for not complying. Even with the millions spent making eligibility lists and authorizations more user friendly, MCOs still have significant IBNR exposure due to continued noncompliance among providers/practitioners with even less labor availability, even to use their computers instead of fax machines. The future for MCOs must recognize that their previous attempts at improving the convenience of authorizations and their subsequent encounter reporting have not nearly been effective enough at minimizing IBNR.

# 8 Managed Care Legal and Regulatory Compliance

## INTRODUCTION

Managed care organizations (MCOs), like the health care industry, are subject to rules and regulations regarding their operations and their relationships with other entities. The various rules and regulations fall into three general categories:

- compliant relationships with regulations of government agencies,
- contracts between MCOs and practitioners/providers, and
- patient rights and member relationships with payers/caregivers (see Chapter 5).

Thousands of pages in books and periodicals have been devoted to the explanation of these relationships and how to manage them. Therefore, it is impossible to cover every legal aspect of MCOs in this chapter. Chapter 8 is intended merely as an overview of the most important and pervasive managed care issues for health care financial managers and is not a replacement for law school or legal counsel.

## FEDERAL REGULATORY COMPLIANCE IN MANAGED CARE

As a result of their participation in Medicare Part C or Medicare Advantage (i.e., Part D), MCOs must comply with the regulations, rulings, and specific interpretations of the Office of the Inspector General (OIG) of the U.S. Department of Health and Human Services (DHHS). MCOs must also comply with regulations to which practitioners/providers have long been held, such as the False Claims Act (FCA), Emergency Medical Treatment and Active Labor Act (EMTALA) and Health Insurance Portability and Accountability Act of 1996 (HIPAA), Stark I and II, as well as the need for a compliance officer.

The compliance officer ensures that medical and surgical decision making are not based on any nonmedical factors (however enticing they may be), such as incentives and disincentives that do not accrue to a patient's benefit.

### PAYER COMPLIANCE

The chief aspect of payer compliance under federal law relates to their marketing activities as well as their contractual relationships with practitioners/providers. Marketing compliance, for example, remains a significant problem in the Medicare program. Prohibited marketing activities include activities that discriminate, confuse, or mislead beneficiaries.

Many beneficiaries inadequately understand the advantages and trade-offs of joining a Medicare MCO (see Chapter 4). At the same time, MCOs spend significant monetary, promotional, and labor resources to market their products under both Medicare risk (pursuant to Public Law 105–33) and Medicare Part C (Balanced Budget Act of 1997) and the subsequent passage of Medicare Part D prescription coverage under the Medicare Advantage program. As Medicare Advantage pays more to MCOs than did the Medicare risk program, this new program created significant competition in subscribing beneficiaries. MCOs try to channel Medicare beneficiaries so that they can subscribe the "right" ones. Healthier beneficiaries generate a lower medical loss ratio (MLR) because they use fewer medical services per premium paid.

MCO marketing activities cannot discriminate by minimizing adverse selection in trying to attract healthier people. The manner in which this discrimination occurs may involve confusing or misleading beneficiaries. The rationale for these strategies to discriminate or mislead is that MCOs might

- weed out new members likely to overconsume health care,
- prevent unhealthy beneficiaries from enrolling, and
- reduce use of expensive health care services attributable to these beneficiaries.

Examples of such discriminatory marketing include

- attracting beneficiaries with a college-level education, as MCOs often equate higher education with lower levels of needless consumption;
- conducting seminars for individuals with high income, as income and health care consumption are also inversely proportional (higher income equates to lower costs); and
- spending more time at places where healthier and wealthier senior citizens are found, such as at golf courses or health clubs, and less time at nursing homes.

DHHS therefore scrutinizes marketing materials prior to their dissemination to Medicare beneficiaries and will deny those that are discriminatory, confusing, or misleading, using a "layperson" standard. Solicitous marketing that is premium driven, such as gift giving, as well as activities that violate a marketer's duty are also contrary to approved marketing for Medicare MCOs.

Medicare beneficiary discrimination is not limited to discriminatory marketing activities. This form of "cherry-picking" can also occur in materials viewed as misleading or confusing, in an opposite manner from those described.

Misleading collaterals involve intentionally confusing all but the most educated or savvy beneficiaries. For example, some marketers have been known to unethically trick desirable beneficiaries, not immediately receptive to the presentation, into enrolling. Which activities are considered misleading? Prohibited examples of misleading activities are those that

- convince beneficiaries that the MCO product is not part of the Medicare program (even though certain add-on products, like zero-copay options, might very well be beyond the scope of the basic product itself); or
- lead beneficiaries to believe that additional information about managed Medicare is available only through the action of the MCO (such as the marketer's presentation) and not through the Medicare program itself.

Which activities are considered confusing? Prohibited examples of confusing activities are those that

- misstate plan and "original Medicare" coverage, or
- verbally offer benefits not approved by the Centers for Medicare and Medicaid Services (CMS).

Which activities misrepresent? Prohibited examples include misleading

- the marketing agent's relationship to the Medicare program (such as suggesting that the agent is a member of the federal government); or
- the relationship of the MCO with the federal government on envelopes or in enclosed marketing materials.

These actions also tend to misrepresent the relationship with DHHS. Giving beneficiaries the wrong impression of their relationship with the Medicare program itself is prohibited for Medicare MCO marketers. Specifically, agents

- are not federal employees;
- have no rights to use the Medicare logo or any other federal copyrights in their promotional materials; and
- must realize that approval of marketing materials by DHHS does not constitute an endorsement of the specific products of the MCO.

Consider the following examples of payer noncompliance:

### Discriminatory Marketing Activity:

Mr. B is a permanently disabled New Yorker who is covered by Medicare fee for service but does not understand English well. His first language is Creole. When an English-speaking health maintenance organization (HMO) marketing agent came to his ESL (English as a second language) class with English language marketing materials, Mr. B signed up, not fully understanding how an HMO works. He only discovered something was up when he received denials for physician bills because he had received care out of his enrolled HMO network. He never received written materials in French or Creole.

What is prohibited in this example is that the marketing activity discriminated based on language. No accommodations were made for Mr. B to make an informed decision. The discrimination was probably not incidental, as the salesperson knowingly presented in English to an ESL class.

### Confusing or Misleading Marketing:

A. In early 2009, Mr. Q was dying of cancer and had lost his retirement benefits. He scheduled an appointment with an MCO saleswoman, who said she could cover him under a Medicare Advantage policy to replace his lost retirement benefits. At the presentation, she told him that the paper he was signing was to insure him for Medicare coverage; the paper was actually an MCO enrollment form. He continued to see his cancer specialists and was admitted to a hospital that was not part of the network of the MCO. When discharged, he returned home to find that he had thousands of dollars worth of unpaid medical bills.

B. Mr. and Mrs. G already were enrolled in a Medicare HMO for 2 years when a sales representative from a competing MCO plan visited their home. Mr. and Mrs. G asked for further information. The agent, who had not brought any printed materials with him, asked them to sign a form, which they believed simply requested the information. Instead, they had unwittingly signed an enrollment form for the competing MCO. Not understanding that he had changed plans, Mr. G, who had a defective heart valve, continued to go to his cardiologist in the former HMO network. He only learned that he and his wife were enrolled in the MCO when the HMO denied payment, and Mr. G started to receive bills for his care.

C. Mr. S was told by a Medicare HMO saleswoman that she would not process the enrollment paperwork he completed unless he gave verbal authorization. However, the HMO subsequently enrolled him anyway, without his specific permission. Mr. S called the HMO three times to make sure that the HMO had *not* enrolled him and was falsely reassured each time that he had not been enrolled.

Examples A, B, and C point to misrepresentation by the MCO marketer of what the beneficiary was signing. These activities are not only prohibited by DHHS but also might be considered criminally fraudulent. These examples also point out the costs to vulnerable beneficiaries of marketing abuse. The beneficiary victims of these prohibited activities, who belong to these MCOs and many of whom are on fixed incomes, are left financially responsible for thousands of dollars of care. Their attempts to obtain new Medigap coverage under Medicare Part D may be more expensive than prior to joining a Medicare Part D HMO. The additional costs associated with correcting situations caused by such marketing practices are reflected in reports MCOs submit to DHHS and the level of pricing they ultimately receive in future years.

Another marketing activity prohibited by DHHS is the offering of improper gifts or payments to induce enrollment. This prohibited marketing activity represents inducements given to desirable beneficiaries who enroll in the plan. If this marketing activity targets everyone attending a presentation—not just those who subsequently enroll—DHHS permits "nominal gifts" to be given, generally those under a specific dollar cap.

Examples of permissible inducements include taglines placed on mass-produced refrigerator magnets, key chains, shoehorns, or pocket combs. According to DHHS, these types of trinkets meet its regulation, in that a promotional shoehorn has little resale value, is not easily convertible to cash, and is well under $10 in retail value. Finally, if the shoehorn is placed in a box in the registration area, available for anyone to take, it fulfills the last requirement that the item not be an inducement given only to enrollees.

Another prohibited marketing activity is participating in improper beneficiary solicitations. This type of marketing activity violates rules of DHHS by soliciting desirable beneficiaries in improper ways. Examples by which prohibited solicitations occur include

- making presentations to targeted households or individuals, not in response to request by a beneficiary or household for a presentation;
- making presentations in a manner that likely violates the beneficiary's right to privacy; and
- accepting enrollment applications at the time of presentation.

The following is an example of this type of prohibited solicitation activity:

Mr. and Mrs. M were watching television one evening when they heard their doorbell ring. Wary of criminals in their neighborhood, Mr. M asked of their visitor's business through the dead-bolted door. The visitor announced that he was a sales representative of a local Medicare HMO and asked if they would allow him to make a presentation as he was "in the neighborhood."

DHHS specifically prohibits such door-to-door Medicare MCO presentations as they are presumed to be unannounced and not as a result of a specific request by a beneficiary for a presentation. Such door-to-door solicitations can also be an invasion of a beneficiary's right to privacy, especially when made at night.

Such types of solicitations are prohibited by DHHS. They are violations because the salesperson made a presentation not as a result of a specific request for one. Regardless of whether the solicitation occurs in a private residence or in a private room of a nonprivate residence (such as a group home or a skilled nursing facility), the presentation itself is unwelcome, not specifically requested, and a potential invasion of privacy. In general, such door-to-door solicitations are considered by DHHS to be a violation of a permitted marketing activity.

Compliant payer activities also include the duty of MCO marketers in not misrepresenting the role of DHHS in preapproving promotional content. This duty of the MCO is to submit all intended marketing materials for approval by DHHS. DHHS disapproves content that is inaccurate or misleading or makes a material misrepresentation. DHHS must approve or disapprove such materials within 45 days of their first submission. Furthermore, any materials that DHHS has not disapproved after 45 days are *deemed* approved. However, the burden of proof is on the MCO to verify that DHHS received the materials submitted and that the 45-day deadline is clearly marked.

Title 42 of the *Code of Federal Regulations* (*CFR*) Regulation 417.428 specifies another marketer's duty. MCOs that violate any one of these duties face penalties that are severe. These duties include the following:

- Offering written language sufficient to make informed decisions of beneficiary enrollment;
- Notifying the general public of annual enrollment periods for managed Medicare MCOs; and
- Informing enrollees that MCO contracts may terminate, and that enrolled beneficiaries in a terminated MCO plan will result in disenrollment from managed Medicare.

Finally, MCOs are strongly urged to use model evidence of coverage, enrollment, and disenrollment forms provided by DHHS. The General Accounting Office continues to press DHHS to replace similar MCO-produced forms with these model documents. A summary of MCO compliance issues is provided as Table 8.1.

Substantial diligence is required of marketing agents of managed Medicare products. Medicare marketers must understand that certain marketing activities are prohibited by DHHS and subject to criminal and/or civil penalties if they are violated. Yet, not every solicitation is clearly prohibited or nonprohibited.

There are types of solicitations that may not be specifically prohibited but may be discouraged by DHHS. Prohibited marketing activities can likely occur as a result of a marketing activity that is, per se, nonprohibited. DHHS refers to these activities as "improper" because their use could result in an illegal action or a prohibited marketing activity.

Sales or marketing agents play a critical role in representing their plans to beneficiaries. Yet, each has different presentation styles, some of which may serve to confuse beneficiaries. What agents say during presentations may misrepresent what DHHS had approved in the marketing materials of the Medicare MCO. Specifically, marketing staff of Medicare MCOs must not engage in fraudulent representations, including

- making intentional misstatements

## TABLE 8.1

### Summary of MCO Managed Care Compliance

In conducting Medicare marketing presentations, pay close attention to the following five types of DHHS prohibitions.

1. **Don't discriminate in marketing activities,** such as:
   - over-selling to high-income areas while under-selling to low-income ones,
   - over-selling in health spas and gymnasiums while under-selling in nursing homes, and/or
   - over-selling to new beneficiaries just turning 65 while under-selling much older adults.

2. **Remember that the purpose of Managed Medicare presentations, as recognized by DHHS, is to teach beneficiaries about all program options and enable them to make informed decisions.** By following DHHS's recommended approach, you will avoid marketing activities which are designed to confuse or mislead, such as:
   - handing out marketing materials written for too-high of an intellectual standard, thereby inviting beneficiary confusion;
   - over-selling plan benefits by slipping in inadvertent misstatements of what DHHS approved, which has the effect of misrepresenting its administration of Managed Medicare; and/or
   - misleading beneficiaries into believing that only marketers, or their fulfillment staffs, can provide information about Managed Medicare plans

3. **Avoid spending significant promotional budget on gifts, as only nominal gifts given to everyone in attendance — not just to those interested in enrolling — are permissible.** Remember that DHHS defines a "nominal gift" as under $10. An example of such a gift would be a refrigerator magnet.

4. **Remember that all Managed Medicare solicitations require prior beneficiary requests.** Door-to-door or "in the neighborhood" cold-call approaches are specifically prohibited by DHHS.

5. **Always obey the marketer's duty to solicit compliantly. Don't use marketing materials that DHHS has not already approved.** Also, don't use materials DHHS has specifically disapproved. If DHHS takes longer than 45 days to issue a ruling on your submitted materials, they are deemed to be approved (if compliantly submitted).

---

- using inaccurate marketing materials,
- distributing nonapproved marketing materials, or
- otherwise violating enrollment or marketing guidelines set by the Managed Medicare program.

Marketing staffs of managed Medicare plans also have an obligation not to take advantage of mentally challenged and cognitively impaired beneficiaries, particularly those covered by Special Needs Plans under Medicare Part D. A marketer's presentation style must be appropriate to the audience's cognition, such as

- Speaking with a microphone or using a loud voice;
- Restricting presentation vocabulary to a sixth-grade level;

- Using standard black-on-white overheads or slides to eliminate discrimination against color blindness that normally occurs with age, such as difficulty reading white text on red or green backgrounds; and
- Distributing large-text versions of marketing materials and using large font sizes on slides or overhead transparencies presented.

DHHS specifically prohibits a marketer from engaging in activities that mislead, confuse, or misrepresent. DHHS does not proscribe specific styles or presentation formats. Rather, it is concerned with generally discouraging marketing that takes away a beneficiary's ability to make an informed choice about enrollment.

- All marketing presentations and mailings to Medicare beneficiaries within 75 days of the end of a calendar year (e.g., October 15) must include a Summary of Benefits for the benefit package information for the successive year. In addition, Medicare Advantage marketers must cease selling current-year benefit packages through any public medium (such as television, radio, billboards, display ads, etc.) that may serve to confuse beneficiaries.

DHHS suggests that the following four marketing practices be adopted by Medicare MCOs:

A. **Use the same professional standards for Medicare marketing staff as for marketers of other managed care products.** For example, if commercial HMO marketers must be licensed by a state agency, then extend that requirement to managed Medicare marketers. Similarly, if commercial HMO marketing positions are filled from among in-house employees, it should attempt to fill Medicare Advantage marketing positions from among in-house or commercial risk employees as well. In fact, DHHS strongly discourages using outside consultants as sales representatives for managed Medicare products.
B. **Establish an enrollment verification system that requires that a different agent visit each potential enrollee at the time the application is received than at the time of original presentation.** Furthermore, DHHS strongly recommends in its HMO manual that plans call each Medicare beneficiary who has applied for enrollment prior to the processing of the enrollment to confirm that the beneficiary understands the HMO restrictions and practices. DHHS, however, does not mandate that this be done.
C. **Analyze disenrollment data, sorted by marketing agent, to determine beneficiaries who enroll and subsequently disenroll within 3 months.** MCOs should apply matches to marketer commission data to identify marketers with a tendency to misrepresent the products being sold. Supervisors should more closely monitor these marketers. This can be more of a challenge for MCO plans that do not require lock-in

of membership for specific periods and can increase the potential for marketers improperly capping using the same groups of enrollees subscribed for multiple plans (and incentive payments) over the same plan year (see item D). This monitoring is required to detect misstatements about Medicare and plan benefits or cause the HMO to be noncompliant with DHHS regulations.

D. **Compensate marketers based on sustained retention (e.g., 90 days) of members enrolled, not just on beneficiaries enrolled per product or per plan year.**

The following is an example of marketing practices not specifically prohibited, but nevertheless discouraged by DHHS:

Mutual Underwriters of Louisiana (MUL) is an insurance company with a new Medicare Advantage product called Senior Health Initiatives (SHI). To sell SHI efficiently while containing costs, MUL decided not to gear up for a large sales staff until sufficient beneficiaries were subscribed to cover the incremental costs. Consequently, MUL signed with Louisiana Health Sales (LHS) to market SHI until a critical mass is achieved such that in-house marketers could be hired for managed Medicare products. LHS marketers were told to sign up as many beneficiaries as possible within 30 days. LHS was paid by MUL on the basis of total number of beneficiaries signed up.

DHHS was unhappy to learn that LHS was engaged to sell only to Medicare beneficiaries and not to sell other MUL products.

## OPERATIONAL COMPLIANCE

The frontline professional to whom hospital managers are responsible is the compliance officer.

## Managed Care Department

At the provider level, the director of managed care (or equivalent full-time employee) has the following managed care operations responsibilities to the compliance officer, all in addition to the basic duties of compliance for a facility:

1. Implement compliant managed care contracting approaches that reflect the assigned responsibilities of the facility assigned per its strategic business plan (and the marketing and promotion plan, if applicable).
2. Be the managed care compliance representative to the compliance officer of the facility, in combination with negotiating managed care contracts in accordance with specific hospital parameters and contracting objectives.

3. Be trained in managed care compliance requirements and receive biannual in-service education of changes to managed care compliance requirements.

4. Provide immediate response to MCO or practitioner contracting approaches that could jeopardize the

   a. continued participation of the hospital in commercial managed care contracts,

   b. continued participation of the hospital in managed care plans administered by CMS,

   c. investigations of the hospital by OIG, as applicable, and

   d. compliance status of the hospital.

5. Represent the defined managed care contracting goals of the hospital in ways that are legally compliant.

6. Provide immediate contact to the compliance officer of the facility of any physician-hospital relationships, rumored or in fact, that might compromise the compliance status of the hospital:

   a. Provide resources to the compliance office of the hospital to review or investigate suspect managed care contracting relationships

   b. When the hospital evaluates a physician practice for acquisition or inclusion on managed care panels, provide appropriate market intelligence, practice characteristics, consumer satisfaction studies, and noncompliant practices or procedures that could put the hospital in jeopardy (as a result of this new relationship).

7. If the hospital does not have a separate department or unit for administering self-funded, MCO, or managed care beneficiary plans, administer all managed care services, including

   a. Enrollee or beneficiary relations, including answering questions;

   b. Practitioner credentialing and continued participation of physician providers in provider panels and networks;

   c. Initiation of disciplinary actions against noncompliant physician practices of panel/network members, in concert with the physician credentialing committee of the hospital;

   d. Assurance of compliant claim management (including coordination of benefits [COB] rules against HMO balance billing) and encounter reporting;

   e. Completion of cost, clinical quality, member satisfaction, or HEDIS (Healthcare Effectiveness Data and Information Set) reporting (for MCOs accredited by the National Committee for Quality Assurance [NCQA]);

   f. Evaluation and outsourcing of any delegated managed care functions to outside contractors, if applicable;

   g. Managing provider claims submission, adjudication, payment, and retroactive audits—including compliance monitoring; and

   h. Managing authorization, claim reporting, and incurred but not reported (IBNR) minimization activities.

These areas are important for providers' managed care compliance because some patients receive differential care based on what their insurance cards say. For example, an important compliance law such as EMTALA was enacted to protect everyone's equal access to lifesaving emergency care. Without strict conformance to managed care aspects of compliance laws such as EMTALA, equal access to emergency health care may be restricted based on the type of insurance maintained or when nonmedical factors encroach on physicians' decision making, sometimes to the detriment of patient care.

In addition, federally qualified HMO (FQHMO) (see Chapter 2) and Medicare certification requirements prohibit provider discrimination pursuant to the Equal Employment Opportunity Commission (EEOC) and the Office for Civil Rights. Therefore, most provider contracts prohibit discrimination on the basis of payment source, race, color, age, sex, religion, disability, national origin, or sexual orientation. Nondiscrimination compliance with these characteristics is also mandated for providers by almost every state and some localities.

## ILLEGAL GAIN SHARING

One of the single most important issues that affects the managed care relationship between providers and practitioners is called "gain sharing," which the OIG first addressed in July 1999. A gain-sharing program involves a contractual arrangement between a hospital and members of its medical staff, generally for a share of cost savings on a contingent basis, based on a reduction of fee-for-service, managed care business the physician performs. The reduction of business to which the physician agrees is frequently requested by managed care payers, such as earlier discharges (e.g., to decrease length of stay) than the physician's previous practice. The business loss the physician sustains (mostly reduced days for which the physician can bill) is partially, or sometimes fully, offset by gain-sharing revenues paid by the hospital (e.g., percentage reductions in overall length of stay), typically tied to quality measures such as medical necessity.

On July 8, 1999, the OIG issued a Special Advisory Bulletin stating that contingency fee gain-sharing programs between hospitals and physicians violate federal law, specifically Sections 1128(b)(1) and (2) of the Social Security Act.

As gain sharing was originally defined and described by the OIG in July 1999, civil monetary penalties (CMPs) could be assessed on capitated Medicare risk physicians (or capitated managed Medicaid) who keep costs down and are paid incentives not for prohibited gain sharing, but for contractually stipulated risk pool overaccruals. Similarly, this interpretation violates the spirit of the gain-sharing alert by ignoring the following facts:

- Capitated physicians have no opportunity costs that need to be compensated;
- Capitated physicians already receive a benefit for spending administrative time in the hospital; and

- The more time capitated physicians spend in the hospital, the greater their "payment per visit," as the monthly capitation payment is spread over a smaller denominator of patient visits (a hybrid of the MLR).

The OIG amended its stated position and created a "safe harbor" for capitated managed Medicare and Medicaid in a letter from the Office of Counsel to the IG on August 19, 1999. According to the assistant inspector general for legal affairs, the creation of such a safe harbor was intended by Congress to include physician incentive arrangements related to Medicare risk-based managed care contracts and similar Medicaid contracts. A similar safe harbor was later enacted under the Affordable Care Act (governmental Shared Savings Program) to apply to gain-sharing incentives paid to physician members of accountable care organizations (ACOs).

The position that capitated managed Medicare practitioners be excluded from gain sharing stemmed from the recognition that physician incentive payments by hospitals were part of the normal practice of any managed care plan, including managed Medicare and Medicaid. The contingent incentives paid are per specific methodologies in the contracts governing appropriate physician practice. The money paid to physicians of managed care beneficiaries by a contracted hospital has a different effect from prohibited gain-sharing arrangements, as the capitated physician makes money, instead of loses money, every incidence when services are consumed.

The OIG appears to be troubled by applying CMP to gain-sharing structures. DHHS recognizes that hospitals are motivated to bill less at the same time that physicians are motivated to bill more. On one hand, cost containment by hospitals is in the best interests of the nation, as is establishing hospital performance standards of physicians with an appropriate cross section of physicians involved in the process. On the other hand, the OIG determined that an illegal inducement still exists to get physicians to increase or maintain their hospital presence as a quid pro quo for the hospital making partially offsetting gain-sharing payments to those physicians. The OIG has stated that compensation formulas that take into account hospital referrals are prohibited under gain sharing, not simply compensating physicians for their time based on a fair market value.

As a form of amnesty for hospitals already making gain-sharing payments to its fee-for-service physicians, the OIG promised in July 1999 that OIG will not prosecute any hospital for entering into a gainsharing program that included incentive payments in the past, provided that:

(1) the gainsharing program does not violate any statute other than the CMP provisions of the Social Security Act;
(2) the gainsharing program has not adversely affected patient care; and
(3) the hospital promptly terminates any impermissible gainsharing program.

Hospitals not taking advantage of the amnesty offer face not only substantial financial penalties of $5,000 to $10,000 per occurrence, plus possible jail time as part of civil monetary penalty (CMP)—even for discontinued unlawful relationships—but also criminal exposure due to violations of fraud and abuse laws, as well as Stark I and II statutes. To repeat, the providers' liability extended not only to current unlawful gain sharing but also to *past violations*. The defendants in these situations are not only the physicians accepting gain-shared money but also the hospitals, many of which initiated this unlawful relationship.

The exposure of hospitals to violations of gain-sharing relationships does not stop there, however. Nonproprietary hospitals with public debt financing may be required to be in compliance with Revenue Procedure 97–13, by which gain sharing involves the use of tax-exempt bond-financed space by "nonqualified users"— such as private physicians. Related federal income tax regulations that regulate the permissible duration and compensation methodologies of contracts entered into by such hospital laws may also apply. In addition to the foregoing, public benefit nonproprietary hospitals can be subject to Internal Revenue Service (IRS) tax exemption laws, including subsequent loss of tax-exempt status.

Unless a hospital knows *for a fact* that members of its medical staff are receiving either straight salary (with no volume-based incentives) or capitated payments from their independent practice association (IPA) or independent medical group, providers are ill-advised to assume that relationships with physicians belonging to capitated IPAs or groups will qualify for the gain-sharing safe harbor allowed by the OIG in August 1999 for capitated managed Medicare or Medicaid physicians.

Finally, if there is no other option but to continue past gain-sharing relationships in a currently compliant manner, providers should remove variable compensation strategies performed by the hospital to the physicians and convert the methodologies to fixed-fee or fair market value as the basis. For example, a hospital could pay its physicians for the actual amount of time provided to the hospital via a fixed hourly sum of money (e.g., hourly salary) tied to both time provided and the fair market value of a physician's time as an alternative to illegal gain-sharing relationships. While the liability may be mitigated by converting the compensation formula, the previous activities would still constitute a violation of the prohibition by the OIG against improper gain sharing.

The penalties associated with illegal gain sharing are severe for a hospital, its compliance officer, or its managed care contracting staff, to risk criminal indictments and civil monetary penalties. One strategy to comply with gain-sharing laws involves restructuring the contracts to continue past gain-sharing relationships in a currently compliant manner, remove variable compensation strategies performed by the hospital to the physicians, and convert the methodologies to fixed-fee or fair market value as the sole incentivizing basis.

Gain sharing need not be an overt attempt by the hospital to pay for continued business by its fee-for-service physicians. Gain sharing can occur in a much more obtrusive manner. The following case demonstrates a real-life example that identifies a less-than-intentional gain-sharing violation.

Robert Noble, the chief managed care officer of St. Evan Hospital, made an announcement to the board of directors today. He reported that the hospital needs to develop disease management protocols to be more accountable to outcomes while making hospital-specialist interactions more efficient to lower variable costs involved in doing so. The rationale he suggested was to both increase its market position with capitated payers and effectively respond to its current capitated payers' demands for better outcomes accountability. Complying with these demands would avoid the steep per member, per month (PMPM) decreases they initially proposed and would impose only a slight decrease.

Mr. Noble suggested that representatives of each of the five hospital-contracted IPAs with these payers be identified. He proposed that each contribute 5 hours per week to assist him and his staff in this effort, but that some equitable arrangement needs to be made to compensate these physicians for their administrative time. After some discussion, the board decided to institute Mr. Noble's recommendation and to incentivize the physicians based on both hospital cost savings due to incremental efficiencies as well as on the hospital-related costs of disease morbidities prevented. The board felt that this decision was compliant because the IPAs are capitated—not fee for service—and qualifies for the August 1999 safe harbor set by the OIG for capitated managed Medicare services.

While a safe harbor does exist for capitated managed Medicare or Medicaid physicians who participate in activities that would otherwise be considered as gain sharing, the decision of the board does not appear to qualify for this relief from noncompliance exposure, such as CMP and exclusion.

Just because an IPA receives a capitation from a payer does not mean that the physician members are not paid on a fee-for-service, or quasi-fee-for-service, basis. In embryonic IPAs, for example, a common inducement to get physicians to belong to the panel is that member practitioners will continue to be paid on a discounted, fee-for-service basis similar to what they receive from preferred provider organizations (PPOs), regardless of how the IPA is contracted with its partner hospitals or MCOs. This type of arrangement is also known as *risk banding*, in which first-year losses (difference between capitation modeled and fee for service actually paid) are absorbed at no penalty to the provider to encourage learning "the art of managed care" medicine, which is not taught in medical school.

Another common practice among IPAs in markets with less than 35% capitation penetration is to compensate its physicians a percentage of PMPM received, weighted according to volumes of service performed and acuities of patient care treated. This methodology, called *contact capitation*, in effect, pays a relatively nominal fee that is weighted according to consumption; in other words, it is based on the same principle as fee-for-service arrangements, namely, of "higher payment for higher care." The only difference between contact capitation and a flat fee-for-service payment arrangement is the amount of discounting the net IPA payment represents.

Either of these common IPA payment methodologies pays physicians on the basis of their consumption of hospital resources and differs significantly from nonconsumptive-related payments truly capitated physicians receive from their group or even their IPA. While this distinction has not yet been the subject of an

OIG ruling or been tested in the courts, it is likely that the safe harbor for capitated managed Medicare and Medicaid does not necessarily apply to this situation.

Finally, the case does not specify whether capitation payments IPAs receive constitute PMPMs that their physicians, in fact, receive. This practice, however, does not appear to apply to this case, as Mr. Noble was talking about increasing capitation business at St. Evan Hospital.

## ILLEGAL DOWNCODING

A corollary issue of gain-sharing arrangements tied to a hospital's reduced costs is a relatively new practice called downcoding. Downcoding itself is not the problem, unlike its opposite, upcoding, which is actually illegal under the FCA. What makes downcoding a potential violation of the FCA (as upcoding already is) is when computerized systems are preprogrammed, without physician purview on a case-by-case basis, to produce UB-04s or CMS-1500s for managed care patients that are just as fraudulent as upcoded federal claims. Thus, any downcoding through manual adjudication of a claim is not the concern of the OIG, as practitioners are legally bound to tie claims to work performed, even if doing so results in a downcode. Rather, the potential FCA violation occurs when downcoding is done automatically and without the interaction of a practitioner.

Illegal downcoding occurs in one of the following three ways:

- To automatically reassign one or more procedures actually performed to a lower diagnosis-related group (DRG), resource-based relative value scale (RBRVS), the federal health care common procedure coding system (HCPCS), *ICD-9 (International Classification of Diseases, Ninth Revision)* or 2011–2012 transitions to ICD-10, *DSM (Diagnostic and Statistical Manual of Mental Disorders)*, or *CPT (Current Procedural Terminology)* code, the effect of which misrepresents the procedure as less costly, lower charged, or not subject to utilization management or review by peer review organizations (PROs);
- To automatically change the description of the procedure actually performed so that computerized grouper or billing software would misinterpret the scope of services actually performed and automatically downcode; and
- To "hard code" into electronic physician practice management or billing software a downcoding of (or even exclusion of) diagnostic codes (e.g., evaluation and/or management (E&M or E/M coding), service codes, professional-based procedures, or products themselves, all of which are submitted as a claim or as managed care encounter data. While the purpose of such hard coding may be to reduce deductions from revenue that certain MCOs disallow, it is nevertheless still an illegal automatic downcoding.

Downcoding is also performed to intentionally and automatically cover up high-cost mistakes, such as services provided within the 72-hour window of Medicare (for which federal law does not allow a separate payment to be made and sets in motion possible fraud investigations) or automatically bundling individual lab tests into a lower-paying overall charge to comply artificially with clinical practice parameters set for providing services to managed care patients. In so doing, the provider who automatically downcodes is submitting a false claim. The applicability of CMP and intermediate sanctions is appropriate because the provider (or practitioner) of record, through no individual action on his or her part, might be found liable for malpractice by undertreating a patient's condition, as evidenced by a false claim filed.

One of the reasons that downcoding is attractive to practitioners is when their encounter data are being evaluated by an MCO for cost-effective care, low utilization of high-cost diagnostics, and integrated delivery system panel selection. Another temptation is to trick practice parameter and outcomes systems into achieving better results for lower-level work that was not actually performed, which is clearly of a fraudulent intent.

Finally, the impetus for physician gain sharing and downcoding—and one of the rationales for referring to hospitalists—is the desire to benefit in ways that hospitals want them to behave. If the remuneration is direct, it is gain sharing; if it is indirect, such as for certain referrals to hospitalists and for automatic downcoding, the benefit is to improve their attractiveness to MCOs as well as receive incentives tied to reducing overall costs.

CMP and sanctions are liable to federally certified MCOs under Final Rules 59 of Federal Regulation 36072 of July 15, 1994, per Statutory Authority 42 USC (United States Code) §1395 mm (6)(a), as amended. The specific language alluding to downcoding is under "Reverse Fraud and Abuse Law," where a provider misrepresents or falsifies information that it furnishes to CMS (or other DHHS units).

## PRACTITIONER COMPLIANCE

Practitioners within MCOs must be careful in their relationships with both payers and providers. Following are some of the most critical issues.

### Physician Marketers

The use of practitioners as MCO marketers may raise a number of conflicts. Such physicians likely have a financial incentive to enroll beneficiaries, typically through provider contracting. DHHS also recognizes that physicians, while clinically trained, typically receive little instruction in sales and marketing, especially for complex managed Medicare products.

A second concern relates to contracted physicians providing marketing services to Medicare MCOs. DHHS tries to discourage the use of physicians as marketing agents for a number of reasons, such as

- the physician may have "insider knowledge" of certain beneficiaries' health status;
- physicians can make health status judgments based on sight alone; and
- Physicians may not be the best source of membership information for their patients as they are not employed by the MCO.

The use of physician marketing agents is particularly troublesome for the beneficiary, who will likely have trouble relating to a physician as both caregiver and sales representative. Beneficiaries may also be confused into believing that subscribing with the physician-agent's managed Medicare plan may constitute a condition of being able to remain his or her patient. Some Medicare HMO enrollees might also feel that they could not disenroll because their physicians prompted them to enroll in the plan. They may believe that disenrollment would result in a gap in their medical care.

DHHS does not advise that MCOs specifically avoid physician marketers. While the employment of physician marketers is not in and of itself a prohibited activity, the use of physician marketers might lessen the ability of a beneficiary to make an informed choice about enrollment. This kind of misrepresentation could result in an illegal marketing activity.

MCOs are not allowed to require beneficiaries to undergo a health screening before enrollment. Preenrollment health screening or asking questions about the health or physical status of beneficiaries is against the law. The physician who has been treating the potential enrollee may already possess health status information that could lead the physician to either encourage or discourage enrollment. The physician likely has a financial incentive to see the HMO make money and may want to discourage, albeit subtly, sicker patients who will consume more resources from enrolling. In addition, a physician's clinical training might encourage a physician serving as a marketing agent to discriminate against those with a higher likelihood of being in poorer health than other seminar attendees. DHHS has taken the position that this discrimination does not have to be overt to be considered improper.

## Illegal Hospitalist Relationships

Another managed care compliance issue for practitioners refers to "hospitalists." A hospitalist is a specialist in inpatient medicine who spends at least 25% of his or her time serving as the principal physician for inpatients who are "handed off" by their primary care physician at hospital admission and "handed back" at discharge. The use of hospitalists is a managed care compliance issue because its use may represent an illegal inducement by capitated practitioners to utilize a provider employing hospitalists.

The use of hospitalists represents a more cost-efficient and cost-effective means of providing inpatient care. By comparison, most primary care providers (PCPs) do not have enough hospital experience to compete with hospitalists. In 1969, for example, 40–50% of a PCP's time was spent in the hospital, caring for 10–12 patients each day; by 1999, in contrast, 10% of a PCP's time was spent seeing 1–2 inpatients each day, who, compared to 1969, were much sicker when admitted and sicker when discharged to outpatient care. Moreover, 71% of PCPs had no more than two hospital cases in the entire year of 1998. In fact, since then it has become no longer practical or efficient for the office-based PCP to do hospital care. Also, it is debatable whether "hospital" skills can be maintained at an average daily census of two or less.

While fee-for-service physicians may view hospitalists as competitors for inpatient care, capitated physicians—who are legally incentivized by their MCOs to reduce provider costs of care—are tempted, via these incentives, to admit to hospitals that employ hospitalists. This temptation is that they would receive higher cost-based incentives to use a hospitalist than to self-provide inpatient care. This incremental cost savings is a form of in-kind remuneration applicable to both civil and criminal remedies under federal antikickback laws.

An additional compliance exposure exists if the capitated PCP fails to notify the patient, prior to admission, that a hospitalist will be used during the inpatient stay. Another exposure is if capitated providers do not disclose the financial incentives they have in referring to a hospital employing hospitalists. These notifications must be in writing and signed by the patient to lessen these areas of compliance exposure.

This improper "cross-referral" relationship is subject to a $100,000 fine, per occurrence, pursuant to Stark I and II. Additional penalties under Stark include refunds to patients as well as $15,000 fines per violated referral. Finally, the absence of prior signed patient authorization of the referral to a hospitalist for inpatient care risks exposure under breach of patient-physician confidentiality. In addition to this federal breach, additional violations can accrue under state medical record custody laws, with additional penalties.

The potential for kickbacks is also apparent in that capitated PCPs would receive no incentive compensation to treat inpatients. Caring for inpatients represents impractical, inefficient, and time-consuming scopes of work for these physicians were hospitalists not available. This potential is plausible because 22.8% of hospitalists are employed directly by hospitals. Hospitals also have antikickback and Stark exposure if their hospitalists receive incentives, even in part, on test utilization. Fortunately, a small number of hospitalists employed by hospitals (less than about 5%) receive incentive based on test utilization.

The following case illustrates the managed care compliance exposure of capitated PCPs:

Dr. Haas is a capitated family practitioner and sends significant referrals to Pleasant View Hospital. Mr. Smith, the president of Pleasant View Hospital, was at a cocktail party and heard that Dr. Haas is thinking about sending her patients to Orange Crest Hospital, a fierce competitor of Pleasant View, because Orange Crest employs hospitalists. The next day, Mr. Smith calls Dr. Haas and says, "I heard a rumor that you're considering moving your business to Orange Crest Hospital because they employ hospitalists. I'll provide you with your own hospitalist for all of your inpatient business; just please continue your practice as usual."

Mr. Smith would clearly be in violation of Stark II antikickback law for using a personal hospitalist as in-kind remuneration for Dr. Haas to continue to direct inpatient business to Pleasant View Hospital. If Dr. Haas thereafter uses a hospitalist employed by Pleasant View Hospital for her capitated inpatients, she is also in violation of Stark II for receiving in-kind remuneration (cost savings accrued to hospitalist use for capitated inpatients) when she refers to this hospital.

The federal government is in the process of initiating compliance investigations to determine if hospitalists are improperly assigned only to managed Medicare patients under specific HMO or MCO contracts. For example, one particular MCO recently forced Medicare risk member-patients into a mandatory hospitalist program. Under such an arrangement, the hospitalist is paged whenever a member of a specific set of capitated health plans requires admission. The hospitalist then makes on-the-spot decisions, similar to a case manager, regarding the appropriate level of care that the patient can medically sustain. The presumption is that disparate levels of care by hospitalists might exist between governmentally and privately paid inpatient stays. In comparing the Medicare risk of an MCO versus its commercial products, DHHS might assert that higher levels of care for Medicare patients of similar DRG and acuity might be a violation of the FCA, subjecting the MCO, provider, or practitioner to

- $5,000 to $10,000 *per* claim,
- treble damages to DHHS, and
- the risk of permanent exclusion from the Medicare program.

### OTHER FEDERAL ISSUES

Regulation of non-HMO MCOs is far less widespread than HMO regulation, although some states have passed laws to make all HMO laws applicable to PPOs as well. A model act for PPOs has been developed, but in general, participants in PPOs are assumed to be regulated under other laws.

PPOs are essentially not regulated, unless a specific state requires licensure, as they are merely a network offered to self-insured plans or a licensed carrier. Since they are essentially only "administering" and not assuming insurance risk, most states have no oversight of them.

Patient rights issues in the managed care arena generally center on medical management/utilization review decisions. The Model HMO Act and state regulations require HMOs to have an established medical management program, which is reviewed and examined in the same way that finances are. Some states have additional, and varying, regulations about utilization review and medical management.

## STATE ISSUES

The extent of regulations impacting an MCO depends on what type of MCO it is and what state it is in. Almost all states regulate HMOs; about half regulate PPOs and utilization management organizations, and a few regulate exclusive provider organizations (EPOs). If a specific type of MCO is not separately regulated, it is covered under state insurance provisions or the federal HMO act. As of publication, states are also gearing up for creating health exchanges when individual health insurance coverage becomes mandatory in 2014, even for "assigned risk" populations such as those requiring lifetime catastrophic care management and those with ongoing high-cost medical conditions (such as cancer patients, ventilator-dependent quadriplegics, and hemophiliacs, to name but three).

States are also involved in initiating compliance-related activities. For example the concept of automatic downcoding referenced is also being picked up by individual states. Florida's Department of Insurance issued a bulletin to Florida HMOs that automatically downcoding medical claims without investigating them is illegal.

The bulletin referenced downcoding performed by MCOs as a means to artificially reduce claim costs and predictions of IBNR (thus reducing the MLR numerator to achieve a set ratio, one way or another). The complaints are made by providers to the Florida Department of Insurance because of the adjudication software used not being in synch with downcoding algorithms. Here is how it works: The HMO automatically downcodes properly submitted claims (with documentation appropriate to the original claim) to achieve lower MLRs, in so doing creating a rejection by the adjudication software when documentation was not provided to support the fraudulently downcoded claim; the providers learn of the false claim when the enrollee is sent an automatically generated HMO letter by the adjudication system to provide documentation to support the false claim within a given timeframe (such as 14 days).

Following are other state-related legal issues.

## TYPICAL STATE REGULATORY REQUIREMENTS OF PROVIDER CONTRACTS

HMOs are generally regulated by more than one state agency, typically the departments of insurance or health. The insurance regulators focus on the financial and consumer aspects of the HMO, while health regulators are responsible for quality-of-care issues, utilization, and providers' ability to provide adequate care. The regulators govern through statutes and regulations, written policy statements, and internal office policies. Increasingly, there is direct legislative action regarding mandated benefits and patient rights at both the state and federal levels.

HMOs are licensed by the insurance department of their state through applying for a certificate of authority. The application also usually includes corporate bylaws, financial statements, financial feasibility plan, description of service area, sample provider and group contracts, evidence of coverage form, internal grievance procedures, and a proposed quality assurance program. There is also a licensing fee. Both freestanding HMO companies and HMO subsidiaries or product lines are licensed.

The licensing and recertifying of HMOs enable the state to ensure that the HMO is operating properly and in compliance with law. An HMO that refuses to cooperate with state oversight will probably be considered to be engaged in the unauthorized practice of insurance and prosecuted accordingly.

After licensing, the HMO will be required to file certain financial documents with the insurance department. A schedule of premium rates, or the methodology for determining them, was initially required under the Model HMO Act. Premiums will normally be approved by the state unless they are excessive, inadequate, or discriminatory or do not meet a state-mandated premium cap. HMOs are also required to update regulators if there are substantive changes in the initially filed documents.

## Variable State Regulatory Requirements of Provider Contracts

Many states still require a certificate of need (CON), which regulates the construction, alteration, or licensing of a medical facility and may also regulate acquisition of equipment and changes in the level of services. Regulatory permission may be needed for these activities. Certain capital expenditure thresholds exceeded may be subject to Section 1122 review for those states that have not eliminated this provision.

Regulators will periodically review sample provider contracts, including those for hospitals, primary care, specialists, and ancillary services. Provider contracts must include a list of covered services, payment terms, contract term/termination, hold-harmless clause, and utilization and quality assurance requirements. Regulators are also interested in risk-sharing arrangements, especially ones that may seem to endanger the solvency of the provider or compromise the quality of care.

## State Insolvency Protections

When a state is guided by the Model HMO Act, the following guidelines have been set, primarily to protect consumers from the bankruptcy of an HMO. These include specific capital, reserve, and deposit requirements. An initial net worth of $1.5 million is necessary before a certificate of authority will be issued. After the certificate is issued, the HMO must maintain a net worth of the greater of

- $1 million
- 2% of the first $150 million in annual premiums plus 1% of annual premiums in excess of $150 million
- Three months uncovered medical costs
- 8% of annual uncapitated medical expenses plus 4% of annual capitated hospital expenses

In addition, funds must be deposited with the state regulatory agency. The deposit is reflected as an asset on financial statements but is intended to protect the interest of enrollees or to cover administrative costs should the HMO go into receivership.

Regulators are allowed to conduct inquiries into the finances, marketing activities, and quality assurance programs of an HMO to ensure its solvency and compliance and to look for potential future problems. The examination may include an on-site visit to evaluate operations and review documents. The Model HMO Act requires that state insurance departments conduct a detailed examination of the finances of an HMO every 3 years to verify the ownership and value of assets and to ensure the adequacy of the net worth of the HMO. The National Association of Insurance Commissioners' handbook (NAIC, 2009) *HMO Examination Handbook* (sometimes referred to as the "Orange book") defines the procedures for examining assets and liabilities.

States are also moving toward requiring a risk-based capital for HMOs that provides other than the arbitrary standard set forth in the Model HMO Act. Risk-based capital requirements are in place for life as well as property and casualty (P&C) insurers and will eventually be in place for HMOs.

If the HMO is undercapitalized, regulators (not barred from doing so by state law) will normally allow time for management to correct the situation. However, the license of an HMO will be suspended or revoked if regulators believe it is necessary to protect consumers. The insurance department could also place the HMO in supervision, rather than suspend or revoke its license (domestic HMOs only).

Most states require HMOs to have contingency plans for insolvency. These plans spell out how benefits will be provided to enrollees for the period for which premiums have been paid. The HMO may also be required to purchase additional insurance, set aside additional insolvency reserves, add contract provisions for continuation of medical services, or obtain letters of credit. As mentioned, most states require provider contracts to include a hold-harmless clause to protect enrollees in case of HMO bankruptcy.

A few states have established guaranty funds that cover the health care liabilities of an insolvent HMO and require that all HMOs participate.

If the financial condition of an HMO threatens its enrollees, creditors, or the general public, regulators may order the HMO to take the actions necessary to remedy the situation, such as increasing the capital and surplus contributions of the HMO, suspending the volume of new business for a period, or reducing potential liabilities through reinsurance.

## COMPLIANCE IN ELECTRONIC TRANSMISSION OF MEMBER RECORDS AND ENCOUNTERS

Most managed care payers as of the 21st century have required contracted providers to submit claims electronically. The frequency and scope of shared information between the plan and the provider can lead to serious compliance issues. Serious compliance issues related to breaches of confidentiality are common to this practice. While breach of confidentiality can, and does, occur in non-managed care situations, the requirements of certain plan and provider contracts mandate significant patient clinical information and demographic data sharing in an electronic format. Such data often consist of pieces of a patient's medical record, such as a discharge summary, operative report, or a transcribed emergency department report.

Managed care providers and practitioners, notwithstanding their contractual relationships with managed care payers, have a duty to protect the physicianpatient privilege by asking for, and obtaining, patients' written authorizations to share all or part of their records with others. When authorized by the patient, the electronic transmission must occur in a highly confidential manner. Violation of this duty is in violation of both the HITECH Act and HIPAA. HIPAA is the federal statute that delineates the rules for electronic transfer of protected patient information (PHI) and HITECH governs HIPAA's enforecement. Such disclosure of a medical record, in breach of this confidentiality and prior patient authorization, likely violates custody laws in every state. Moreover, the HIPAA statute suggests that electronic authentication and encryption might be the best method for protecting patient-physician confidentiality.

HIPAA embodies standards on compliant electronic health information and its transmission over phone lines. Intended HIPAA standards for electronic transmission of confidential patient information by providers was published in the May 7, 1998, Federal Register. The final rules for HIPAA compliance, including provider electronic transmission standards have been in effect for more than a decade.

These electronic transmission compliance standards for managed care affected the business office, medical records, case management, and especially the information systems department, as seen in the following case. A summary of strategies to ensure HIPAA compliance is also provided as Table 8.2.

---

**TABLE 8.2**

**Seven Key Aspects of HIPAA Compliance (per American Health Insurance Management Association [AHIMA] Recommendations)**

1. Informing key internal stakeholders about HIPAA and its impact on information systems and processes

2. Up-to-date information on the industry's approach to HIPAA compliance

3. Develop resources (e.g., publications, seminars, Web sites, professional associations) to assist in developing a compliant approach to HIPAA requirements

4. Meet with key staff in information services to discuss the requirements, identify the people who need to be involved, and develop a plan of action

5. Perform a gap analysis of existing policies and procedures compared to the requirements of the compliance standards

6. Have individuals needing to be involved submit copies of their policies and procedures that address the requirements

7. Develop a checklist to help identify those policies and procedures needed for compliance

---

Dr. Robert Lewis is sitting on the sofa enjoying a rare morning off from his internal medicine practice. At 8:45 a.m., he receives an urgent phone call from the surgical scheduling department at Great West Medical Center. It seems that Ms. Glinda Gold, a Medicare risk patient of Dr. Lewis's medical group, is scheduled for a 9:00 a.m. preauthorized surgery to remove a Kaposi's sarcoma (a complication of advanced AIDS). (This procedure was needed because of a mistake the surgeon had made on a prior surgical procedure.) The immediate problem, Dr. Lewis is told, is that she is now in preoperative care, and the operative report of her first procedure, which is part of Ms. Gold's medical record, has not yet arrived. Dr. Lewis asks to speak with the anesthesiologist or surgeon, but both are involved with an ileostomy procedure and are unavailable. Dr. Lewis calls his office, speaks with Martin Lyons, his nurse, and directs that Ms. Gold's medical record be located, the operative report scanned, and the scanned report e-mailed to Great West's administration department, which will print the report and e-mail it to surgery scheduling using the local-area network of the hospital.

If Martin Lyons followed Dr. Lewis's verbal requests, the practice would compromise the confidentiality of Ms. Gold's medical records, in turn violating the patient-physician privilege that Ms. Gold placed in Dr. Lewis. Mr. Lyons and the hospital would escape liability for noncompliance with these laws if transmission software (at Dr. Lewis's office and in the administration office) met the then-current encryption standard for e-mail and access to the patient records database of DHHS.

Related compliance issues concern the use of facsimile capabilities as well as communication protocols that upload and download information to or from the Internet. It should be noted that facsimile transmissions without additional encryption are compliant, as long as reasonable steps are taken to protect confidentiality. The inherent risk of faxing confidential patient information is that the person retrieving the facsimile might not be privileged to view such data.

Some specific strategies to limit facsimile risk are

- Calling a recipient prior to sending a fax to make the recipient aware that a facsimile transmission is imminent, and that the recipient should wait by the machine to receive the fax immediately;
- Calling a recipient as soon as possible after transmission to verify that the fax, in its entirety, both was received and was received legibly; and
- Attaching a cover sheet to the transmission indicating both the number of pages being sent as well as a confidentiality disclaimer indicating that the fax includes personal and confidential information intended only for the named recipient.

For the best protection, it is recommended that highly sensitive patient information, such as for patients with HIV/AIDS, be used cautiously because unauthorized disclosure can occur. Such disclosure occurs because it is not possible to know who receives the information on the other end without practicing these rules religiously.

Internet-based transmissions, or any other modem-based transfers, require adherence to a higher security level than fax because such use does not require the intended recipient to be available at the time that confidential patient information is sent. A transmission via File Transfer Protocol (FTP), for example, is strongly discouraged by the American Health Information Management Association (AHIMA) because of the high risk of viruses, hacking, and general violation of copyright laws and because file transfers outside the organization may result in disclosing confidential patient information and HIPAA- and HITECH-protected PHI.

Providers who contract with managed care plans must provide detailed and thorough information in a timely and efficient fashion. New methods for supplying this information, including e-mail and encrypted modem transmissions, have emerged. Not only are standard compliance requirements, such as obtaining proper authorization, important, but also today the compliant provider must ensure they conform to HIPAA statutes. While this issue is not unique solely to managed care information requests, it is much more likely to occur when a patient is covered under such plans.

## CAPITATION CONTRACTUAL ISSUES

Issues that should be included in a capitation contract include

- When are capitation payments made?
- Who collects copayments, if any?
- Who is responsible for payment for unauthorized or uncovered services, and how is authorization obtained?
- Is a claim form needed? If so, in what form are claims submitted, and what information must be included with claims?
- What are the time limitations on claims submission and on adjustments to claims?
- When will "clean" claims be paid, how will contested claims be handled, and what is the definition of a *clean claim*?
- What is the responsibility of the MCO as a secondary carrier in a COB situation?
- Who is responsible for specific tasks if a third party is involved (including Medicare situations)?
- What kind of fraud prevention program is in place in each organization? Who is responsible for payment for services obtained under false pretenses?

Since volume is the reason many providers enter into managed care contracts, the effect of volume on payment should be spelled out in the contract.

Risk-sharing and risk pool arrangements must be spelled out carefully in contracts, a good reason for keeping them simple. Complicated and hard-to-understand arrangements have caused confusion and distrust among contracting organizations. Terms and conditions, administration, and the funding of risk pools should be included in all contracts. Illustrations of possible risk pool distributions under various circumstances are suggested.

## MODEL HMO ACT

Nationwide, the NAIC is a major force in HMO regulation. The Model HMO Act was adopted in 1972 and has since been updated. It is a model bill that authorizes the establishment of HMOs and provides a system for ongoing regulatory monitoring. Over half of the states in the United States have adopted the Model Act or parts of it. The NAIC and the National Association of HMO Regulators continue to develop regulatory guidelines, including the most recent updates to the former's "Orange Book."

The Model HMO Act specifies the information that enrollees must receive. This information includes

- Copies of the individual and group contracts, which must cover term of coverage, eligibility requirements, covered benefits, limitations and exclusions, out-of-pocket expenses, termination or cancellation procedures, continuation of benefits, conversion rights, claims processing, grievance procedures, subrogation rights, and grace period for nonpayment of premiums. These documents must be filed with, and approved by, the appropriate regulatory body.
- Evidence of coverage, which describes the essential features and services of the HMO.
- Information on how services are obtained and a telephone number at which questions can be answered.
- On enrollment or reenrollment, a list of providers.
- Within 30 days, notice of any material change in the plan that affects enrollees.

The Model HMO Act also requires a grievance procedure to deal with enrollee complaints, and state regulations may cover how these complaints are handled as well. Usually, HMOs are required to form a grievance committee and to inform enrollees of their right to a hearing on enrollment. The decisions of the committee may be appealed internally, and the state may also step in to review the complaint. A regular report of complaints received and processed must be submitted to state agencies.

Regulators will review the documentation and effectiveness of a quality assurance program of an HMO, including program administration, accessibility of care, preventive health care, provider credentialing, utilization review procedures, risk management, provider payment methods, medical records, claims payment procedures, and management information systems. An increasing number of states are requiring HMOs to have their quality management program reviewed by such agencies as the NCQA and URAC (formerly Utilization Review Accreditation Commission) (see Chapter 4).

## CONCLUSION

The regulatory aspects of managed care are growing considerably, primarily because MCOs have shirked their responsibility to their members to address their health status. As a result, members are especially dissatisfied with their health plans, their capitated practitioners, and the provider organizations in which they practice. Recent legislative changes in many states, with increasing pressure at the federal level, are precluding MCOs and self-funded employers from hiding behind ERISA (Employee Retirement Income Security Act of 1974) law in defending themselves against charges of malpractice or outright managed care fraud. As litigants emerge to exact some form of "punishment" against MCOs, the legal and regulatory landscape in managed care is sure to change rapidly during the first part of the 21st century. Rough waters are definitely ahead.

# 9 Innovative Managed Care Modeling for the 21st Century

## PART A: MODELING FOR ACCOUNTABLE CARE ORGANIZATIONS FOCUSING ON MEDICARE

Per the new §1115A(a)(1) of the Affordable Care Act, Congress created the Centers for Medicare and Medicaid Innovation (CMI) to test innovative payment and service delivery models *to reduce program expenditures* under the applicable titles while preserving or enhancing the quality of care furnished to individuals under such titles. In selecting such models, the secretary of the U.S. Department of Health and Human Services (DHHS) shall give preference to models that *also* improve the coordination, quality, and efficiency of health care services furnished to applicable individuals defined in paragraph (4)(A). One such modeling approach can be to improve coordination and efficiency of serving Medicare members of managed care plans, with these plans attempting to transition to accountable care organizations (ACOs) before 2012.

Per the current Request for Proposal (RFP) for CMI program administrative services, the broad outline of how §1115A is anticipated to be implemented is described as follows:

> Research and development for the Medicare and Medicaid Programs involves the detection of health care delivery problems and issues, the discovery of new program ideas and concepts to solve these problems, the development and testing of programs based on these hypothesized solutions, the evaluation of trials of these new programs, and based on the findings, the formulation of new policy proposals to successfully implement new program initiatives within Medicare and Medicaid (RFP #HHS-CMS-DRCG-SS-10-002, effective June 16, 2010).

The construct follows the FOCUS-PDCA process improvement model initially developed in the 1950s in Japan by W. Edwards Deming (also known as the "Deming Cyok"):

**Find** a health care delivery problem or issue needing to be improved;
**Organize** a team to address the problem or issue to be improved;
**Clarify** the problem or issue and rationales for improvement;
**Understand** sources of process variance and root causes of problem;
**Select** a specific new process to implement—and then

**Plan** for procedure refinement and planned rollout,
**Do** the implementation procedures planned,
**Check** that the planned improvements actually occurred,
**Act** on findings and repeat PDCA as needed.

## NEEDS IDENTIFICATION FOR PROCESS IMPROVEMENT ("FIND" PHASE)

As passed by Congress per the new §1899a on March 23, 2010, ACOs that lack a demonstrated primary care component that is patient centered and available to be deployed on a fee-for-service (FFS) basis will not be able to contract in such a capacity beginning January 1, 2012 (occurring subsequent to the date of publication). Because many of the players vetted to form ACOs lack the experience to do so or to structure other appropriate at-risk managed care modeling approaches, innovation from new sources is needed for the managed care industry in America.

While they have a proven model to assist this industry, optometrists, who are able to positively and cost-effectively improve the primary care design and implementation for ACOs, were unfortunately excluded by Congress from providing needed and enhanced primary care services at documentable high quality, with measurably improved access and patient volition, all at a fraction of the cost of comparable care performed by MDs (medical doctors) or DOs (osteopaths). In so doing, ACOs are already being set up to fail, perpetuating primary medical care provided to both the 60% of Medicare beneficiaries not enrolled in Part C or D, as well as the additional 31 million Medicaid lives, for all of whom such care is:

- Inappropriately fragmented,
- Provider focused (rather than patient centered),
- Illness based (rather than prevention or wellness based),
- Absent development of Healthcare Effectiveness Data and Information Set (HEDIS)-certifiable medical homes,
- In already short supply of eligible physicians, and therefore
- Of artificially higher cost to the Medicare program.

## ESTABLISHING A TEAM APPROACH FOR PROCESS IMPROVEMENT ("ORGANIZE" PHASE)

A relatively small complement of the some 45,000 American optometrists even recognizes what an ACO is, let alone truly understand what the Affordable Care Act provides to Americans. In my private consulting, I have had the pleasure of helping the field of optometry to address innovative models to improve access of optometrists within the governmental and private sectors and appropriate to a CMI-approved model to implement a workable solution to the specific problem.

## ESTABLISHING RATIONALES FOR PROCESS IMPROVEMENT ("CLARIFY" PHASE)

When Congress enacted ACOs under the new §1899(b)(1) of Title 18, it limited ACO formations to medical group practice networks (subpart A, most of which are currently capitated for primary care risk); independent practice associations (IPAs; per subpart B, nearly all of which capitate their primary care risk to some extent); hospitals (all of which already employ clinical nurse specialists, if not hospitalists, physician assistants, or nurse practitioners); and to the joint ventures and collaborations among them, per subpart C. *The basic problem* in enacting §1899(b)(1)(A)–(D) is that few, if any, approved entities within emerging ACO formations have any experience *actually providing*

- High-acuity primary medical care services [§1899(d)(3)],
- Of sufficient service coverage by physicians [§1899(b)(2)(D)],
- On a Part B FFS consumption basis [§1899(h)(3)], and
- In a manner demonstrating patient centeredness [(§1899(b)(2)(H)].

By contrast, optometric physicians have practiced for years providing patient-centered care, on a FFS basis, and to high-acuity patients with diabetes and glaucoma, many of whom in such poor health status to have developed vision-threatening co-morbidities. However, Congress has excluded non-MDs and non-DOs, such as optometric physicians, from being "ACO Professionals" [per §1899(h)(1)(A)].

### Primary Care Access of All Medicare-Certified Physicians

Despite the well-documented shortages of primary care practitioners (MDs, DOs, physician assistants [PAs], nurse practitioners [NPs], and clinical nurse specialists [CNSs]) vetted by the American Medical Association (AMA), Congress inappropriately excluded the full range of physicians already legislated per Title 18 §1861(r)(1–5), per Title 42 regulations in §410.20(b)(1–5), and subject to regulatory limitations per §§410.21–410.25. Since the work of CNSs is limited to that where they receive medical direction [per §410.76(c)(3)(i)], they are legally unable to extend services when the MD or DO to provide direction is unavailable to extend care; because they require master's level preparation, CNSs are almost always employed in hospital settings. As PAs and NPs are primarily employed by existing MDs/DOs and clinic providers, few are truly able to address the current primary care shortage because the MDs/DOs who employ them are already in short supply and cannot appropriately extend their care to accommodate the 31 million Americans to be covered under ACOs on January 1, 2012. Without elasticity of MD/DO supply to meet incremental demands of well over 100 million Americans, Congress is further exacerbating the current shortfall of approved ACO professionals by excluding four other types of physicians already overseen and certified by DHHS.

What are these four physician types? What primary care services can they legally provide now per the resource-based relative value scale of Part B for ambulatory supplemental care services?

- First are doctors of dental medicine [defined in §1867(r)(2) and §410.20(b)(2) with licensure limitations per §410.24], who can perform some aspects of primary care, but are limited mostly to the teeth and surrounding nerves and tissues.
- The second are podiatrists [defined in §1867(r)(3) and §410.20(b)(3) with licensure limitations per §410.25], who are able to perform aspects of primary care, but only those that MDs/DOs would do and primarily limited to the feet and ankles.
- Chiropractors [defined in §1867(r)(5) and §410.20(b)(5) with additional limitations per §410.21] are the third type but are able to perform neither diagnostic primary care services nor order any ancillary tests, and approved treatment under Part B is limited to manual manipulation only to correct spinal subluxations.
- The fourth type of primary care practitioner excluded is the optometric physician [defined in both §1867(r)(4) and §410.20(b)(4) with limitations per §410.22 only to licensure of their respective state]. Like all of the aforementioned physician types, optometric physicians have been included within the Physician Quality Reporting Initiative (PQRI) of DHHS since it began.

## INAPPROPRIATE PRIMARY CARE EXCLUSION OF OPTOMETRIC PHYSICIANS

The difference between the field of optometry and the aforementioned other excluded physician types is that optometric physicians' licensed scopes of practice *include* primary care diagnostic and therapeutic services to the eye, but *not exclusively so*. For example, nothing in California's Business and Professions Code statutes or Board of Optometry regulations specifically prevents any optometrist from following standard primary care practices performed by MDs and DOs (at more than twice the cost):

1) Taking detailed patient and family histories, particularly of diabetes, hypertension, and glaucoma;
2) Surveying patients' health risk as well as other risk statuses;
3) Performing measurement of vital signs, including assessing anatomical structures and neurological aspects of the eye (which Congressionally vetted primary care providers (PCPs) are not properly trained to perform);
4) Ordering a variety of laboratory tests (even to include venipuncture to collect blood samples) consistent with medical necessity requirements of §1862(a)(1)(A) of the Social Security Act;
5) Performing comprehensive eye examinations, consistent with HEDIS and *Current Procedural Terminology* (*CPT*) II criteria, and only as

medically necessary and compliant with Centers for Medicare and Medicaid Services (CMS) regulations (such as §410.23 of the *Code of Federal Regulations* for glaucoma screening);

6) Performing advanced diagnostics and therapeutics, either in office or referred to other physicians for follow-up (according to the California Optometric Association, optometrists already refer 9.5% of their patients to appropriate MDs/DOs for such follow-up care); and

7) Providing personalized patient care plans, with specific strategies to enhance health status, prevent chronic disease comorbidities, and prevent injuries.

To the contrary, schools of optometry in America train optometrists to be diagnosticians and to perform treatment at a primary, rather than specialty, level of care. Yet, current medical insurance underwriting could be halved, including for Medicare and Medicaid, if optometric physicians were not relegated to specialty care status and allowed to perform the full scopes of their primary care training and certification (in full compliance of §410.22) as both FFS primary care physicians as well as bearing risk for primary medical eye health status within Medicare Advantage and its Special Needs Plans, managed Medicaid plans, federally qualified health clinics (FQHCs), and especially for disease management aspects of ACOs.

Also within the intent of clarifying understanding of the problem is the nature of optometrists being classified by underwriters as providing specialty care. Even from the standpoint of what constitutes specialty care, such an assertion is indefensible. In most states, for example, optometrists are not allowed to puncture the skin, with the sole exception being venipuncture or capillary blood draws to order medically necessary diagnostic tests (I reiterate: diagnostic tests). Other than psychiatry, one is hard-pressed to name a single specialty that cannot perform surgery, repair a laceration, or order advanced therapeutics. And, from the standpoint of the optometrist, nothing they do constitutes specialty-level care (other than prescribing corrective lenses),

Consider a parallel in the managed care industry. Before the enactment of Medicare in 1965, there was no formal profession of family practice; all medical care for nonpediatric patients was performed by internists. With the evolution of health plans, and the move to the types of health maintenance organizations (HMOs) that continue today (or at least as of publication), medical underwriters came to a similar conclusion that we see unfulfilled today with optometrists: By bifurcating the risk then given solely to internists—relegating internists and pediatricians more specialty underwriting and creating family practitioners to capture the primary care risk—the health plan could save tremendously on underwriting, thereby improving plan profitability with little actual change to its scopes of practice. With more of an internist's payment dollar given over to family practitioners at a fraction of the servicing costs, health plans improve their profitability.

This same change in underwriting can again create a profitability bump for health plans if eye care risk is bifurcated for the ophthalmologists (who are surgeons and true specialists). Let us do the math: In a typical Medicare Advantage network, the health plans carve out eye care risk at approximately $6–$10 per member, per month (PMPM) and subcontract directly with ophthalmology-directed eye care networks at 80% of the underwritten risk (essentially taking their allowable 20% administrative component off the top), which now brings the amount subcapitated to the ophthalmologists at $4.80 to $8 PMPM, even though this amount fully indemnifies the health plan from paying for eye care costs, whether optometric, retinological, surgical, or simply corrective lens prescribing (and an allowance for frames, which are carved in or out depending on plan benefit design). Since Medicare patients are much more likely to require surgery (such as cataract repair and laser therapy), ophthalmologists keep that risk and subcapitate to optometrists only for vision care of commercial risk (which is typically less than 20% of Medicare PMPM). At this level of care, most optometrists battle their fellow providers to capture subcapitation risk contracts with ophthalmologists at 6–10¢ PMPM, or roughly 1% of the original underwriting for eye care risk under Medicare Advantage.

Without arguing the inequality of ophthalmologists competing with optometrists for primary medical eye care services or optometrists forced into money-losing subcapitation agreements with their medical counterparts, it is obvious that "where there's smoke, there's fire." Let us say that a 6¢–10¢ PMPM for routine optometric care is commensurate with the level of risk and cost structure relative to the $6–$10 originally carved out for medical eye care (both primary and surgical in scope). This relationship would suggest that bifurcating eye care risk, and assigning optometrists to provide nonsurgical medical eye care, could be as low as 1% of the underwriting costs carved out for undifferentiated medical eye care.

Put another way, it means that health plans are *overpaying* medical eye care risk performed by ophthalmologists at roughly 1,000% compared to providing comparable care by optometrists. Yes, it is not a simple syllogism because routine vision care provided by optometrists to commercial risk populations is substantively different from performing wellness-oriented primary medical eye care to Medicare Advantage members that they do not yet get to treat. Maybe the relationship is not 1% but 20%—either way, though, the health plan stands to dramatically improve its profitability and reduce its need for specialty care underwriting, and again with no direct impact to the scope of operations or clinical decision making of the health plan.

This inappropriate exclusion of optometric physicians from performing similar services as AMA-vetted physicians—absent much of the service fragmentation as currently exists in primary medical care and at less than half the costs experienced by insurance carriers, including Medicare and Medicaid—is hardly a new phenomenon. There is also a misperception that optometric practice is limited to refractive studies and fitting lenses, almost entirely on a referral basis, and within a specialty scope of practice, as perpetuated under Medicare Advantage, the FQHC Act, and in many private health plans.

# ROOT CAUSE ANALYSES OF RATIONALES FOR PROCESS IMPROVEMENT ("UNDERSTAND" PHASE)

## Biases Against Optometry

There is a long-standing bias among AMA-affiliated physicians in limiting or excluding specific scopes of medical eye care practice that optometric physicians are licensed to perform and can do so in the appropriate primary care settings. California ophthalmologists, first with the California Medical Association and then with the AMA itself, represented a party to litigation to stall the enactment of a new law approved by the California legislature. This law, implemented in Summer, 2011, allows optometric physicians to become certified to diagnose primary wide-angle glaucoma and manage aspects of it without ophthalmologists' oversight. The arguments for and against this statute had been made repeatedly in the legislature, over many years, and the law was enacted via the democratic process, yet this ridiculous and inequitable bias persisted in California for a number of years, and similar biases exist in many other states in America.

But, this unwarranted bias against optometrists is a long-standing feud with the AMA, and persists at the federal level, even within DHHS itself. Despite the reporting by the American Optometric Association that two-thirds (67%) of all annual eye exams in the United States are performed by optometrists, the abstracted estimates by the Centers for Disease Control and Prevention (CDC) of annual ambulatory care utilization in the United States (per National Health Statistics Reports [NHSRs]) continue to be based on combining data from the National Ambulatory Medical Care Survey (NAMCS) and National Hospital Ambulatory Medical Care Survey (NHAMCS). The obvious bias is that both the NAMCS and NHAMCS continue to exclude optometrists from physician inventories and the optometric care they provide from all tabulations simply because their field is *not "recognized" by the AMA*.

As has now become evident with the current critical shortage of ACO professionals for emerging ACOs, both Congress and the American people have been provided misinformation for years, particularly in assuming that optometric care has been included in eye care visits and optometrists within the supply of primary care practitioners in the United States.

So, in the most recent NHSR, reported on August 6, 2008, that there were some 46,292 nonhospital eye care visits provided in 2006, the CDC likely underestimated true demands by an additional 53,116, of a total 99,408,000 eye care exams, 67% of which were provided by optometrists.

This bias also extends to the interrelationship between primary-level eye care exams and MD-provided general medical exams, the latter reported by NHSR at 27,506 such preventive health visits. Of the 46,292 eye care exams that NHSR reported, there was no disclosure that they were performed only by ophthalmologists or subspecialists, and that these visits comingled primary medical and specialty surgical eye care, even if all such eye care was underwritten or compensated at specialty surgical rates. The data inappropriately portrayed that 31.6%

more eye care services than preventive health services were performed, when the real relationship is that 3.6 times as many eye care visits as general medical visits actually occur each year. This misrepresentation, born purely of bias, ignores the obvious role that optometrists have been performing for years in America: Americans are 260% more willing to have their eyes examined each year, two-thirds of which on a primary medical eye care basis, than to be evaluated by an MD for a general medical examination.

## IGNORING THE WELLNESS MODEL PARADIGM

This same bias in continuing to malign optometrists ignores the fact that Americans' pattern of usage is to treat with an optometrist on a fixed, annual or biennial cycle, *while asymptomatic,* or to seek care with an optometrist or ophthalmologist at the very first signs of eye problems. What this pattern describes is the wellness model, which is the entire presumption of a shared savings program for Medicare and the basis of insisting on a patient-centered primary care core for ACOs. The wellness model not only is one that few other physicians practice, even in capitated managed care plans, but also is the entire business model of optometric physicians. In fact, optometry is one of the only forms of medical care in America that does not perpetuate the opposite "illness model" of care (by which is delayed until it is bad enough to miss work, with the underlying problem becoming so severe that more expensive, high-acuity intervention is necessary at infinitely greater provider, payer, and societal costs with increased chances for suboptimal outcomes). Moreover, few, if any, managed care professionals are currently aware that any physicians are currently treating patients via the wellness model, let alone that Americans are more than three times as likely to entrust their primary eye care needs to optometrists than most all of their other primary care needs to MD- or DO-licensed primary care physicians.

## UNDERUTILIZATION OF EYE EXAMINATIONS FOR SYSTEMIC DIAGNOSES

One consequence of perpetuating biases against optometric physicians and corresponding misperceptions that the field of optometry is limited to vision testing and lens fitting is the corresponding underutilization of eye exams specific to specialty care settings. The value of eye examinations to diagnose a variety of systemic diseases has largely been wasted when performed by ophthalmologists, who mainly use the findings to support or refute the need for specialty care services, such as surgery or the need for subspecialty referrals. This is because ophthalmologists mainly treat the specialty eye care needs of their patients, while largely ignoring all of the other types of systemic diagnoses that optometrists would address if organized biases against their profession were not allowed to persist. In fact, most ophthalmologists simply follow their capitation agreements, presuming that noneye systemic diseases have already been diagnosed by the patients' PCPs or that their contracts prevent them from treating eye care patients that way.

The specific utility of eye examinations by optometrists, for systemic primary *medical* care purposes, includes the following conditions:

1. **Diabetes Mellitus**, with 17% of cases diagnosed via eye exam.
2. **Death**, at an excess risk ranging from 34% to 89% in patients with proliferative or nonproliferative diabetic retinopathy, after 16 years of follow-up, but only for type 2 diabetes.
3. Presence of early-onset **diabetic retinopathy**, present in 6.1% of adults 65 and older and in 29.5% of those 65 and older with diabetes. Eye examinations of those with retinopathy can also diagnose the following systemic conditions:
   a. *Coronary heart disease* (CHD) and predictors for CHD mortality.
   b. *Cerebrovascular accidents* (stroke), both clinical and subclinical (independent of cerebrovascular risk factors), particularly for 33% of symptomatic strokes attributable to disease of small arteries/arterioles of the cerebral circulation, for which little is otherwise known about these smaller-vessel pathologies, especially for those with diabetes.
   c. *Microalbuminuria and clinical nephropathy*, independent of hypertension and other shared risk factors.
   d. *Gross proteinuria* and *progression of renal impairment*, associated with retinopathy independently.
   e. *Silent myocardial ischemia* is clinically indicated by diabetic retinopathy.
      - Retinopathy is a valuable prognostic predictor for diabetic patients undergoing *cardiac revascularization procedures.*
      - Retinopathy is a more predictive indicator of *adverse cardiac events or complications* (e.g., death, myocardial infarction (MI), congestive heart failure, in-stent restenosis) of percutaneous coronary intervention or CABG (coronary artery bypass graft) surgery.
   f. More severe forms of *diabetic polyneuropathy* are associated with retinopathy and other microvascular diseases.
   g. *Lower-extremity amputation* risk is associated with severe proliferative or nonproliferative diabetic retinopathy.
   h. *Cognitive decline* is associated with retinopathy lesions.
   i. *Cerebral atrophy* associated with retinopathy detected by magnetic resonance imaging.
   j. *Cognitive dysfunction* and *dementia*, modestly associated with retinopathy.
   k. *Myocardial infarction*, at a twofold higher risk when associated with retinopathy.
   l. *Coronary arterial disease*, at a twofold higher incident risk and threefold higher risk of fatality, when associated with retinopathy and Type 2 diabetes, but not Type 1.

    m.  *Congestive heart failure*, at a fourfold higher risk when associated with retinopathy, but independent of diabetes duration, glycemic control, smoking, lipid profile, and other risk factors.
- Population-attributable risk of CHF to retinopathy is 30.5% among diabetics with no previous history of MI and hypertension.

    n.  *Systemic vascular complications* secondary to early signs of retinopathy, including
- Impaired vascular tone autoregulation,
- Vascular inflammation, and
- Endothelial dysfunction.

    o.  *Atherosclerosis* secondary to inflammation common to diabetic retinopathy.

    p.  *Diabetic cardiomyopathy*, which is causally linked to diabetic retinopathy but is a complex and unique disease that is independent of atherosclerosis disease and hypertension.
- Diabetic retinopathy is associated with *left ventricular concentric remodeling*, a known precursor for heart failure development.
- Diabetic retinopathy is strongly associated with *clinical CHF* among diabetics.
- These factors are believed to link diabetic retinopathy to widespread systemic microcirculatory (resistant-vessel) disease, creating excessive loads that compromise cardiac performance (such as ventricular emptying and cardiac contractility) and lead to diabetic cardiomyopathy.

4. **Cardiovascular risk assessment** incorporating retinal assessment improves precision of risk prediction for cardiovascular disease among patients both with and without diabetes.
5. **Nondiabetic retinopathy**, diagnosed via direct ophthalmoscopy, is of high incidence (6–10%) and prevalence (up to 14%) and is associated with the following systemic disease processes:
   a. *Stroke,*
   b. *Ischemic heart disease,*
   c. *Congestive heart failure,*
   d. *Renal dysfunction,* and
   e. *Diabetes risk* consistent with significant family history of diabetes.
6. Currently available risk prediction tools for **systemic vascular diseases**, which lack precision for diabetics, are optimized and microvascular health *personalized* by incorporating screening for retinopathic lesions on *digital fundus photographs.*
   a. These *personalized* findings (presence or absence of retinopathy) lend to even closer correlations with systemic vascular diseases.
   b. Eye care professionals relying on direct ophthalmoscopy miss up to 50% of retinopathic lesions when digital fundus photographs are not taken and graded.

7. Causal link between *anisocoria* (unequal pupil size) and one or more systemic diseases, such as
   a. Brain membrane infection due to *meningitis* or *encephalitis,*
   b. *Subdural hematoma,*
   c. *Brain tumor or abscess,*
   d. *Brain aneurysm,*
   e. Excess pressure in one eye secondary to *glaucoma,*
   f. *Migraine headache,* or
   g. *Upper chest or lymph node tumor or mass* causing pressure on a nerve (such as with *Horner syndrome*).
8. **Leukemia**, evidenced by *Roth's spots* (small hemorrhages with small yellow dots in their centers) detectable during eye exam.
9. **Acquired immunodeficiency syndrome (AIDS)**, which is associated with eye infections, retinal detachment, eyelid tumors, and neuro-ophthalmic disorders. AIDS-related infections can lead to blindness, and abnormal retinal circulation is one comorbidity of AIDS.
10. **Sarcoidosis** has a 15–50% prevalence of ocular involvement, typically in the form of anterior granulomatous uveitis, an eye inflammation diagnosed during an eye exam.
11. *Proptosis* (protruding eyeballs), secondary to **Graves disease**, also involving limitations of eye movement, diplopia, corneal disease, and optic nerve damage in severe cases.
12. **Cancer**, while rare for tumors to start in the eye, is indicative during an eye exam of metastases that start elsewhere and spread to the eyes.

## ABILITY OF EYE EXAMINATIONS TO REDUCE PRIMARY CARE FRAGMENTATION

In current primary care medicine practiced by most MDs and DOs, a single episode of care rarely results in the appropriate diagnosis and treatment of any condition, especially for a general medical examination. One exam is often accompanied by a variety of laboratory and radiographic testing. The same is true while continuing to ignore the value of the primary medical eye examination to diagnose noneye systemic conditions. Such ignorance poses an additional risk for the future of diagnostic medicine in less-fragmented, lower-cost care settings.

Moreover, little is medically known—other than via eye examinations—of the 33% of strokes caused by small-vessel arterial involvement, given that medical research has focused primarily on large-vessel arteries (like the carotid and aorta) and hypertension as proximal causes. Unlike the expensive testing needed to diagnose such large-vessel causes, the 33% small-vessel causes can be diagnosed simply via eye examinations, *which ophthalmologists do not routinely perform* (except if the results lead to the need for eye surgeries or subspecialized therapeutics, which is not the case).

There are at least two noneye diagnoses that are problematic for MDs/DOs today, and hold future promise for detection via eye exams:

1. **Multiple sclerosis (MS)**, which is expected to be quickly and reliably diagnosed by measuring retinal thinning via optical coherence tomography (OCT), despite sample size being small and not of sufficient study length to be considered statistically valid (UT Southwestern Medical Center, 2010, June 8. *Simple Eye Test Measures Damage from Multiple Sclerosis, Researchers Find.*). MS is currently assessed during eye examinations in terms of changes in eye movement, vision, and optic nerve function (*Eye Facts* of University of Illinois at Chicago School of Medicine, 2006).

2. **Alzheimer's disease**, which is reliably diagnosed only via autopsy—and recently 90% associated with specific protein signatures in cerebrospinal fluid obtained via spinal tap (CNN, August 11, 2010)—shows promise for simple early-stage diagnoses via eye examinations involving a specialized ophthalmoscope that detects fluorescent markers of early neurological disease, in effect using the retina as a real-time barometer of brain cell death (*Cell Death and Disease*, 2010, 1, e3, doi:10.1038).

The potential for both of these conditions so problematic to MDs/DOs in America today to be diagnosed via a simple eye examination during a single primary medical care visit to an optometrist would be surely wasted if eye examinations continue to be performed simply to validate or refute the need for eye surgeries and specialty eye procedures by ophthalmologists and their subspecialists.

## SELECTION OF IMPLEMENTATION APPROACH TO IMPROVE CARE DEFICITS AND COST SAVINGS ("SELECT" PHASE)

The purpose of the CMI and other approaches to improve service delivery and other core economics is to test innovative payment and service delivery models to reduce program expenditures while preserving or enhancing the quality of care furnished to individuals under such approaches. In selecting CMI models, for example, DHHS gives preference to models that also improve the coordination, quality, and efficiency of health care services furnished to applicable individuals.

Primary care populations of capitated managed care plans looking to become ACO patient-centered medical homes (PCMHs) and/or to compete more effectively is one such defined population facing care deficits. Their care needs are currently indemnified via risk contracting, rather than actually provided. Moreover, capitation involves delaying or withholding all care that would otherwise be demanded on a FFS basis. To implement FFS from a capitated model, substantial innovation is required to attract members to be seen for care, as is possible with optometry-, rather than MD-based, primary care physicians.

## Care Deficits Leading to Potentially Avoidable Expenditures

Optometrists have a completely different perspective on eye care and primary care than comparable care performed by MDs or DOs. Current MD-based care is highly fragmented, duplicative in scope, and highly uncoordinated among providers, who do not tend to convert their practices to EHR (which ACOs require in conjunction with PQRI participation for accountability of care and performance benchmarking). In fact, little nonpharmaceutical treatment actually occurs in primary care settings, instead requiring their patients to be referred for follow-up testing or therapeutics among more specialized caregivers.

All of these practices result in excess expenditures to payers, often for duplicative, non-value-added services. In fact, excess copayments and travel-related costs are also borne by patients and their families, as well as by informal caregivers invested in their clients' actual care and support needs, not to mention time off from work or avocation, both for the member/patient and his or her support network. This system is frankly broken, and optometrists should be given the opportunity to find appropriate fixes, if they can.

Much of the perpetuation of the current lack of coordinated, cost-effective care could also be eliminated by implementing chronic disease-stratified patient-centered medical homes (PCMHs; see Chapter 5), which emerging ACOs lack the vision or capability to implement, let alone attract their current members to be initially evaluated and appropriately assigned to one.

A specific aspect of care that this selected innovation addresses is early assessment, intervention, and management of type 2 diabetes mellitus and of glaucoma, both diseases for which poor coordination and care deficits are well documented in the literature as leading to excess expenditures by the Medicare program.

## Promoting Greater Outpatient Service Efficiencies and Timely Access

Improving the capabilities of emerging ACOs to establish compliant primary medical care on a FFS basis, per §1899(a) standards or utilizing optometrist-designed PCMHs (with pathway to NCQA or URAC accreditation) serve to improve service efficiencies. In addition, availability of optometrists to supplement key aspects of a nationally-depleted primary medical care delivery system also improves service access, and at substantially less costs.

## Selected Process Improvement To Implement

The selected process improvement to implement involves a new primary care model of primary medical eye care examinations and limited primary medical diagnostics, all performed by medically-certified optometrists. The process improvement also involves optometrist-assignment of a significant segment of Medicare beneficiaries to select PCMHs.

## PLAN AND PROGRAM DEVELOPMENT TO IMPLEMENT SELECTED PROCESS IMPROVEMENT ("PLAN" PHASE)

The end result of the FOCUS process, and the starting point for the PDCA cycle (Deming Cycle) is to fully describe a plan to implement the selected process improvement. This plan is more fully fleshed out in Table 9.1.

### PROGRAM DEVELOPMENT TO IMPLEMENT SELECTED PROCESS IMPROVEMENT

### Medically-Necessary Eye Examinations

Appropriate eye exams (if any) are performed only after optometric physicians establish medical necessity to do so per CMS guidelines, to eliminate the need for service referrals at triple the expense and delay. Note the mention of "if any": where medical necessity for eye exams is not demonstrated, an optometrist can't perform it at public expense.

### Optometrist Conformance to State Licensure Restrictions

Eye exams are performed by only state-certified optometric physicians to ensure such services are furnished by health professionals authorized to do so under existing state laws.

### Establishment of Wellness Components to Individualized Care Plans

In order to establish a regular process to monitor and update individualized patient care plans, all initial primary care and primary medical eye care evaluations include wellness plans that:

- Schedule future eye care visits per appropriate guidelines,
- Create initial individualized patient care and wellness plan,
- Establish and monitor progress toward 5-year wellness/treatment goals,
- Establish interim performance objectives to meet goals,
- Assess objectives attainment at each subsequent visit,
- Develop appropriate incentives for objectives attainment.

### Integrating Optometric Diagnostics with Respective PCMHs

Integrating Optometric PCPs with optometrist-designed PCMHs, particularly for chronic conditions that affect the eye, promotes patient centeredness (plus family and caregivers) of the care team.

### Importance of Integrating Optometrists with PCMH Team Conferences

Semiannual PCMH team conferences with patient and caregivers establish in-person contacts with patient, family, and caregivers.

**TABLE 9.1**

**Proposed Primary Care Exam Framework and Rationale**

| What Is Done | Why It Is Done | Differential Diagnosis (Dx) |
|---|---|---|
| *Detailed intake*, including initial preventive physical exam components (such as personal and family history, functional health status, depression screen), materials on eye health and injury prevention, current Rx (prescriptions), PCP contacts, and legal disclosures | Detailed data are input at point of care into ACO EHR; family Hx (history) crucial to establish medical necessity; personal health symptoms, medical, and Rx Hxs assist in differential diagnoses; legal disclosures (such as HIPAA [Health Insurance Portability and Accountability Act]) protect rights | Personal symptoms or direct family Hx are key criteria to diagnose diabetes, hypertension, or glaucoma. Other treating physicians using same EHR improve care coordination and reduce potential for medical errors. |
| Bilateral, two-image *digital fundus photos* (centering on macula and optic nerve), using evidence-based lesion grading, with both local and EHR-linked image archival. On patient's return to eye clinic, future DFPs trended to previous and baseline images | Bilateral, two-image digital fundus photos (and using grading criteria such as Airlie House or modifications of it) establish baseline and periodic indicators of retinopathy, its more severe forms, and its progression. Retinopathy is a significant factor among older adults (causal link) | Eye care professionals relying on direct ophthalmoscopy miss up to 50% of retinopathic lesions when digital fundus photographs are not taken and graded, thus potentially underestimating the true disease progression and missing indicators of more severe acuity. |
| Measurement and grading of *body mass index* (BMI), via conversion grid, per measurements of weight (via scale) and height (standometer), and EHR input using standard clinical grading: BMI < 25; BMI ≥ 25 ≤ 29; BMI ≥ 30 ≤ 34; BMI ≥ 35 ≤ 39; BMI ≥ 40 | Older women are 68.6% likely (78.4% for men) to be measured as clinically overweight (BMI ≥ 25), equating to 34% prevalence rate of hypertension (a causal risk factor for diabetes) at this BMI. Prevalence of diabetes, all adults at BMI ≥ 25, = 23.7% and = 5.7% at BMI ≥ 30 (grade I obesity). At BMI ≥ 35 (grade II obesity), a diabetes diagnosis is an 83% certainty. | BMI determinations (overweight [**25–29**] and obesity [**≥30**]) associated with Excessive death, Excessive disability, Hypertension, Type 2 diabetes, Diabetic retinopathy, Coronary arterial disease, Stroke, Cancer (breast, prostate, colon, endometrial, rectal, gallbladder, cervical, ovarian), Gallbladder and liver diseases, Osteoarthritis, Congestive heart failure, Sleep apnea, Binge eating disorders, |

(continued)

## TABLE 9.1 (Continued)
## Proposed Primary Care Exam Framework and Rationale

| What Is Done | Why It Is Done | Differential Diagnosis (Dx) |
|---|---|---|
| | | Polycystic ovary syndrome (PCOS), Dyslipidemias, Depression, and Serotonin syndrome |
| Measurement of *blood pressure* (automated, 3–4 readings ≥ 5 minutes apart, varied positions) | Hypertension (BP ≥ 140/≥90 for nondiabetics; for diabetics ≥ 130/≥ 80) has 70.8% prevalence (ages 65+) | Prevalence of untreated hypertension among adults 65+ is 40% and causally linked to both diabetes and glaucoma |
| Measurement of *hemoglobin A1c* (via glucometer-type device using capillary blood, 5-minute results, 99% lab accurate; CLIA-waived, CMS Part B-approved) **(Note: HbA1c will be done instead of glucometer.)** | Per 2010 revised standards of the American Diabetes Association, diabetes is now defined as either self-report of prior diabetes (excluding gestational) or HbA1c result ≥ 6.5%. | Type 2 diabetes. Comorbid retinopathy prevalence for diabetics age 65+ is 29.5% and 5.1% for severe forms that threaten vision; comorbid glaucoma prevalence is 11%. Comorbid diabetes with Dx'd 18+ hypertension prevalence is 18.4%. |
| Bilateral *tonometry* (serial tonometry with initial glaucoma Dx) | Elevated IOP can cause irreparable damage to optic nerve. | Rule out (R/O) glaucoma; R/O macular edema and other retinopathy forms |
| *Refractive evaluation* (maximum FFS cost in 2011 was $22), *excluding* **both** *DME* (durable medical equipment; such as spectacles, lenses, and lens fitting/handling) and *presbyopia evaluation* (given that ~100% of adults 65+ have this refractive condition) | *While not a covered benefit under Title 18*, tested refractive errors are associated with falls, depression, and social isolation; decreased functional health status and quality of life; and excessive morbidities. | R/O fall risk secondary to refractive error; R/O depression (per intake screening) R/O restrictions in functional health/activities of daily living (ADL; per intake screening) Assess improvements to quality of life (per social intake screening) |

(continued)

## TABLE 9.1 (Continued)
## Proposed Primary Care Exam Framework and Rationale

| What Is Done | Why It Is Done | Differential Diagnosis (Dx) |
|---|---|---|
| Diagnostic laser tomographic evaluation (e.g., GDX®, HRT®) | GDX/HRT detects early-onset glaucoma for at-risk diabetics or hypertensives, while asymptomatic, and can allow earlier interventions to preserve vision and slow disease progression. OCT measures effects and severity of retinopathy; OCT has been shown in small studies to measure the corneal thinning effects of MS & Dx MS. | GDX/HRT is the "gold standard" to diagnose primary wide-angle glaucoma while still asymptomatic. OCT is the gold standard to diagnose macular edema and other severe forms of diabetic retinopathy and monitor disease progression and structural changes of internal eye structures. OptiMap, while costly, creates real-time three-dimensional (3D) eye images without dilation. |
| Complete dilated eye examination (diabetic retinal or glaucoma with intraocular pressure (IOP) testing and slit lamp), if medically necessary | Detection of diabetes, retinopathic comorbidities, and glaucoma statuses | Diabetes<br>Diabetic retinopathy<br>Glaucoma |
| Visual fields testing, if medically necessary | Detection of loss of fields secondary to glaucoma or retinopathy | Blindness secondary to glaucoma, diabetes, or acute forms of retinopathy |
| Personalized wellness planning, including 5-year goals and interim objectives setting, as well as eye health prevention strategies and schedule for future wellness visits | Patient-centered approach to health maintenance, disease management, injury and comorbidity prevention, protecting vision and eye health + MD/DO follow-up | Wellness and disease management<br>Preventive health |
| Assignment and referral to an appropriate PCMH | PCMHs improve personal primary care access via a multidisciplinary team with shared EHR | Multidisciplinary team approach to primary care, disease management, care accountability, and wellness education/adaptation |

## Integrating Optometric Diagnostics with Traditional EHR Archival Data

Use of electronic health records (EHR) and remote patient monitoring, over time and care settings, incorporate all of the following program elements:

- All digital fundus photographs, locally archived and EHR accessible
- All 5-year and updated annual wellness plans being EHR accessible.
- All intake, exam findings, and diagnostic data updated to EHR of the ACO
- All PCMH originating intake, exam, education, diagnoses, prognoses, satisfaction and evaluation, and outcomes data uploaded and updated to EHR of the ACO.

### IMPLEMENTATION PLAN OF SELECTED PROCESS IMPROVEMENT

The following elements constitute the appropriate performance of primary medical eye examinations by medically-certified (or other comparable state licensure classification) of optometrist involved in implementing this plan.

1. The use of topical pharmaceutical agents for the purpose of the examination of the human eye or eyes for any disease or pathological condition
2. Through medical treatment, infections of the anterior segment and adnexa, excluding the lacrimal gland, the lacrimal drainage system, and the sclera in patients under 12 years of age
3. Ocular allergies of the anterior segment and adnexa
4. Nonsurgical ocular inflammation, limited to inflammation resulting from traumatic iritis, peripheral corneal inflammatory keratitis, episcleritis, and unilateral nonrecurrent nongranulomatous idiopathic iritis in patients over 18 years of age
5. Traumatic or recurrent conjunctival or corneal abrasions and erosions
6. Corneal surface disease and dry eyes
7. Removal of foreign bodies from the cornea, eyelid, and conjunctiva with any appropriate instrument other than a scalpel or needle
8. Lacrimal irrigation and dilation, excluding nasal lacrimal tract probing, only for patients over 12 years of age
9. Ocular pain, nonsurgical in cause
10. Therapeutic pharmaceutical agents during examination, including:
    a. Topical miotics
    b. Topical lubricants
    c. Antiallergy agents (excluding topical steroids)
    d. Topical and oral anti-inflammatories
    e. Topical antibiotic agents

    f.  Topical hyperosmotics

    g.  Nonprescription medications used for rational treatment of ocular disorders

    h.  Oral antihistamines

    i.  Prescription oral nonsteroidal anti-inflammatory agents

    j.  Oral antibiotics for medical treatment of ocular disease

    k.  Topical and oral antiviral medications for medical treatment of the following:

- Herpes simplex viral keratitis
- Herpes simplex viral conjunctivitis
- Periocular herpes simplex viral dermatitis
- Varicella zoster viral keratitis
- Varicella zoster viral conjunctivitis
- Periocular varicella zoster viral dermatitis

    l.  Oral analgesics that are not controlled substances

    m.  Codeine and hydrocodone, both with compounds and maximum 3-day supply

11. Corneal scraping with cultures
12. Nonsurgical punctual occlusion by plugs [per Title XVII§861(s)(1) and California Business and Professions Code §3041(e)(10)]
13. Debridement of corneal epithelia, including:

    a.  Mechanical epilation

    b.  Administration of oral fluorescein to diabetics with suspected retinopathy

## PHASED ROLL-OUT OF IMPLEMENTATION PLAN SELECTED FOR PROCESS IMPROVEMENT ("DO" PHASE)

In addition to the diagnostic elements of the above-enumerated implementation plan, the next phase of implementing it requires participating optometrists to be able to impact patients' health status, health care services demands, care continuities, and service economies in a more positive manner than exists in the current health care delivery system, and especially in a team-oriented and patient-participative approach. Throughout this book, and especially in consideration of NCQA's and CMS' standards to implement shared savings provisions of the PPACA, the concept of patient-centered medical homes (PCMHs) has been shown in early-2000s medical and health economics literature as preferable to assigning primary medical practitioners alone to patients in need of primary care management. In general, the one-physician approach has many limitations, as have been shown in the rapid rise of hospitalists managing inpatient care, the shortage of MD/DO primary care physicians that the PPACA is exacerbating in its Medicare Shared Savings Program, and the complete inability of MD/DO physicians to perform even basic-level diagnosis and treatment of eye health.

As has also been demonstrated amply in the more recent literature, the PCMH model is designed to reduce service fragmentation by assigning each member a particular "medical home" of appropriate, multi-disciplinary medical, allied health, nursing, and support professionals who can treat each person holistically, relative to each patient's health status. In order to align the right professionals for different patients' health statuses, PCMHs are more optimally organized as "centers of excellence" for specific groupings of assigned patient by the most high-cost-variance chronic medical conditions, as well as for groups of patients requiring specialized differential diagnostic procedures to rule-out those chronic medical conditions. And those patients who are otherwise healthy, and lacking familial predisposition to those chronic medical conditions, can also be managed in their own PCMHs that focus on healthy living, including supportive care to reduce stress and improve mental health. This type of PCMH focus has a demonstrated effect on health status improvement (even for people with chronic diseases at-risk for life-threatening or disabling, socially-expensive disease co-morbidities) and even in reducing the incidence of certain chronic diseases, like hypertension, dyslipidemia, and Diabetes Mellitus.

Let's consider non-Type-I (so-called "non-juvenile") Diabetes Mellitus, whether first occurring with pregnancy (gestational diabetes) or after age 30 (Type-II, so-called "age-onset"). Diabetes Mellitus, as shown in the "Check" and "Understand" phases and "Plan" phase of the Deming Cycle, is not only one of the most problematic diseases to diagnose, the most socially-expensive and medically-disabling when sub-optimally managed or where management is reliant solely upon patient volition, but one that is already well-suited for optometrists, as patients are already 3.4 time more likely to treat with optometrists than allopaths or osteopaths, and as optometrists are already responsible for diagnosing 17% of America's initially-diagnosed diabetics.

What is most surprising about the 17% statistic is:

1. How few medical eye patients are actually referred to optometrists in capitated managed care settings, given that pervasively-errored underwriting classifies optometrists as "specialists" and requires optometric patients to be initially-referred to their ophthalmologists;
2. How even fewer optometrists are able to participate at all in Medicare risk plans where ophthalmologists receive health plan carve-outs or subcapitation from larger IPAs or IMGs that is typically not subcapitated to optometrists; and, as a corollary to both,
3. How ophthalmologists are failing to diagnose initial cases of Diabetes Mellitus for 1 of every 6 of their Medicare patients!

For purposes of rolling out the classifications of PCMHs well-suited for referral by medically-certified optometrists, to implement the above-selected process improvement for Medicare beneficiaries, this roll-out is focused on those eye and systemic medical conditions that optometrists are well-suited to refer for appropriate PCMH follow-up. Not only can optometrists refer to PCMHs, but they are also well-suited to go at-risk for a portion of PCMH capitation dollars (such as contained in CMS' March 31, 2011 draft ACO regulations, and which hadn't been finalized as of manuscript edits prior to this book's publication) for non-surgical management of diabetic retinopathy, glaucoma, cataracts, and other eye-related conditions; preventing eye-related injuries; and for preventing incidence of eye-related co-morbidities of their assigned diabetic and hypertensive patients. The numbering and classification of these proposed PCMHs suitable for optometrists to assign are shown in Table 9.2.

## VALIDATION OF PROCESS IMPROVEMENT ("CHECK" PHASE)

Models are subject to termination or modifications per 1115A(b)(3)(B) if they do not (i) improve the quality of care without increasing spending; (ii) reduce spending without reducing the quality of care; or (iii) improve the quality of care and reduce spending. These criteria represent the means to check whether the implementation was successful. Additional means of evaluating this innovative managed care model are shown below.

**TABLE 9.2**

**Classification of PCMHs Suitable for Initial Assignments by Optometrists**

| PCMH # | PCMH Classification for Appropriate Referral of Members for Follow-Up |
|---|---|
| 1 | Diabetes Mellitus—Type I |
| 2 | Diabetes Mellitus—Type II |
| 3 | R/O Diabetes (Random Blood Glucose >200 mg/dL, HbA1c<6.5%) |
| 4 | Newly-Diabetic (HbA1c ≥6.5%) |
| 5 | Pregnant, Elevated Blood Glucose (R/O Gestational Diabetes) |
| 6 | R/O Diabetes (Previously-Diagnosed Gestational Diabetes) |
| 7 | R/O Diabetes (Obese (BMI>30) or Other Diabetes Risk Factor) |
| 8 | New Hypertensive Diabetic (BP ≥130/≥80 & HbA1c ≥6.5%) |
| 9 | Hypertensive Diabetic (Prior Hypertension & Diabetes Diagnoses) |
| 10 | Glaucoma, per Previous Diagnosis |
| 11 | At-Risk for Glaucoma (Diabetic, Ethnicity) with Negative GDX |
| 12 | Early-Detected Glaucoma (Positive GDX®, HRT®, OptiMap® or OCT), Non-Diabetic |
| 13 | Early-Detected Glaucoma (Positive GDX®, HRT®, OptiMap® or OCT), Diabetic |
| 14 | All Other Members (Needing More Advanced Primary Care Follow-Up) |
| 15 | All Other Members (Needing Behavioral Health or Specialty Medical Consultation) |

### ADDITIONAL CRITERIA FOR PROGRAM EVALUATION

1. Graded reviews of digital fundus photographs of each optometrist' patient against other quality benchmark measures, such as proportion of diabetics with comorbid retinopathies, glaucoma, and hypertension;

2. Cost to diagnose performance ratios, such as trended FFS cost to derive diagnoses of chronic diseases that can comparatively be benchmarked against costs for similar diagnoses by MD/DO FFS PCPs; and

3. Multiple diagnosis profiles to be tracked and trended, with estimates of cost savings to Medicare based on earliness of diagnoses, such as both positive and negative confirmations of the following:

   a. High cost-variance chronic diseases (including diabetes, glaucoma, and hypertension),

   b. Observable conditions (such as Roth's spots, Horner syndrome, proptosis, and anisocoria) that are causally linked to other systemic diseases, and

   c. Medical findings that are documented in the literature in conjunction with diagnostic benchmarking (such as HbAlc, BMI, averaged blood pressure, presence or absence of both diabetic and nondiabetic retinopathy, diabetes and glaucoma as comorbidities of other diagnoses, and vision-threatening forms of retinopathy).

The results of the evaluation criteria during the "Check" Phase of the Deming cycle represent a validation of whether the plan achieves its goals and objectives. The aspects that don't achieve objectives become inputs under the "Act" (phase of the Deming cycle) to repeat the PDCA cycle, thereby adjusting the previous plan accordingly.

## ACTION STEPS TO RE-INITIATE THE DEMING CYCLE ("ACT" PHASE)

Results of program evaluation that demonstrate suboptimal attainment of program goals and objectives in the Deming Cycle's "Check" Phase can be fine-tuned for subsequent model phases.

## PART B: AN AT-RISK DISEASE MANAGEMENT APPROACH FOR SSI RECIPIENTS

### BACKGROUND

Managed Medicaid in most American counties is specific to beneficiaries of the Personal Responsibility and Work Opportunity Reconciliation Act of 1996 (PRWORA), formerly the Aid to Families with Dependent Children (AFDC) program, and as enacted by Congress as PL104-193. Capitation payments associated with this line of business are also reflective of actuarial mathematics and underwriting to indemnify for the probability of losses occurring.

In other words, the money is to be spent on preventive care and care required to avoid acute and chronic medical conditions that cost more money. The other Medicaid line of business, chronic and catastrophic acute care to recipients of Supplemental Security Income (SSI), is not part of Managed Medicaid and is paid directly by CMS. And the Medicaid portion of Medi-Medi (i.e., Special Needs) plans also falls into this same line of business. PRWORA recipients who develop chronic or catastrophic diseases, but do not qualify for SSI, are paid no differently even though costs go up.

The US DHHS is paying for SSI-related care on a FFS, and not managed care, basis primarily because few providers—and even fewer health plans—are contracting with CMS or any state for these public aid recipients. As such, there is tremendous flexibility in approaching a state, to bear responsibility for SSI patients. The At-Risk model included herein can be structured to help implement and manage these win-win opportunities.

## RECOMMENDED ACO (OR OTHER AT-RISK APPROACH) FOR SSI-FUNDED CHRONIC DISEASE PATIENTS

It is important to structure a win-win business relationship, especially where no standards exist and where potential competitors will not be savvy enough to do the hard work to satisfy all parties, even if some dilution of profitability would occur. In other words, any such ACO that is first in the door can set the bar very high, such that any subsequent bidders must either jump that bar or cede more business in the future. At the same time, most government agencies are not structured to perform actuarial studies to cost this level of risk appropriately or to outsource such risk for subcontractors to perform.

That said, and given that SSI patients are not being treated via managed care already for their chronic, disabling conditions, an actuarial model does not apply here. Rather what could apply is as follows:

### Medicaid Costs

The true costs of Medicaid to treat these people—with no price guarantees and nothing to show for the money being spent (e.g., improved outcomes, better medication compliance, reduced hospital charges for comorbidities, etc.)—can be divided by patient load to derive a capitated price per patient per month (PPPM).

### Cost-Structuring for Capitated Assumption of SSI Risk

Structuring a capitated price tied to average of patient expense for full medical management (possibly in the range of 90–95% of the average per patient expense), aggregated by specific disease state (e.g., diabetes mellitus, congestive heart failure, positive for human immunodeficiency virus [HIV+], acquired immune deficiency syndrome [AIDS], etc.). Exclusivity for management within defined zip codes and International Classification of Diseases, Tenth Revision (ICD-10), serves to normalize a state's SSI risk on a PPPM basis that guarantees a 5–10% off the top saving with a fee cap.

This approach is not being done now, but was the recent suggestion by CMS to chief executive officers (CEOs) of Southern California health plans and provider networks to structure fixed payments for Medi-Medi patients using innovative service approaches that do not require gatekeeping, referrals, and traditional primary care management approaches—which means a window for funding has remained open all these years and remains "ripe for the taking."

This author specifically test marketed this approach to Medi-Cal (California's Medicaid program) in 1996 for meningomyelocele (exposed-spine spina bifida), in conjunction with both the UCLA School of Medicine and the UCLA Medical Center, and it was well received by all state agencies except California Children's Services (CCS), the state agency that was performing so-called case management at the time. CCS refused to give up its case management function under a prior medical director, even though it represented less than $10 per patient. This alone was a deal killer for patients who could have been capitated for roughly $75,000 per patient per month (which, incidentally, represents a cap on the liability of the state and was actually 20% less than the cost borne at the time, mostly for improperly managed cases for which cerebral shunts were not implanted in time to prevent severe, expensive and crippling comorbidities over the first 5 years of each child's life).

This structure is not new. Medi-Cal published its per patient costs to treat AIDS patients in January 1993 as $1,873 per patient per month—then—including hospitalization, medical care, and pharmaceutical care; but even nearly two decades later, no health plan has yet stepped up to the plate to offload SSI AIDS patients at or near that average cost and in any manner to cap this level of SSI Risk in California.

What is even more telling is how this pricing compares to market-based PMPM subcapitation pricing for undifferentiated immunology risk. In other words, this PMPM indemnifies AIDS-related losses paid to immunologists on a subcapitated basis, representing a piece of full-risk capitation pricing for commercial populations. Even in late-2011 this PMPM is roughly the same price as it was in 1993, at between 8¢ and 10¢ PMPM (remember that this subcapitation is paid for undifferentiated populations that may include AIDS patients, even though the pricing presumes that the level of risk is homogeneous).

Immunologists to whom this author had presented both scenarios—10¢ PMPM for an undifferentiated population that may include AIDS patients versus $1,686 (90% of the published $1,873 rate) per defined AIDS patient per month—prefer the disease management-based pricing because the revenue is tied to costs of care, regardless of the fact that such a rate was probably severely understated in 1993 for non-Medi-Cal provider networks, given that utilization in the public sector is at least 50% less than in the private sector (given less efficiency in provider referrals, contracting, contract hospitals, pharmacy formularies allowing antiretroviral drugs to treat HIV/AIDS, and DME).

## Positively Impacting Disease Adaptation

Understanding the optimal management of each disease, including providing supportive services that may inexpensively improve the probability of successful disease adaptation—specific to each disease state—that positively correlates to better disease adaptation or outcomes (e.g., better medication compliance, healthier lifestyles to reduce the probability of disease morbidities and comorbidities [e.g., diabetic retinopathy or blindness resulting from macular degeneration, both tied to poor glucose control over time], weight reduction and behavior modification to reduce obesity in diabetics). A second phase—probably a deal killer in phase 1—could add first-degree relatives of these SSI patients who are most at risk for developing the disease, particularly apt for diabetes, cancer, CHF, stroke, and HIV.

Examples of such supportive services are shown below:

1. Minimal-cost memberships in national support organizations (e.g., $28 online rate for American Diabetes Association consumers) to receive magazines and support networks to improve disease adaptation, reinforced by the contractor (approximately $310),
2. Low-cost/volume-purchased memberships in local gymnasia/health clubs for healthy lifestyles to reduce obesity/prevent comorbidities,
3. Negotiated pricing for duodenal sleeve or laparoscopic band gastric surgeries (with graduated cost sharing for noncompliance with this relatively expensive treatment, even though collateral benefits—including putting diabetes in remission—are well documented with evidence of patient compliance and volition),
4. Offering capitated pricing for chiropractic, especially those coupling therapeutic massage with supervised exercise to address obesity/exercise needs as well as to improve circulation and use touch to identify problems at their earliest stages, and
5. Internet accounts to *Web*MD® or private-labeled intranet to help keep track of blood glucose readings and address disease-specific questions or concerns, that can be integrated with EHR (see Chapter 7) and lifestyle improvement contracts (LICs; see Chapter 5).

There is flexibility to tie any covered supportive service to specific performance objectives or comorbidities that the ACO model tries to avoid by disease state (sort of a Poka Yoke approach, as addressed in Chapter 7, to disease management errors), such as:

1. Getting preferential ad space or "fluff articles" in national support organization magazines [see a(i)] tied to hitting targets for new membership in their respective organizations,

2. Incentivizing contracted health clubs [see a(ii)] with bonuses for each patient-member achieving 10% reduction in BMI, 10% more musculature, or every 10% reduction of weight relative to his or her "ideal weight,"

3. Tying capitation pricing [see a(iii)] to avoiding the contracted comorbidity (e.g., ensuring that 80% of surveyed patient-members have less-perceived pain each quarter and rescinding contracts if perceived pain scores do not improve by at least 10% each quarter)—nobody is capitating these providers now, and they are the ones who continually second guess allopaths, and

4. Apportioning a percentage of administrative fees, such as on a quarterly accrual, to give cash bonuses to all providers when patient-members achieve disease management objectives tied to low comorbidity risk (e.g., HbA1C scores of < 6.5% for diabetics, evidencing tight glucose control over time).

5. Service delivery to SSI patients can be further enhanced at less cost by creating optimal disease management networks to address as many comorbidities as possible with providers/contractors willing to avoid them and go at risk via capitated pricing on a full-risk level (e.g., contracting podiatrists to prevent/manage diabetic foot neuropathies, contracting cardiologists to reduce/manage heart pain of CHF patients, contracting registered dieticians to ensure compliance with customized meal plans specific to disease state and cultural sensitivities)

6. In addition, it is possible to utilize the contractor's utilization management department for case management, community-based medical/nursing care (e.g., visiting patient-members in their homes to ensure compliance with treatment and lifestyle improvement objectives for themselves and their families, as appropriate, possibly through the use of *promotoras* discussed in Chapter 5), electronic records management (as available, or by separate grant application), management reporting, outcomes data gathering and reporting to Medi-Cal (or other state Medicaid agency), and other such objectives.

7. In conjunction with contractor's marketing department and in consideration of being willing to offload states' SSI risk, contractors should be able to negotiate with state Medicaid offices the following:

   a. Zip code exclusivity, by disease state, for all SSI patients specific to disease states such as CHF, oncology, diabetes, hypertension, CVA (cerebrovascular accident), chronic obstructive pulmonary disease (COPD), and so on. One approach may be to identify primary service area of the target market of the health plan and utilize its contracted clinics as a quasi-PCP for the disease state.

   b. Help Medicaid determine the average cost for treating each specific disease state and calculating an appropriate capitated price to indemnify Medicaid from paying more than that average cost in the future and ensure a 5–10% reduction in that expense on a not-to-exceed basis.

c. Remove purview of CCS (or other states' case management functions for SSI or developmentally disabled populations) for the case management responsibilities of any SSI children (with or without excluding the budgeted fees of CCS for those respective children, as politically feasible), to give the contractor's comparatively better case managers (in most cases, at least) more complete autonomy in improving outcomes

## INTENDED OUTCOMES OF INNOVATIVE SSI RISK APPROACH

Intended outcomes of offloading state SSI risks are:

1. Contracting health plan gains revenues tied to improving the management of diseases of its defined market area (see 7a), as well as improving community health status in innovative ways for public health crises including obesity, HIV, diabetes, and CHF;

2. Contractor gains revenues tied to SSI patients it does not get now as well as improving compensation for the same patients they see now (any subcapitation for specialty risk for current SSI patients among other managed Medicaid MCOs is a drop in the bucket compared to the costs tied to actual care for these people);

3. Contractor builds its Medicare business by spreading out the denominator (see Chapter 1) to essentially reduce its medical loss ratio (MLR) for each such disease state, albeit now with contracts that incentivize based on disease adaptation and not for simply withholding needed care;

4. This approach can bring capitated pricing to new network participants, such as capitated chiropractic tied to chiromassage and compliant exercise, which can be a model to sell to capitated PCPs to improve patient compliance and provide crucial medical information in a pleasurable way;

5. Contractor positions itself with state Medicaid agency as an innovative health plan and gains a reputation for saving significant money for the state, which puts it ahead of its competitors for future demonstration projects and for providing an innovative model to move SSI to managed Medicaid as well (perhaps gaining market advantage over other managed Medicaid plans, particularly those in the public sector); and

6. Contractor has the opportunity to pilot an innovative model that may represent the future of managed Medicaid projects within the CMI.

## CONCLUSION

This chapter demonstrates that there are measurable, implementable, and cost-effective solutions to the lack of primary care physicians organizing as ACOs under the Affordable Care Act that have not yet been tried. It seems unfortunate that optometrists have been ignored by Congress during the enactment of the Affordable Care Act and that managed Medicaid plans continue to cherry-pick their members by avoiding SSI recipients, especially as states continue to manage these people on an expensive FFS basis not tied to any value-added service delivery.

# 10 Innovative MCO Financial Modeling for the 21st Century

## INTRODUCTION

So much of the applications in the health care industry of advanced managed care models, like taking a capitation approach to implement sophisticated weighted indices to make otherwise-fixed payments more variable and controllable, are unfortunately coupled with poor understanding of the rationales for taking such approaches in the first place. We saw, in the case of Colombia, where well-connected consultants with poor understanding of managed care and the insurance industry knowledge on which this field rests, made horrendous recommendations that had disastrous fiscal impacts on the medical care entitlements of the citizenry of an entire nation. If the consultant has a flawed understanding, then unsophisticated clients (typical in the public and governmental sectors) will have even poorer knowledge from the outset.

In summer 2010, I had my déjà vu moment from two decades earlier, when a provider who claimed to have sophisticated knowledge of managed care acknowledged accepting the long-standing subcapitation payments he was receiving from a particular independent practice association (IPA) but understood only that the methodology for computing them was "complex and very confusing." While the methodology involved specific "contact capitation" modeling (see Chapter 6), the provider had no cogent idea how he could increase the amount of subcapitation he was receiving by influencing the weightings applied to his payments, except to acknowledge that they were "very low." I did not have the heart to ask him, "Too low for what?" given that doing so would have been merely rhetorical; the provider assumed that he was already being "compensated" for the work he contracted to perform. Of course, if that were the case, there would have been no appropriate need to weight anything because the subcapitation paid per referred service provided would have been entirely fixed and more akin to an all-inclusive case rate than to a recurring subcapitation payment.

Should it be of any surprise that this provider is an optometrist who is two levels down on the managed care "food chain" of an ophthalmologist-owned specialty eye care IPA that itself receives subcapitation from one or more medical practices, with some of *them* already receiving subcapitation? With each level of subcapitation received, the subcontractor takes his own profit chunk (typically 15–20%, in the guise of "administrative allocation") from subcapitation payments the subcontractor would then offer to lower-level providers. Can you imagine how little is left by the time the lowly optometrist is subcapitated? In this particular case, the optometrists are paid approximately 8¢ per member, per month (PMPM) for limited scopes of vision-related eye care (such as refractions and lens fitting for only commercial vision-risk lives), with no access to Medicare-paid patients, to primary medical eye care services, or even to perform specialized diagnostics (such as GDX®/HRT® screening for asymptomatic glaucoma) that few ophthalmologists perform, or even have an interest in performing, especially if the end result will not appreciably increase any demands for surgery (that is, except for LASIK surgery). A more thorough exploration of the case for utilizing optometrists more effectively to fill unmet managed care needs in the second decade of the 21st century is presented in substantially more detail in Chapter 9.

## FUTURE VALUE OF MANAGED CARE CONTRACTING: PART 1

Before we consider new innovations in managed care service delivery, I would like to pick up on a disturbing trend to which I just alluded. The transformation of fixed per capita pricing inherent in capitation to a semifixed or entirely variable methodology (such as in case rates or indexed per diems) through either straightforward contracting or sophisticated modeling involving weighted capitation payments is a fundamental difference between care payments in the late 20th century and the first decades of the 21st century. In fact, it is a complete reversal of the trends in managed care contracting starting in the 1980s and the first half of the 1990s, when entirely variable payments (such as fee for service and percentages of charges) gradually transformed to more fixed payments (such as by paying per diems that were gradually front-loaded and eventually indexed or by paying case rates that were initially subject to substantial carve-outs but eventually reaching parity by carving-in many of those same exclusions) and eventually to entirely fixed forms of capitation. We saw in the early 1990s how entire hospitals entered into subcapitation arrangements for general acute care by members of certain payers' Medicare risk plans, even though they had absolutely no mechanisms in place to control demand—in short, they were always "surprised" by every census day consumed under any capitated agreement. We even saw the rise of regional referral hospital services, such as in academic medical centers, negotiating tertiary capitation (subcapitation agreements for quaternary services) such as liver or heart transplantation services. As such, high-end services were typically sold as an add-on service to a wide variety of health plans looking to reduce reinsurance and loss ratio liabilities by carving-in high-end hospital services into a subcapitation relationship.

In my previous work, *Capitation*, I sincerely questioned the wisdom of health care providers obviously invested in serving managed care populations, regardless of various commitments to exclusivity, by eschewing capitation when pricing was more generous or in nonmature markets. Those who missed that boat by holding on to less-differentiated variable-pricing methodologies (like preferred provider organization [PPO] networks paying 90% of negotiated in-network charges) were typically subject to such hot competitiveness that contracted pricing opportunities for them not only reached parity but also began to be discounted more heavily than might have been experienced. The case in point is the PPO that kept the 90% of in-network charges but substantially reduced the contracted differential between the "in-network price list" and the provider's allowable charges per unit of service. I saw firsthand how some in-network hospitals accepted a 90% contractual adjustment for certain commercial insurance HMO/PPO network coverage, at a time when many negotiated case rates would have yielded at least twice the net income for the same services rendered.

Incidentally, every indication points to a recurrence of such a mad scramble in late 2011—when CMS was due to finalize its accountable care organization (ACO) contracts with providers, health plans, and practitioners who met very specific and difficult-to-implement selection criteria, and an even madder scramble predicted in late 2014/early 2015 if the ACO program successfully documents substantial cost savings to the Department of Health and Human Services (DHHS) at equal or greater benchmarked quality. Just like in the case of "fence-sitting" PPOs unwilling to make the move to capitation before the window of opportunity closed, I see an expanded cadre of players who have waited too long to join an ACO (such as waiting for nearly a year for CMS to release regulations that were clearly going to conform to the Affordable Care Act [ACA] statute) and who run the risk of being excluded from the Medicare/Medicaid program in 2015, presuming the ACOs are successful in transforming the program to an accountable care model, presumably with only those contractors with their 3 years of experience contracting with ACOs.

There is also a fundamental lack of perceptiveness about what any provider contract actually means. A good friend of mine, and a knowledgeable colleague in this area, Mr. Lawrence Lievense, FHFMA, FACMPE, argues that the price of any health care service is its true value. This witticism seems simple enough, but I will illustrate why its seeming simplicity is actually deceptively complex. Say a hospital prices daily hospital services (DHSs) at $10,000 per day on its charge description master (CDM or simply its "chargemaster") but negotiates with a PPO to offer that exact service at $2,500 per day. What is the value of each DHS charge to that PPO? While you may be tempted to say that the value to the PPO is the monetary price paid per unit of service ($2,500 in this example), the real value is actually $10,000. So, where did the other $7,500 per DHS charge go? It went to a combination of the following (please note that I use the words *tangible* and *intangible* strictly on the basis of how they would be recorded on financial statements):

- Tangible monetary benefits (such as prompt-pay discounts and accruals to risk pool bonuses) that help reduce receivables,
- Intangible monetary benefits (such as payer goodwill associated with contracting a higher-priced provider with better quality or patient satisfaction benchmarks),

- Tangible in-kind remuneration (such as payers allowing scanned claims rather than digitally created ones, payers making their member eligibility and coverage data online-accessible to contracted hospitals via their own intranets, or automating denials and claim tracer procedures to save hospitals' collection staff valuable time and expense, to name but a few), and

- Intangible in-kind remuneration (such as cascade effect on hospitals being able to recruit medical staff based on negotiated contracts, such as hospitalists, or the intangible benefit of insured members selecting a particular medical or hospital provider for referred care needs when such contracts were not negotiated from the outset).

Of course, payers do not typically itemize all the tangible monetary and in-kind benefits that are packaged into a particular contract, and providers do not typically view the intangible monetary and in-kind benefits (or most any of the tangible ones, for that matter) as contributory to the discounted price negotiated.

Another déjà vu moment is that such thinking is really no different from unsophisticated primary care providers (PCPs) thinking they were awarded a capitation contract based on their prowess at the negotiating table, their self-perceived quality relative to their competitors (even in the same medical group), or simply a windfall on their balance sheet. In my previous books, I warned such unsophisticated providers that they were awarded a capitation contract based on substantial number crunching on the part of the actuary for the plan, reflecting an assumed capability to provide all of the needed services more cost effectively than the health plan could accomplish alone, at incrementally better quality, and to a larger population of members than the experience (such as operating a staff model health plan) of the contracted HMO.

The same is analogous to the conundrum raised by Mr. Lievense. Hospitals mistakenly believe that the $2,500 payment is the true value because they do not consider that the in-kind and nontangible monetary payments—which do not have a direct impact on their cash flow or bottom line—count at all. The perceived benefit of the $2,500 paid–especially if competitors engaged in similar negotiations with the same payer are paid less—is attributed to the skill of the contract negotiation team and may even be a basis for giving performance bonuses to those employees. Likewise, if the $2,500 compares unfavorably to competitors, again the contract negotiators become the focus, but this time of criticism, demotion, and possibly job loss. The providers and their employees/physicians might bad-mouth the payer for reducing their monetary payment by 75% of the CDM charge and instead believe that 75% of the CDM gross charge represents a "contractual disallowance."

Just the term *contractual disallowance* is a misinterpretation of the composition of any CDM charge, as it assumes that the provider's finance departments (whether reimbursement, patient accounting, controller's office, or even the chief financial officer [CFO]) understand the composition of charges and which aspects of benefits received constitute a true deduction from revenue. If all of the $7,500 of a single DHS unit gross charge is a contractual disallowance, then how does the hospital value the physician/member marketing benefits built into each charge, the operational cost savings by the payer that benefit the revenue cycle or patient financial services (PFS) staff of the provider in servicing each individual CDM charge, and the risk pool/bonus contributions that are all built into the $7,500 that is misclassified *en masse* as a contrarevenue? There is a distinct trade-off, either assumed or implied, in each contract between any payer and any provider, between how much of each charge contributes to

- A monetary payment to the provider in terms of value-added service like higher-quality indicators and achieving key cost efficiencies (a contra-liability to the payer);
- A monetary payment to the payer in terms of covering pro rata operating expenses (i.e., risk pool, quality benchmarking, authorization process infrastructure, its actuarial risk of incurred but not reported IBNR), a payer's contrarevenue; and
- Nonreimbursable component of each charge in terms of non-value-added services by both parties (such as providers filing encounter reports, payers supplying case managers to oversee utilization and reduce bed days, and both participating in required audits), both a payer's liability and a provider's true contractual disallowance.

In short, every aspect of the relationship between the payer and the provider—as well as any or all public perceptions of each participant—contributes to equate to the full value of every charge on the CDM—*quod erat demonstrandum*.

## Veracity of Charges in Managed Care Contracts

So, what, you might ask, is so important in understanding all of the elements that go into the negotiated price of a service or product relative to its full actual value? Consider the obvious, if you will. With payers able to compartmentalize all aspects of each charge, and providers stuck on the misperception that anything not received in cash from a particular contract is a contractual disallowance, who has the distinct advantage at any bargaining table for future contracts?

Since the payer negotiated the pricing, chances are the payer understands the pro rata costs to it of every monetary and in-kind benefit offered to the hospital in any per unit of service, case-priced episode of care, or capitation-type payment offered. The hospital, unfortunately, has little idea of its pro rata or total costs, except for the charges in its CDM, and that is excluding the 1% of hospitals nationwide that employ any appropriate activity-based costing methodology. When hospitals must consider their costs only in the context of their allowable charges (if they, like most in the industry, rely on a ratio of costs to charges, typically at a cost of approximately 70% of charges), how can they differentiate *different types* of costs? Without such differentiation fomented by a simple ratio of costs to charges, how would any hospital be able to track in-kind benefits received against specific operating and nonoperating costs per unit of service? The answer is none.

When a hospital underbills for services actually rendered (also covered in more detail in this chapter), what is the effect on its operations? Do not be so aghast at the suggestion, as few bills are hand verified before they go "out the door" and typically are never reviewed except as part of a random sampling (typically far less than 10% of total claims) by a clinical auditor or firm and then after more time has passed than within the allowable statutes of limitation to rebill for missed charges. Any otherwise-recoverable underbilling becomes an expensive education, as the audit occurred outside of payer statutes of limitation. (And, since claims reviewed are part of 5–10% retrospective audits, any such undercharges uncovered might never be recognized as "common-cause" problems but rather just a function of "sampling error.")

The entire focus of revenue cycle operations remains on improving the throughput of services that were billed, to be collected and posted as quickly as possible, with absolutely no concerns for services that were not billed. While the types of undercharging errors are obvious—like billing for days of intravenous therapy but not billing to set the intravenous line in the first place, or billing for a second chemotherapy drug without billing for the first one—it is finding these needles in haystacks that is vexing for hospitals that do not rely on computerization to flag the applicably errored patient accounts and rebill them accordingly.

The obvious issue for the managed care organization (MCO) is that it does not even know that any undercharge problems exist, whether common cause or special cause, such as would be revealed during the analysis DMAIC (define, measure, analyze, improve, control) phase of a Six Sigma project (see Chapter 4). And, since they do not know any such problems exist, they would not have even started to investigate the causality of these problems. In essence, every hospital should assume it is underbilling by at least 10% of gross charges each year, unless proved otherwise, and begin Six Sigma DMAIC programs focusing on their revenue cycle operations. (To define the problem—the "D" in DMAIC—MCOs will have to undertake undercharging analyses and benchmark their true error rate and the financial impact of such errors on their bottom lines.)

The undercharging errors typically fall into one of three types: common cause, special cause, and other. Most of these billing errors may be of common-cause origin, such as

1. Known computer glitches or delays due to staffing, new system implementation, limitations on programming certain numbers of line items for a particular charge code, and so on;
2. Departments failing to manage or post their charges within the respective bill-hold cycle of the hospital (typically 72 hours from date of discharge, a revenue cycle stage known as work in progress or simply WIP);
3. The problems faced by overworked PFS staff, whose claims for a particular service do not pass charge edits per the bill scrubber of the MCO (or whose paper claims are rejected by the payer as "unclean"), and they might downcode the service just to get the claim submitted as clean; or where

4. Certain surgical implants or new services are not hard coded into the CDM and require a manual "soft coding" of the charges, which drastically increases the probability of missed charges if those implants include such items as implanted atrial defibrillators or permanent pacemakers (which are extremely expensive charges in and of themselves).

Special-cause problems are not typically tied to a facility-wide problem, such as rejected claims, computerization problems, and department-wide late postings. They are tied to individual people, random errors due to lack of automation and 100% prebilling reviews, as well as specific charges (such as pharmacy billing off a payer's formulary). Finding these root causes is typically impossible if common-cause problems have not already been identified and addressed for causality. A perfect example of such a special-cause problem is from a consulting client: A certain admitting staff member was improperly trained in using the patient accounting software of the hospital and routinely checked a box during patient registration that was not to be checked, resulting in suppression of these patient charges from appearing on revenue cycle accounts aging reports and not assigning these charges to patient financial services collectors for any follow-up whatsoever. Only during the course of a management engineering interview with the admitting supervisor present was the training error revealed; by the time all of the suppressed patient accounts were identified, the hospital had identified an additional $1.3 million in aging charges that had yet to be followed up for collections and subsequent posting.

A third type of underbilling error is attributable to other charges. Examples include

- employee theft or embezzlement,
- providing inappropriate "courtesy" discounts (which are actually fraudulent) to family or friends or other physicians and their families,
- disgruntled employees (such as those making demonstrated statements on behalf of the uninsured),
- union activity (such as employee disobedience in protesting cuts in hours, wages, or benefits), and
- substandard or inappropriate computer error reporting.

So, yes, let us get back to the original question: How do these undercharges affect an MCO?

1. *Financial*: In my own consulting, I have documented that hospitals leave approximately $45,000 in unbilled or underbilled charges, per licensed bed, per year. This ratio equates to an additional 10% of the annual gross charges of a hospital being "left on the table." Since a typical hospital will generate at least $100 million in gross charges per year, the math is easy ($10 million left on the table), and this remains a largely untapped source of operating income, particularly for hospitals close to insolvency.

Undercharging affects the profitability bottom line of a hospital, its balance sheet assets and asset turnover ratios, its deductions from patient service revenue and gross margin ratios on its profit and loss statements, as well as cost structure overall—in the absence of activity-based costing—given that costs are estimated on the basis of charges.

2. *Payers*: Payers truly love hospitals that leave claim dollars on the table because that represents increased bonus potential for them. Moreover, and given the extent of undercharging among hospitals, payers come to expect that a given percentage of authorized claims accruals will not be reported (which is a weird variation of IBNR, except this IBNR accrues to a payer's financial benefit). Payers come to expect that these undercharges will generate a "float" for the accruals they do take (and provide additional cushioning for routine loss of accruals due to IBNR liabilities), which still generates a windfall at the end of each fiscal year. Payers especially love the fact that every single undercharge reduces the payer's medical loss ratio (MLR), which makes them appear to be better-performing health plans than they actually are, and entirely on the backs of MCOs that do not even know that they are undercharging in the first place. Even more troubling for MCOs is that payers know more than they do about their true costs for a given contract, including the undercharged proportion. This represents a true negotiating disadvantage for MCOs (and advantage for payers) at the bargaining table, especially when the payer understands more of a provider's cost and charge behaviors than the MCO does. This is a key reason why MCOs often find it difficult to negotiate higher capitation or fee-for-service rates, as the other party to the negotiation knows far more data than does the provider organization. And, if the MCO does "clean up its act" and maintain better control of its undercharges, the payer can always stand to get it back by initiating a retrospective claims audit with allegations of contractual noncompliance (see item 4).

3. *Physicians*: Physicians, particularly surgeons, are extremely well versed in what care costs in all care settings (the operating room [OR], the postsurgical intensive care unit [ICU], and medical/surgical wards, the rehabilitation facility, home care, clinic care, durable medical equipment costs, and physical therapy, to name but a few). When a hospital undercharges for a surgical procedure, the surgeon is the first to realize it (especially when all surgical patients tend to feign sticker shock when they see their hospital bill). So, what exactly does the surgeon realize? The hospital gave this patient a discount that was not extended to any of the physician's other patients. In the case of common-cause problems, the physician will perceive that the hospital has officially lowered its prices for that particular surgery. Not a big deal? How about when the physicians' cash-paying patients seeking price quotes from revenue cycle staff are told the charges would be higher than their physicians' understanding of what is truly charged? Then, the physicians

go to hospital management and ask why *their* cash-paying patients are being charged *more*? (Of course, since this phenomenon results from common-cause undercharges, hospital administration will have no idea what the physicians are complaining about.) The end result is that these physicians will begin referring their cash-paying patients (the ones most desirable to health care providers) elsewhere. And, as for special-cause errors—mostly attributable to human error due to lack of 100% prebilling audits and lack of automation in general—the complaint to hospital administration is more sinister: "Why do you intend to charge my cash-paying patient more than Dr. X's patients undergoing the same procedure?" That end game could result in the complaining doctor taking *all* of his surgical cases elsewhere. Last, it needs to be said that fluctuations in common-cause undercharges attributable to late postings from ancillary departments hit physicians particularly hard, as it may be perceived that a physician's patients are being charged "extra," especially when the MCO has no idea that late postings are a common-cause problem affecting undercharges that they probably do not know even exist.

4. *Regulatory*: Failure to charge for items can be seen by regulators as "selective free care," which undermines "most-favored nation" clauses of most managed care contracts. Moreover, and particularly when rejected claims may be inadvertently downcoded to pass claim edits, MCOs must be ready to explain why their undercharges (which few realize they have) are not to be construed as illegal downcoding. (Does civil monetary penalty ring a bell?) MCOs must also be ready to explain why selective free care might be inconsistent with their own indigent care policies and their records in providing charity care versus selected free care due to missed or undercharges. This may be particularly difficult, and expensive, to explain from within the context of bond obligations, not to mention Hill-Burton requirements for charity care. For example, MCOs must be ready to explain why charity care applications are denied at the same time that at least 10% of allowable charges are either undercharged or not charged entirely. When the undercharges of any MCO, particularly those resulting from common-cause problems, are for governmentally paid patients—such as administered by CMS (Medicare or Medicaid), Department of Defense (Tricare), or state health care exchanges—the repercussions are that certain types of patient procedures are excessively discounted for certain patients and overcharged for every other such patients, all in violation of their managed care contracts. Under CMS, these perceived violations could trigger referrals to the Office of the Inspector General, covering not only most-favored nation provisions of their contracts (like in the private sector), but likewise triggering Internal Revenue Service (IRS) investigations of inurement violations for MCOs operating as nonprofit public benefit entities. It also increases the potential, particularly for special-cause problems, of extending unexplained pricing discounts

to certain payers that are not extended to governmental payers (who maintain most-favored nation clauses in their managed care contracts).

5. *Employees*: Undercharging directly affects the bonus potential of managers and incentive compensation for hospitalists. It is particularly demoralizing for employees when known "deadwood" employees are allowed to stay without disciplinary action, and their undercharging errors are perceived as being covered up or otherwise condoned. Undercharging exposes poor managerial controls in revenue cycle function, particularly if full-time employees (FTEs) are wasted correcting WIP errors, particularly with late postings and failed billing edits at the bill scrub revenue cycle stage. The math is not difficult: If 10% of the charges of a hospital are being left on the table, and the hospital uses a 70% ratio of cost to charges for estimating its operating expenses (or 7% underreporting of costs due to money left on the table), and given that employee-related costs are typically 60% of total operating costs, then SW&B (salaries, wages, and benefits) are expected to be at least 4% lower for every dollar of charge left on the table. Thus, for $10 million of such charges left on the table, there will exist an insufficiency of approximately $4 million to pay employee-related costs. How would that affect the MCO? Consider the increased potential for unionization activity as well as for reductions in force to make up for a 4% cost overrun in SW&B expenses. And, what is the exposure of at least one hospital measured to have left 24% of its billable charges on the table?

So, the original question raised by Mr. Lievense still stands: If the true value of a claim is its full-retail billed charges, then what exactly does a managed care contract represent? And, let us add our new corollary: If MCOs are leaving a minimum of 10% of their billable charges on the table, isn't the true value of the claim the combination of what was billed at full retail *plus* the services that should have been billed at full retail but were not? The latter is how payers and regulators would define the true value of each claim.

## FUTURE VALUE OF MANAGED CARE CONTRACTING: PART 2

So, let us start by addressing Mr. Lievense's original question. The true value of a managed care contract is simply to shift the proportion of full-retail charges paid as cash remuneration relative to in-kind remuneration. The managed care contract itself does not alter the nature of charging for services based on their costs (controllable or noncontrollable, fixed or variable, direct or indirect, fully loaded or incremental, operating or nonoperating, or even known or unknown) plus an allowable markup. Incidentally, this is one of Mr. Lievense's major contentions in a number of personal injury cases in which he has testified and which is serving to overturn the *Hanif* decision that has inappropriately limited the liability of a hospital in personal injury (PI) or Medical malpractice litigation to the value of its "contracted" discounts from full-retail charges. (Congratulations to Mr. Lievense for all he has done to set the judiciary straight on the true value of managed care contracts relative to the full value of services actually rendered.)

To be sure, the issue of adding the money left on the table to the true value of a claim is one that has yet to be brought up in court. But, since discussing this chapter with Mr. Lievense, I am certain that it will come up soon enough. Consider the perspective of the hospital. One of its contracted members incurs costs as a result of a particular tort, and the hospital has believed that its liability for inpatient costs is limited to the 25% net of billed charges that it was paid for that patient's care. With *Hanif* no longer applicable, the tort can be litigated not only for the full value of the services incurred per the CDM (irrespective of actual cash remuneration paid) but *also* for the 10% under- or missing-charge billing ratio experienced by the hospital. Consider the math: If a litigant incurs $150,000 of full-retail hospital charges that were reimbursed by a payer at $37,500 (in cash), the "true charges" represent not only the $112,500 paid to the hospital in in-kind or "intangible" reimbursement (such as goodwill), but also an allowance for an additional $15,000 in undercharged claims per the experience of the hospital. Thus, the mix of charges reflective of the tort includes $37,500 paid in cash, $112,500 paid in intangible and in-kind remuneration, and a $15,000 accrual for cash and in-kind remuneration attributable to the claim but never actually billed. The numbers are even more eye opening when the litigant is covered under a Medicare Advantage plan for which the health plan pays capitation to the hospital.

So, what is the value of the managed care contract, especially if it no longer shields a defendant from liability under a tort? In the truest sense of billing and contracting, this was never an intended benefit of covering MCOs under such contracts. Rather, it simply represented an unintended financial benefit due to misinterpretation of the billing process under *Hanif*. Are there future legal and regulatory implications from those hospitals receiving relief under this statute at the point that it is officially overturned in the judiciary? While that has not yet happened (and the first test case of Mr. Lievense's testimony related to *Hanif* in a PI case was first reviewed by the California Supreme Court in May 2011), I expect that there will be such repercussions that the courts will also have to consider if (or, most likely, when) *Hanif* is formally overturned.

## THE ELEPHANT IN THE ROOM: HOW HEALTH PLANS CAN COMPETE WITH STATE HEALTH EXCHANGES

Of course, the "elephant in the room" is the true value of health plans and managed care contracting when the ACA establishes state health care exchanges starting in 2014, and for which employers already know that the act has so far (as of publication, at least) underallocated resources to enforce provisions requiring employers to offer health insurance to their employees. Some employers, as of this publication date, truly believe that it will be less expensive to pay a fine (that likely will not be enforceable) rather than comply with the ACA and make sure all of their employees are covered by their own health insurance carriers rather than force them to join public health exchanges. Thus, the value of the managed care contract is truly in flux, as are the nature and market shares of existing private-sector health plans. However, I do believe that the largest health plans are not going away with ACA implementation.

I do believe, however, that health plans must fundamentally change to protect their future market shares and benefit marketability starting in 2014. A key differentiator is by changing their underwriting practices. Not only must they reengineer their underwriting in the case of bifurcating eye care risk into a combination of primary eye care (both medical and vision only) and specialty eye care (covering both medical and specialized vision correction), but also they must move from community-based rating to experienced-based rating. Let me explain the latter in this chapter, as the former has already been presented in some detail in Chapter 9.

The problem with community ratings is that they are too easy to implement and result in far more expensive underpredictions of true utilization and cost behaviors. Consider a community rating based simply on family size: With only three population-based tiers, rates can be set simply on adding to the denominator of the MLR with absolutely no knowledge of its numerator. The other problem with community ratings is that an entity has to be large enough to spread its denominator as high as possible to reasonably predict or fall under a given MLR.

But, community ratings represent a security blanket for health plans that is about to get very wet. Since large HMOs continue to spread their denominators and sell their plans to new customers, they have overlooked any rationale to change to experience ratings. After all, experience ratings require not only size but also specific experience in paying claims, analyzing member utilization and provider performance, benchmarking claims performance against outcomes and specific balanced scorecards, and spending the money on actuaries and underwriting to translate these experiences into specific changes to premiums, provider compensation formulas (capitation, carve-outs, copays, coinsurance, etc.) and budgetary accruals, and then to both rewrite respective DoFRs (divisions of financial responsibility) and evidences of coverage and republish marketing collateral to aid their sales efforts. This cannot be done at the last minute but is part of a multiyear effort to transition from community ratings and adjusted community ratings (ACRs) to full experience-rated formulas.

Consider what is about to occur with state health exchanges. For example, consider what types of underwriting state health exchanges will need to undertake to create standard benefit designs and premium pricing and to formulate compensation formulas for their provider network and specific benefit offerings and add-on premiums. The kicker is this: This is for populations that they know nothing about. Of course, the state health exchanges can therefore not rate their product offerings on the basis of experience ratings. They will start off with a community rating because they lack both the access to encounter data and the economies of scale to start with experience ratings. Experience-rated plans have the underwriting to undercut their premiums relative to community-rated ones.

Of course, experience-rated health exchanges will take years to come to fruition, which presents a competitive advantage for existing health plans that will be competing with state health exchanges, provided they actually transition their products to experience ratings. So, what exactly does an experience-rated plan yield that a community-rated or ACR plan cannot? Variable pricing is an obvious advantage but that does not cut both ways: Any adverse-selected membership base may have much higher charges and poorer records in lifestyle improvements to represent a competitive advantage under experience ratings.

While that may be true, the current health plans have the advantage of time: time to address root causes for overconsumption relative to benchmarks and time to employ different population management techniques to improve problem members' consumption of health care services. There are numerous population-based health and disease management tools in the private sector that health plans should have been utilizing. Health exchanges have no comparable luxury of time, primarily because they cannot subscribe membership until late 2013 for a January 1, 2014, "go-live" date. As a result, a health plan in 2012 can identify every member of the plan, all relevant claims and health status benchmarking results, and all practitioner encounter reports for each such individual over the course of many years, and they still have an 18-month head start over state health exchanges that have not even subscribed new membership.

The advantage of experience ratings means that overconsumers of services might pay higher premiums, while otherwise-healthy members might pay lower premiums. That is not to say that the health plan would discriminate against members with chronic medical conditions. This is the key factor differentiating a community-rated policy, for which simply the occurrence of a chronic disease would have rated the member and branded him or her as having a preexisting medical condition for which policy exclusion was a possibility (at least prior to enacting the ACA). In an experience rating, patients with a chronic disease who manage their condition appropriately would be higher rated than the same type of patients who are not (but incur expensive tests, pharmaceuticals, and hospitalizations just the same). And, since a larger proportion of members do not have chronic medical conditions, especially at younger ages, experience ratings will have a positive impact on premiums for most people.

As mentioned in Chapter 5, a move by health plans to experience ratings would have the added advantage of finally making individual members accountable for their own health status, with the actual translation of lifestyle improvements into lower premiums. This is a significant factor as the entirety of managed care contracting will become more transparent with the introduction of health exchanges. There is nothing transparent about extending lower premium pricing to less-healthy employees of larger employers, based solely on the fact that the policies are underwritten on the basis of a community rating. If two members who are otherwise healthy are covered by different plans—one being a health exchange rated on a tiered community methodology and the other a long-standing health plan utilizing an experience rating—where is the transparency if the experience-rated plan offers premiums for comparable coverage at a much lower rate?

Health plans also have to realize that the purpose of the ACO project starting January 1, 2012, is to gather enough experience-related data on the 31 million

Americans to be newly covered by Medicaid (again, for whom the federal government knows nothing about) to be able to capitate them (rather than pay providers on resource-based relative value scale [RBRVS]) and transition this population to an experience-rated benefit plan. This initial phase of the ACO project is expected to end after 3 years (by December 31, 2014). The ACA therefore lets current health plans know that the federal government anticipates being able to transform a population for whom it knows nothing about to one that can be experience rated or capitated after only 3 years. Private-sector health plans should not need as long to transform populations about whom they already know nearly everything to experience-rated premium pricing. And health exchanges—which will not have the luxury of engaging providers who would be 100% compliant with EHR and PQRI (Physician Quality Reporting Initiative) participation, as well as having 50 states' worth of population to measure and benchmark—should reasonably expect to be able to transition to experience ratings over the first 3–5 years of going live.

A 3- to 5-year transition period for health exchanges moving from community to experience ratings is an advantage for health plans only if they see the need to compete with them and to leverage this critical head start in moving to experience ratings. I know one of the barriers all along is public perception of health plans dictating wellness strategies. Hello? That was their exact role in operating staff model HMOs before selling populations for capitation in the 1980s. Yes, dear reader: History will soon be repeating itself, with managed care coming full circle in our lifetimes. There is a clear difference between health plans self-managing wellness in the 20th century and in the 21st century. Last time, they really did not know what they were doing when dealing with open populations of members (that is, not within EPO [exclusive provider organization] or staff model HMOs, for whom health plans had an abundance of data), and they were quite likely well before their time, given that there really was no Internet then, and the level of computerization was incomparable to what exists today. In addition, the concepts of population-based algorithms for resource prediction of members were also virtually nonexistent then and are truly coming into their own in the second decade of the new millennium.

## COMING CLEAN ABOUT "HEALTH MAINTENANCE"

Another key difference for health plans transitioning to self-management of membership via experience ratings is that the health care industry—with populations remaining capitated to it all these years for commercial risk—has, in truth, failed to manage its respective covered lives via the "wellness model" and embodied the true goals of "health maintenance." In the truest sense of contracting transparency, when will the health care industry acknowledge its failings in performing health maintenance and transforming its health care delivery infrastructures solely to the wellness model? It would also mean that hospitals have to acknowledge that secondary acute, tertiary, and quaternary models of hospital care are completely incompatible with the wellness model, except for their distinct-part ambulatory care (nonsurgical) clinics.

So, as long as the health care industry is "coming clean," let us get to one of the two true culprits: physicians. Hospitals were part of the care continuum because nonprimary medical care needed to be accommodated as health plans started to contract for full risk. But do not be fooled. In most markets, the health plans fully intended to separately contract medical and institutional risk and actually did so for many years. There were some markets, like Southern California and Pittsburgh, Pennsylvania (much later on), where physicians insisted on top-dollar capitation and unmanageably high stop-loss attachment points, and where some health plans were only too happy to speed up the timetable and contract for full-risk coverage in nascent markets. This culprit was so inept in population management that they accepted underpriced capitation rates for both medical and institutional risk in return for price and market exclusivity guarantees. That was the sole upside, incidentally.

## CONCLUSION—A FINAL (?) STROLL DOWN MEMORY LANE

We all know the rest of this journey back in history. The physicians knew about wellness, true, but hospitals were (and still are) organized to treat illness. Did anyone contracting for the first full-risk contracts have any clue how to improve wellness and keep people out of the hospital? Yes, the hospitals did initially want more business, particularly when they were paid by the full-risk integrated delivery network on a fee-for-service or per-diem basis, but they also wanted more business when the payment model started to shift to capitation. Yes, I know this is unbelievable, but hospitals were so eager to keep their census days up (and inexplicably, still are) that they initially did not care that they were prepaid for the capitated patient who started showing up in their emergency rooms (ERs). Of course, that attitude changed pretty quickly, but the hospitals do share a portion of the culpability for entering into ill-advised capitation deals.

And, of course, the other true culprit is the health plan. Sorry to say, but the level of senseless greed extends not only to the clueless physician looking for the highest capitation for the largest exclusivity of membership, but also to the health plan that sold the contract. In retrospect, I think most health plans that made the premature shift to full-risk capitation believe that they should have stuck to their original game plans and eschewed the dollar-hungry physicians who wanted everything from the outset, but obviously lacked the wherewithal to meet their standards for health maintenance and health status management. To this day, I wonder about those negotiations. Why didn't the health plan "kick the tires" more vigorously, such as asking about physicians' strategies to get members to seek care when they were not sick, or to ensure patients' compliance with physician instructions, or simply to understand when it was appropriate to seek ER care? Had health plans been more selective in selling these member populations, I truly believe that many of the problems the managed care industry has been facing in recent years could have been avoided, especially if ratings could have moved from community to experience based far sooner.

I also still wonder why the health plans contracted with physicians like they were having a "fire sale: everyone must go." I have no doubt that redlining was occurring, and there is ample evidence from key markets, like Southern California, that less-affluent zip codes were capitated first and very affluent ones contracted last. But, the necessity of contracting for full risk before contracted providers had the demonstrated capability of managing their respective risk loads escapes me. The greed rested not only with the purchaser but also with the seller. After all, should we blame the seller for offering a product that the buyer wants to buy and fully intends to buy?

I see this as analogous to a bartender who serves the most expensive drink to an obviously drunk patron, whose only demand was for more alcohol. Did the bartender have a higher duty to refuse to serve more alcohol to a drunk? Did the health plan have a higher duty to refuse to contract for full risk to a practitioner network with no cogent plan or demonstrated capability to manage primary care risk appropriately for a health maintenance model? And, did the bartender have a duty—beyond the opportunities of a free-market economy—not to serve the most expensive booze to the patron who could not tell the difference between the quality of a premium label and a "well drink"? Did the health plan have a duty to insist on a much lower stop-loss attachment point for the practitioner organization that was willing to accept the most risk, even though it obviously did not fully realize the difference between a $50,000 stop-loss and a $1-million one?

I am going to go on a limb and say that there was ample blame to go around on both sides of the negotiation table. If health plans did not see themselves as having what we in health care consider a "duty," they clearly had to have been negotiating on behalf of the members they were capitating—the employees and family members of their client employers—to have acted in good faith. Just the same, the physicians sitting on the other side of the table had a duty to both their prior patients (discussed in greater detail in *Capitation*) and to their future members to know what to do with them. The obvious first tip-off, again as detailed in *Capitation* and here in Chapter 5, was the fact that physicians truly believed that they could have self-managed health maintenance based on data comprising simply name, address, Social Security number, and date of birth. Such thinking was always lunatic. Based on an ACR-rated policy, that may truly have been all that the payer was forthcoming in sharing, but they also had claims experience that was not being factored into their ratings. Still, physicians clearly blew the test when they did not inquire, even while sitting at the negotiation table, whether any other data were available for managing health maintenance. If I were the health plan and a practitioner organization truly believed that they could manage at the standard of health maintenance without any medical experience data (or even patient phone numbers), I would have refused to sign my members to such a physician practice that had obviously misrepresented its true experience in managing via the wellness model. And, the managed care industry as a whole would have been much further along relative to health exchanges if just a few had been just a bit more selective of their full-risk-contracting practitioner organizations (and even just for medical risk also).

I remain truly bullish about both the managed care industry and the health care delivery industry, especially as it appears that growing pressure for health plans to finally move to experience-based rating could allow the entire framework to come full circle: health plans themselves encouraging strategies to enhance wellness and improve disease management outcomes, all positively affecting experience ratings. I also am convinced that health plans have a future under the ACA, especially relative to state health exchanges, provided they transform themselves to compete effectively and take advantage of their head start, relative to health exchanges, to offer lower-cost premiums in conjunction with experience ratings and better innovations in capitated managed care (particularly at the level of resource prediction for specific risk-stratified populations of members).

I also believe that employers will ultimately do the right thing and continue to offer health coverage to their employees through current MCOs or ERISA (Employee Retirement Income Security Act of 1974) plans. Doing so will preserve commercial risk products and offer better, less-expensive choices for employees considering joining a state health exchange. In my heart of hearts, I believe that employers do not cheat on their income taxes, do pay their employees fairly, and will comply with ACA provisions regarding offering commercial health insurance to their employees. After all, it is the right thing to do.

# Index